Prai

Mark Noll, in his book *The Scandal of the Evangelical Mind*, raises concern about a lack of contemporary Christian intellectualism. *Finding Home* is a refreshing piece of work which addresses that concern.

Russ Bowers' writing is at once clear, poetic, and intensely well-informed. It achieves in a substantive way what C.S. Lewis began in the final pages of *The Abolition of Man*, where he describes threads of commonality in human thought which he calls "the Tao."

Finding Home is an indispensable map to understanding the powerful flow of ideologies that, though ancient, still drive people's thoughts and actions in the twenty-first century. This book is a must-have for Christian pastors, teachers, and thinkers.

—STEVE DEGEORGE, EdD, dean of the School of Education,
Oakland City University, Oakland City, Indiana

In a time when differences, division, fear, and ignorant caricatures of religion hold great sway, the alternative paradigm for how we view each other, found in Russell Bowers' most recent book, *Finding Home*, is a breath of fresh air.

Finding Home provides a sorely needed framework and rationale recognizing our common quest for truth and meaning across a broad spectrum of religions. Bowers does not promulgate mere platitudes of acceptance, nor champion a dull and ineffectual tolerance of diversity. Instead, he engages the reader with extensive citations and rich analysis of a broad swath of religious texts, building a strong rationale for appreciating the rich wisdom and truth that can be discovered, even in surprising places.

By drawing on primary and secondary sources from within each religion, and listening critically yet fairly, Bowers identifies a wonderfully overwhelming range of common themes, principles, and fundamental beliefs—discovering foundations of our shared humanity and quest for truth and meaning. This book thereby lays the foundations for a more appreciative community, made up of various religions living peacefully together and calling forth the best in each other, without asking readers to make logically specious leaps of faith into false statements that all religions are the same. Bowers' intellectual precision, hard head, soft heart, and open mind combine to bring a unique and refreshing voice in a world where, too often, intellectual sloppiness, ill-informed judgment, and armchair criticism of those who are different have added fuel to the fires of fear, hatred, and violence.

Finding Home is refreshingly entertaining and interesting, as Bowers guides the reader into a fascinating range of religious texts and commentaries with a spirit of respect, of listening, and of discernment. I am inspired as a Christian by the discovery of resounding and eternal truths within the guiding beliefs of people from extremely different backgrounds, and encouraged to persist in my own faith, in my pursuit of truth, and in my appreciation and recognition of the sincerity and richness found in the theology and practice of people from other faiths.

I strongly commend this book to people of all faiths, so that we might be better able to live out our various beliefs among the clamorous media and religious voices of hatred and empire, while building the peace which any concept of a loving God would surely compel us toward.

—**BILL FORBES, director of the Child Protection, Child Development and Rights Team, World Vision International**

Finding Home is a brilliantly-written book that is easy to read and yet scholarly in content, written by a true scholar and God-lover, Dr. Russell Bowers Jr. The book does not suggest that all religions are the same, or that all equally bring us to God. But it does urge that each argues at least one point that is right. How could anyone follow them if they contained nothing true? What the book does is find some significant good in each, and strings these points together into a path that can lead us Home.

This approach is not syncretism, since it views the religions presented neither as authoritative nor as true in their entirety. Each chapter could have been argued as well from the Christian scriptures; however, Russ brilliantly accomplishes the task of getting readers to see that Christianity is not entirely foreign to the understanding and aspirations of many thoughtful people throughout time and around the world. What distinguishes Christians is Jesus—who we understand him to be, and the reality of his cross, resurrection, and coming. All these are brilliantly presented within the fabric of the tapestry of this scholarly book.

Sometimes we hear only snippets from other faiths, cut out for critical purposes by our own apologists. And, sad to say, many non-Christians are similarly acquainted with only an inadequate version of our faith presented through skewed, spotty, out-of-context biblical quotations. But *Finding Home* employs extensive quotations from non-Christian scriptures and writings to accomplish its task, so readers may glimpse what others believe as they themselves believe. We are increasingly finding people of all faiths around us, and as we interact with them it is important to learn more about what has shaped their worldview. *Finding Home* provides a forum where readers can interact in a fashion that is more leisurely, dispassionate, and perhaps objective.

A highly recommended book for every believer to have in their personal library and to also recommend to their friends.

—**DR. RAVI I. JAYAKARAN**, catalyst for integral mission, The Lausanne Movement

Finding Home is not the predictable Christian apologetic in which the truth of Christianity is pitted against the errors of human religion. Dr. Bowers has ingeniously and artfully woven his way through several of the major and minor world religions by way of their own texts, periodically concluding that there are some elements of truth, similarities, and yet differences between them. In so doing, he has also uncovered the longing heart of all these persuasions in their respective quests to find relief from the reality in which they find themselves engulfed and in their attempt to make sense of the world in which they live. In a delightful way, the author has distilled the basic philosophical beliefs of several far eastern and western worldviews, perceiving where their aspirations intersect with one another. Yet, the uniqueness of biblical truth is not lost in the survey, but also weaves its way gently through the book. This writer can highly recommend *Finding Home* for an enjoyable, informative, and persuasive read.

—**DR. FORREST S. WEILAND**, professor of biblical studies and director of the master of arts in biblical studies program, Veritas Evangelical Seminary

FINDING HOME

Mile Markers
Among the World Religions

Russell H. Bowers, Jr.

Russ Bowers
John 17:3

Deep River Books

Finding Home

Published by
Deep River Books
Sisters, Oregon
www.deepriverbooks.com

ISBN: 9781940269870

Library of Congress: 2016941268

Cover photo: Trekking among unusual formations at Bryce Canyon National Park, Utah, USA.

Cover design by Jason Enterline

Printed in the USA

GOIN' HOME

lyrics by William Arms Fisher

music by Antonín Leopold Dvořák

Goin' home. Goin' home. I'm a-goin' home.
Quiet-like some still day, I'm just goin' home.
It's not far, just close by, through an open door.
Work all done, cares laid by, goin' to roam no more;
Mother's there 'xpecting me, father's waiting, too,
Lots of folks gathered there, all the friends I knew.

Morning star lights the way, restless dream all done.
Shadows gone, break of day, real life just begun.
There's no break, there's no end, just a-living on;
Wide awake, with a smile, going on and on.
Going home. Going home, I'm just going home.
It's not far, just close by, through an open door.

CONTENTS

A cabin in the north woods accessible only by foot. It is good to catch this first glimpse of Home after an hour on the trail.

THE MAP

Most of us like to travel: see strange sites, meet different people, escape the routine. Not only geographical but also philosophical treks awaken wonder. New vistas of thought can convince the wanderer that—despite what she has always been taught—Podunk Hills does not in fact represent the apex of civilization. On the other hand, even extensive engagement with others may assure us that there's no place like home—novelties of Oz notwithstanding. Either way pilgrims return from their rovings and ramblings enriched.

No wonder the epic journey remains a favorite literary motif. From *Odyssey* and *Ramayana* to *Star Wars* and *The Life of Pi*, perilous peregrinations through waste and wilderness toward noble ends resonate with our souls. We struggle, sink, succeed, and celebrate with the sojourner.

Danger as well as delight saturates such sagas. While trying to regain his beloved Ithaca, Odysseus needed to navigate the needle's eye between the original rock and hard place:

> One crag thrusts into the vaulting sky its jagged peak,
> and halfway up that cliffside stands a fog-bound cavern.
> Scylla lurks inside it—the yelping horror.
> She has twelve legs, all writhing, dangling down,
> and six long swaying necks, a hideous head on each,
> each head barbed with a triple row of fangs, thickset!
> Holed up in the cavern's bowels from her waist down
> she shoots out her heads, out of that terrifying pit.
> No mariners yet can boast they've raced their ship
> past Scylla's lair without some mortal blow—
> with each of her six heads she snatches up
> a man from the dark-prowed craft and whisks him off.

> The other crag is lower—you will see, Odysseus—
> though both lie side-by-side, an arrow-shot apart.
> Beneath it awesome Charybdis gulps the dark water down.
> Three times a day she vomits it up, three times she gulps it down,
> that terror! Don't be *there* when the whirlpool swallows down—
> not even the earthquake god could save you from disaster.
> No, hug Scylla's crag—sail on past her—top speed!
> Better by far to lose six men and keep your ship
> than lose your entire crew.[1]

Central to our species' soul is a search for significance. Though we may ramble without destination through many a lazy Sunday afternoon, most of us hope at life's end to have accomplished more than aimless wandering. We seek a meaning and goal that are truly there. They are. We may order our route, adapt our pace, and opt to either enjoy or ignore the scenery. But in the final analysis humanity has an identity, a calling, a destination. Some roads lead to it; others detour us until we recognize our wrong turns and correct our course. Odysseus longed not for an odyssey but for Ithaca and Penelope; Rāma sought Sītā and Ayodhyā. Even Steinbeck, who crossed the continent simply "in search of America," found that the joys of the road had evaporated miles from the destination for which he suddenly longed:

> [My journey] was over before I returned. I know exactly where and when it was over. Near Abingdon, in the dog-leg of Virginia, at four o'clock of a windy afternoon, without warning or good-by or kiss my foot, my journey went away and left me stranded far from home. I tried to call it back, to catch it up—a foolish and hopeless matter, because it was definitely and permanently over and finished. The road became an endless stone ribbon, the hills obstructions, the trees green blurs, the people simply moving figures with heads but no faces. All the food along the way tasted like soup, even the soup . . .
>
> Up to Abingdon, Virginia, I can reel back the trip like film. I have almost total recall, every face is there, every hill and tree and color, and sound of speech and small scenes ready to replay themselves in my memory. After Abingdon—nothing. The way

> was a gray, timeless, eventless tunnel, but at the end of it was the one shining reality—my own wife, my own house in my own street, my own bed.[2]

Traveling is fun. It opens the eyes, massages the mind, soothes the soul. "He that has traveled acquires much cleverness."[3] But in the end we all want to get . . . home.

The world's religions all offer to lead us there. They do so by providing both a destination at the end and purpose and meaning along the way. These ultimate and immediate senses infuse, for example, Buddhism's saṃsāra-*sive*-nirvāṇa, and the New Testament's "eternal life," a concept concerned as much with the quality of life as with its duration.

Different religions posit different "homes" within this life, and some beyond it. Since several assume that the present is all we possess, they advocate attitudes and actions only for here and now. Others so value a proposed future that the now is all but ignored. Bin Laden described the difference between himself and his enemies, real or imagined, as "You value life; we value death." Or as Khalid Khawaja put it, "You value life, we consider worldly existence a transition."[4] If that is how someone thinks, present life can be discarded with little compunction. The traditional toast "l'chaim!" reflects an opposing mindset. Clearly, different ideologies propose disparate ideas on defining and enjoying—let alone reaching—home. We cannot pretend that under various facades all religions teach the same things; they do not. Increasingly, religious scholars urge that they do not. But neither does one faith alone promote truth and beauty, while lies and ugliness are all that others peddle. Valuable guidance may be found in all, though sometimes buried beneath débris.

A word about the objective nature of "home" and our route there. While both postmodernism in literature and philosophy and quantum mechanics in physics urge the crucial role of the observer, there still remains something "out there"—a preexisting text or physical reality. Any interpreter or scientist must conform her thoughts to this if she is to understand and articulate truth about it. Water is H_2O and neither H_2O_2 nor H_2SO_4 nor anything else, and she must recognize that should she wish to understand water and exploit its properties. Water is what it is, not what anyone dreams or wants it to be. Though we may not be able to know it exhaustively, we can know some things about it truly. Stating its chemical formula is therefore not a power play by chemists but a statement of reality. Mohandas Gāndhī was born in India on 02 October 1869, not in France on 25 July 1753. Two plus two equal four. What we seek is "true truth," *yathā-bhūta-ñāna-dassana,* "knowledge of things as they really are." We may concur with the Christians or the Buddhists that this is our goal without necessarily agreeing that either the gospel or the dharma captures it.

The idea of a route we must follow to understand and practice that truth, however, need not culminate in cookie-cutter conformity for humanity's billions. Anything that flies must obey the laws of aerodynamics, either intuitively or consciously, or it cannot remain aloft. But within the framework of those laws may be found an amazing array of both things that fly and manners of flying—from bumblebee to space shuttle to helicopter to mosquito to hawk. Similarly, a certain metaphysical and spiritual reality exists in this universe and is what it is. Human life must conform to that reality if it is to "fly." But that one framework supports a variety of legitimate expressions.

The primary job of an ideology, then, is to understand reality and encourage its adherents to embrace it. The universe is thus and not other. Religion's *first* function is not to make people feel good, though we may reasonably hope that peace and purpose will proceed from practicing truth. A good religion draws a map of the world the way it is, not the way its members want it to be. Only to the extent that it succeeds at this does it help the traveler find his way home. "[A]ny interference with the truth is immoral . . . So the Christian [or Buddhist or Muslim or atheist] . . . should not be inhibited in the smallest degree from following the line of truth."[5]

Some examples: Either there is or is not a transcendent, creator God. Either spacetime and matter/energy are all that exists, or there is more. Either God spoke to Muḥammad through Gabriel or he did not. Either Kṛṣṇa is an *avatāra* of Viṣṇu or he is not. Either one who dies in *jihād* is greeted in paradise by forty virgins or he is not. Either Jesus of Nazareth physically rose from the dead or he did not. These are not "ideas" or "values" or "beliefs" or "spiritual metaphors." These statements purport to describe the actual state of affairs. Neither what anyone believes about them, nor how many believe, nor how hard they believe, nor what belief makes them do makes these assertions either true or false. Belief may mold the believer's attitude and behavior, but attitudes and behaviors do not establish the veracity of what a believer believes.

Most if not all religions draw maps that prove helpful for at least one section of the path home. If they did not—if they taught nothing that corresponds with reality—few people could practice them very long. The accuracy of one quadrant, however, does not certify the correctness of the whole. Sometimes a smudged, torn, or distorted map provides at least a rough idea of the lay of the land and benefits a wanderer more than no guidance at all, though trusting incorrect details could culminate in reaching a cliff or quagmire. Maps are meant to represent and orient to the actual terrain; where they do not, the wise traveler opts for physical reality over printed misrepresentation. It might serve us well to recognize "that each philosophy has some truth to it and a wholly adequate philosophy will draw upon the positive resources which all of the other philosophies exploit."[6]

Each chapter of *Finding Home* proposes one metaphysical or spiritual reality of our universe, followed by explanatory and supportive passages from a selected world religion. Sometimes many faiths urge the chapter's proposal, in other cases only one or two. For example, many advocate similar ethical guidelines. But whereas Islam requires the existence of a transcendent God, Buddhism denies any such entity. So this book does not imply that all religions teach the same thing. They don't. *Finding Home* suggests, rather, that each draws a more or less reliable map of one section of the world as it is, and consequently of our path home.

The choice of which assertions to include is mine. These choices naturally reflect my own background, since no one thinks or writes with unbiased, detached objectivity. My roots grew and remain planted in Protestant Christian soil. It is therefore not surprising that the basic thesis of each chapter is Christian as well as (except for chapter 8) part of another faith. In this book, however, I try to allow the various religions to speak for themselves, not skewing them to say other than what they wish. My desire is that both author and readers can thus sample the truth, goodness, and beauty found in faiths other than their own. On some points I will agree with those faiths, on others agree with modifications, and on still others demur.

Where I do agree, it will not be because that faith's sacred Scripture endorses the chapter's assertion. Various religions invoke incompatible authorities—written and oral—to substantiate their claims. For Hindus the Vedas are *śruti*, "heard" from the gods and therefore infallible. Muslims believe the Qur'ān to surpass Jewish and Christian Scriptures, so definitively revealed that it cannot be translated. Cao Dai posits revelation from the spirit world. And on it goes. Since the world's faiths differ on core issues, not all can be true. But we still can read with profit what each says. If adherents of one faith refuse to even listen to another out of prior, uncritical commitment to their own, they can never hope to recognize any errors their system might embrace. Even a disastrously faulty faith will be clasped to the breast to the grave. Since there could thus be neither conversion nor modification nor enrichment nor confirmation, we may as well all go home and practice our prejudices in private. It is healthy, by contrast, to examine what one believes in the light of reality. If one's faith—Christian, Hindu, Sikh, Muslim—is true, it has nothing to fear from such testing; if deficient or false, the time to discover that is now. This approach does not deny the possibility that authoritative texts exist. It simply does not start with an a priori adoption of one.

Since one religion or another rejects the theses of most of these chapters, nothing compels us to accept any given one or the collage that emerges from collating them. Nevertheless, I believe the resultant map to be a reasonable representation of reality. Significant scholars through the centuries have urged its various assertions. What follows, then, is a map for the reader's consideration. Sometimes a religion was chosen to elaborate an idea because that faith articulates it in a unique, classic manner. On other occasions the idea represents the selected religion's central thesis. On still others several faiths speak similarly. However it may be, when stitched together these ideas suggest that *there is a home* that humanity can enjoy, both in this life and beyond, and *there is a path* to follow. *This* is who we are, and not that. *Here* is where we should try to be and go, and not there. But again, the objective existence of home and path neither requires nor urges a monochromatic, straitjacket uniformity for all of us. There is great room for and joy in variety—all within the parameters of the way we and the universe happen to be. One can fly in amazingly different ways, but each way must obey the laws of aerodynamics.[7]

Why the format of this book? Why so many lengthy readings from the core writings of the world religions? Several reasons. Reading them is part of our "traveling" process. Many adherents of one faith have never pondered the propositions of another—sometimes out of fear of getting drawn in, sometimes out of disinterest, sometimes out of not knowing where to start, sometimes out of inertia. Or if they have looked at anything, it has only been phrases snipped by their compatriots for critical or apologetic purposes. But it is good to get to know our neighbors, and doing so includes acquainting ourselves with what they believe. We need to give them a fair hearing—to listen to their faiths as they believe them, not as others (mis)represent them. How they say things can be as informative as what they say. We are stretched as we work through both a new set of ideas and a novel way of expressing them. In a day of sound bites and one-line zingers we should remember that ancient sages pondered long to understand life and the universe, so for us today it also might take effort to unearth life's nature and *summum bonum*.

> To read well, that is, to read true books in a true spirit, is a noble exercise, and one that will task the reader more than any exercise which the customs of the day esteem . . . That age will be rich indeed when those relics which we call Classics, and the still older and more than classic but even less known Scriptures of the nations, shall have still further accumulated, when the Vaticans shall be filled with Vedas and Zendavestas and Bibles, with Homers and Dantes and Shakespeares, and all the centuries to come shall have successively deposited their trophies in the forum of the world. By such a pile we may hope to scale heaven at last.[8]

Reading the world's religious literature perhaps need not precede scaling heaven. But acquaintance may at least encourage appropriate humility as we observe that, though we may not buy all they say, others outside our own faith communities express some true, interesting, and important ideas. Finally, "History, to be above evasion or dispute, must stand on documents, not on opinion."[9] The same is true if we substitute "Understanding of another's religion" for "History." On, then, to the documents.

The Tian Tan Buddha in Hong Kong.

1

THINGS COULD BE BETTER

(Theravāda)

In 1759 Voltaire published his popular *Candide.* The novel satirizes German philosopher Leibniz's notion that, despite all its ills, ours is the best of all possible worlds. Pangloss insists to Candide that Leibniz's optimism is true. However, after surviving multiple catastrophes, Candide rejects Pangloss's Pollyannaism. He retires to the country to tend a garden and live out a more realistic philosophy.

If today someone were to urge with Leibniz that divine providence peers beyond present pain to the paradise it will produce, he might nevertheless admit that for now life has its stresses and sorrows. These often arrive capriciously and remain interminably. To acknowledge this—let alone reiterate Candide's rejection—is simply to restate the first of four principles proposed centuries ago by Siddhārtha Gautama.

Son of a petty king in southern Nepal, Siddhārtha was raised in comfort. His father knew that the physical marks of greatness lay upon his son—he would become powerful either politically or spiritually—and preferred that Siddhārtha pursue the political option. In time, however, and particularly after seeing the suffering outside the palace walls, Siddhārtha's pampered life palled. He abandoned home and sought serenity in self-denial. Six years taught him that meaningful life is not the child of asceticism, just as it had not been born of plenty. The mendicant-prince sat under a fig tree and vowed there to remain until he awoke to the *true* nature of reality. Upon doing so Siddhārtha became the Awakened One, the Enlightened One, the Buddha. He summoned five *bhikkhus* who had followed him before his enlightenment, and for them he first set in motion the Wheel of Dhamma (that is, he preached his first sermon).

Four Noble Truths comprise the core of this sermon. These summarize the Buddha's understanding of the existence, origin, cessation, and path leading to the cessation of suffering, and they remain central to all forms of Buddhism practiced today. Here is the Buddha's exposition of the first of these—the Noble Truth of Suffering:

> And what, monks, is the Noble Truth of Suffering? Birth is suffering, ageing is suffering, death is suffering, sorrow, lamentation, pain, sadness and distress are suffering. Being attached to the unloved is suffering, being separated from the loved is suffering, not getting what one wants is suffering. In short, the five aggregates of grasping[10] are suffering.
>
> And what, monks, is birth? In whatever beings, of whatever group of beings, there is birth, coming-to-be, coming forth, the appearance of the aggregates, the acquisition of the sense-bases, that, monks, is called birth.
>
> And what is ageing? In whatever beings, of whatever group of beings, there is ageing, decrepitude, broken teeth, grey hair, wrinkled skin, shrinking with age, decay of the sense-faculties, that, monks is called ageing.
>
> And what is death? In whatever beings, of whatever group of beings, there is a passing-away, a removal, a cutting-off, a disappearance, a death, a dying, an ending, a cutting-off of the aggregates, a discarding of the body, that, monks is called death.
>
> And what is sorrow? Whenever, by any kind of misfortune, anyone is affected by something of a painful nature, sorrow, mourning, distress, inward grief, inward woe, that, monks is called sorrow.
>
> And what is lamentation? Whenever, by any kind of misfortune, anyone is affected by something of a painful nature and there is crying out, lamenting, making much noise for grief, making great lamentation, that, monks, is called lamentation.
>
> And what is pain? Whatever bodily painful feeling, bodily unpleasant feeling, painful or unpleasant feeling results from bodily contact, that, monks, is called pain.
>
> And what is sadness? Whatever mental painful feeling,

mental unpleasant feeling, painful or unpleasant sensation results from mental contact, that, monks, is called sadness.

And what is distress? Whenever, by any kind of misfortune, anyone is affected by something of a painful nature, distress, great distress, affliction with distress, with great distress, that, monks, is called distress.

And what, monks, is being attached to the unloved? Here, whoever has unwanted, disliked, unpleasant sight-objects, sounds, smells, tastes, tangibles or mind-objects, or whoever encounters ill-wishers, wishers of harm, of discomfort, of insecurity, with whom they have concourse, intercourse, connection, union, that, monks, is called being attached to the unloved.

And what is being separated from the loved? Here, whoever has what is wanted, liked, pleasant sight-objects, sounds, smells, tastes, tangibles or mind-objects, or whoever encounters well-wishers, wishers of good, of comfort, of security, mother or father or brother or sister or younger kinsmen or friends or colleagues or blood-relations, and then is deprived of such concourse, intercourse, connection, or union, that, monks, is called being separated from the loved.

And what, monks, is not getting what one wants? In beings subject to birth, monks, this wish arises: "Oh that we were not subject to birth, that we might not come to birth!" But this cannot be gained by wishing. That is not getting what one wants. In beings subject to ageing, to disease, to death, to sorrow, lamentation, pain, sadness and distress this wish arises: "Oh that we were not subject to ageing . . . distress, that we might not come to these things!" But this cannot be gained by wishing. That is not getting what one wants.

And how, monks, in short, are the five aggregates of grasping suffering? They are as follows: the aggregate of grasping that is form, the aggregate of grasping that is feeling, the aggregate of grasping that is perception, the aggregate of grasping that is the mental formations, the aggregate of grasping that is consciousness. These are, in short, the five aggregates of grasping that

> are suffering. And that, monks, is called the Noble Truth of Suffering.[11]

In the remaining three Noble Truths the Buddha proposes the reason why we suffer (because ignorance leads us to selfishly crave things and pleasures), the way we can stop suffering (recognize the true nature of reality and abandon such cravings), and the path that leads to the abandonment of cravings and cessation of suffering (the wisdom, morality, and meditation of the Noble Eightfold Path). The sūtra that reports the Buddha's first sermon underscores the importance of these Truths:

> "So long, bhikkhus, as my knowledge and vision of these Four Noble Truths as they really are in their three phases and twelve aspects was not thoroughly purified in this way, I did not claim to have awakened to the unsurpassed perfect enlightenment in this world with its devas, Māra, and Brahmā, in this generation with its ascetics and brahmins, its devas and humans. But when my knowledge and vision of these Four Noble Truths as they really are in their three phases and twelve aspects was thoroughly purified in this way, then I claimed to have awakened to the unsurpassed perfect enlightenment in this world with its devas, Māra, and Brahmā, in this generation with its ascetics and brahmins, its devas and humans. The knowledge and vision arose in me: 'Unshakable is the liberation of my mind. This is my last birth. Now there is no more renewed existence.'"
>
> This is what the Blessed One said. Elated, the bhikkhus of the group of five delighted in the Blessed One's statement. And while this discourse was being spoken, there arose in the Venerable Kondañña [sic] the dust-free, stainless vision of the Dhamma: "Whatever is subject to origination is all subject to cessation."
>
> And when the Wheel of the Dhamma had been set in motion by the Blessed One, the earth-dwelling devas raised a cry: "At Bārāṇasī, in the Deer Park at Isipatana, this unsurpassed Wheel of the Dhamma has been set in motion by the Blessed One, which cannot be stopped by any ascetic or brahmin or deva or Māra or Brahmā or by anyone in the world." Having heard the cry of the

> earth-dwelling devas, the devas of the realm of the Four Great Kings raised a cry: "At Bārāṇasī . . . this unsurpassed Wheel of the Dhamma has been set in motion by the Blessed One, which cannot be stopped . . . by anyone in the world." Having heard the cry of the devas of the realm of the Four Great Kings, the Tāvatiṃsa devas . . . the Yāma devas . . . the Tusita devas . . . the Nimmānaratī devas . . . the Paranimmitavasavattī devas . . . the devas of Brahmā's company raised a cry: "At Bārāṇasī, in the Deer Park at Isipatana, this unsurpassed Wheel of the Dhamma has been set in motion by the Blessed One, which cannot be stopped by any ascetic or brahmin or deva or Māra or Brahmā or by anyone in the world."
>
> Thus at that moment, at that instant, at that second, the cry spread as far as the brahmā world, and this ten thousandfold world system shook, quaked, and trembled, and an immeasurable glorious radiance appeared in the world surpassing the divine majesty of the devas.
>
> Then the Blessed One uttered this inspired utterance: "Koṇḍañña has indeed understood! Koṇḍañña has indeed understood!" In this way the Venerable Koṇḍañña acquired the name "Aññā Koṇḍañña—Koṇḍañña Who Has Understood."[12]

This first sermon clearly focuses upon suffering—its pervasiveness and cure. For the next forty-five years the Buddha reiterated his proposals in many ways to multitudes of people. To the consternation of his followers, because of this preoccupation he often declined to discuss metaphysics. On one occasion the *bhikkhu* Mālunkyāputta chafed over the Buddha's refusal to do so and threatened to abandon monastic life. The Buddha replied:

> "How then, Mālunkyāputta, did I ever say to you: 'Come, Mālunkyāputta, lead the holy life under me and I will declare to you "the world is eternal" . . . or "after death a Tathāgata neither exists nor does not exist"'?'—"No, venerable sir."—"Did you ever tell me: 'I will lead the holy life under the Blessed One, and the Blessed One will declare to me "the world is eternal" . . . or "after death a Tathāgata neither exists nor does not

exist'"?"—"No, venerable sir."—"That being so, misguided man, who are you and what are abandoning? . . .

"Suppose, Mālunkyāputta, a man were wounded by an arrow thickly smeared with poison, and his friends and companions, his kinsmen and relatives, brought a surgeon to treat him. The man would say: 'I will not let the surgeon pull out this arrow until I know whether the man who wounded me was a noble or a brahmin or a merchant or a worker.' And he would say: 'I will not let the surgeon pull out this arrow until I know the name and clan of the man who wounded me; . . . until I know whether the man who wounded me was tall or short or of middle height; . . . until I know whether the man who wounded me was dark or brown or golden-skinned; . . . until I know whether the man who wounded me lives in such a village or town or city; . . . until I know whether the bow that wounded me was a long bow or a crossbow; . . . until I know whether the bowstring that wounded me was fibre or reed or sinew or hemp or bark; . . . until I know whether the shaft that wounded me was wild or cultivated; . . . until I know with what kind of feathers the shaft that wounded me was fitted—whether those of a vulture or a heron or a hawk or a peacock or a stork; . . . until I know with what kind of sinew the shaft that wounded me was bound—whether that of an ox or a buffalo or a deer or a monkey; . . . until I know what kind of arrowhead it was that wounded me—whether spiked or razor-tipped or curved or barbed or calf-toothed or lancet-shaped.'

"All this would still not be known to that man and meanwhile he would die. So too, Mālunkyāputta, if anyone should say thus: 'I will not lead the holy life under the Blessed One until the Blessed One declares to me: "the world is eternal" . . . or "after death a Tathāgata neither exists nor does not exist,"' that would still remain undeclared by the Tathāgata and meanwhile that person would die. . . .

"Therefore, Mālunkyāputta, remember what I have left undeclared as undeclared, and remember what I have declared as declared. And what have I left undeclared? 'The world is

> eternal'—I have left undeclared. 'The world is not eternal'—I have left undeclared. 'The world is finite'—I have left undeclared. 'The world is infinite'—I have left undeclared. 'The soul is the same as the body'—I have left undeclared. 'The soul is one thing and the body another'—I have left undeclared. 'After death a Tathāgata exists'—I have left undeclared. 'After death a Tathāgata does not exist'—I have left undeclared. 'After death a Tathāgata both exists and does not exist'—I have left undeclared. 'After death a Tathāgata neither exists nor does not exist'—I have left undeclared.
>
> "Why have I left that undeclared? Because it is unbeneficial, it does not belong to the fundamentals of the holy life, it does not lead to disenchantment, to dispassion, to cessation, to peace, to direct knowledge, to enlightenment, to Nibbāna. That is why I have left it undeclared.
>
> "And what have I declared? 'This is suffering'—I have declared. 'This is the origin of suffering'—I have declared. 'This is the cessation of suffering'—I have declared. 'This is the way leading to the cessation of suffering'—I have declared.
>
> "Why have I declared that? Because it is beneficial, it belongs to the fundamentals of the holy life, it leads to disenchantment, to dispassion, to cessation, to peace, to direct knowledge, to enlightenment, to Nibbāna. That is why I have declared it.
>
> "Therefore, Mālunkyāputta, remember what I have left undeclared as undeclared, and remember what I have declared as declared."
>
> That is what the Blessed One said. The venerable Mālunkyāputta was satisfied and delighted in the Blessed One's words.[13]

Similarly, Sunakkhatta decided to leave monastic life because the Buddha performed no miracles. The latter responded that these were unrelated to his main message:

> "What do you think, Sunakkhatta? Whether miracles are performed or not—is it the purpose of my teaching Dhamma

> to lead whoever practises it to the total destruction of suffering?" "It is, Lord." "So, Sunakkhatta, whether miracles are performed or not, the purpose of my teaching Dhamma is to lead whoever practises it to the total destruction of suffering. Then what purpose would the performance of miracles serve?"[14]

The Buddha's single-minded preoccupation with suffering and its cure prompts some, when they first hear of his teaching, to conclude that it is pessimistic. That is not how Buddhists understand it.

> The First Noble Truth *(Dukkha-ariyasacca)* is generally translated by almost all scholars as "The Noble Truth of Suffering," and it is interpreted to mean that life according to Buddhism is nothing but suffering and pain. Both translation and interpretation are highly unsatisfactory and misleading. It is because of this limited, free and easy translation, and its superficial interpretation, that many people have been misled into regarding Buddhism as pessimistic.
>
> First of all, Buddhism is neither pessimistic nor optimistic. If anything at all, it is realistic, for it takes a realistic view of life and of the world. It looks at thing objectively *(yathābhūtaṃ)*. It does not falsely lull you into living in a fool's paradise, nor does it frighten and agonize you with all kinds of imaginary fears and sins. It tells you exactly and objectively what you are and what the world around you is, and shows you the way to perfect freedom, peace, tranquillity and happiness.
>
> One physician may gravely exaggerate an illness and give up hope altogether. Another may ignorantly declare that there is no illness and that no treatment is necessary, thus deceiving the patient with a false consolation. You may call the first one pessimistic and the second optimistic. Both are equally dangerous. But a third physician diagnoses the symptoms correctly, understands the cause and the nature of the illness, sees clearly that it can be cured, and courageously administers a course of treatment, thus saving his patient. The Buddha is like the last

physician. He is the wise and scientific doctor for the ills of the world (*Bhisakka* or *Bhaiṣajya-guru*).

It is true that the Pāli word *dukkha* (or Sanskrit *duḥkha*) in ordinary usage means "suffering," "pain," "sorrow" or "misery," as opposed to the word *sukha* meaning "happiness," "comfort" or "ease." But the term *dukkha* as the First Noble Truth, which represents the Buddha's view of life and the world, has a deeper philosophical meaning and connotes enormously wider senses. It is admitted that the term *dukkha* in the First Noble Truth contains, quite obviously, the ordinary meaning of "suffering," but in addition it also includes deeper ideas such as "imperfection," "impermanence," "emptiness," "insubstantiality." It is difficult therefore to find one word to embrace the whole conception of the term *dukkha* as the First Noble Truth, and so it is better to leave it untranslated, than to give an inadequate and wrong idea of it by conveniently translating it as "suffering" or "pain."

The Buddha does not deny happiness in life when he says there is suffering. On the contrary he admits different forms of happiness, both material and spiritual, for laymen as well as for monks. In the *Aṅguttara-nikāya*, one of the five original Collections in Pāli containing the Buddha's discourses, there is a list of happinesses (*sukhāni*), such as the happiness of family life and the happiness of the life of a recluse, the happiness of sense pleasures and the happiness of renunciation, the happiness of attachment and the happiness of detachment, physical happiness and mental happiness etc. But all these are included in *dukkha*. Even the very pure spiritual states of *dhyāna* (*recueillement* or trance) attained by the practice of higher meditation, free from even a shadow of suffering in the accepted sense of the word, states which may be described as unmixed happiness, as well as the state of *dhyāna* which is free from sensations both pleasant (*sukha*) and unpleasant (*dukkha*) and is only pure equanimity and awareness—even these very high spiritual states are included in *dukkha*. In one of the *suttas* of the *Majjhima-nikāya*, (again one of the five original Collections), after praising the spiritual happiness of these *dhyānas*,

> the Buddha says that they are "impermanent, *dukkha,* and subject to change" (*aniccā dukkhā vipariṇāmadhammā*). Notice that the word *dukkha* is explicitly used. It is *dukkha,* not because there is "suffering" in the ordinary sense of the word, but because "whatever is impermanent is *dukkha*" (*yad aniccaṃ taṃ dukkhaṃ*).
>
> The Buddha was realistic and objective. He says, with regard to life and the enjoyment of sense-pleasures, that one should clearly understand three things: (1) attraction or enjoyment (*assāda*), (2) evil consequence or danger or unsatisfactoriness (*ādīnava*), and (3) freedom or liberation (*nissaraṇa*). When you see a pleasant, charming and beautiful person, you like him (or her), you are attracted, you enjoy seeing that person again and again, you derive pleasure and satisfaction from that person. This is enjoyment (*assāda*). It is a fact of experience. But this enjoyment is not permanent, just as that person and all his (or her) attractions are not permanent either. When the situation changes, when you cannot see that person, when you are deprived of this enjoyment, you become sad, you may become unreasonable and unbalanced, you may even behave foolishly. This is the evil, unsatisfactory and dangerous side of the picture (*ādīnava*). This, too, is a fact of experience. Now if you have no attachment to the person, if you are completely detached, that is freedom, liberation (*nissaraṇa*). These three things are true with regard to all enjoyment in life.
>
> From this it is evident that it is no question of pessimism or optimism, but that we must take account of the pleasures of life as well as of its pains and sorrows, and also of freedom from them, in order to understand life completely and objectively. Only then is true liberation possible.[15]

When the Buddha examines suffering in his Four Noble Truths, he intends neither to deny that life has pleasures nor to sink into cynicism. His assessment is not pessimistic but realistic: this is simply the way things are. Suffering is "the central problem of human existence."[16] Whether or not we adopt his analysis of its root cause and cure, we can probably agree that even life's finest moments are often tinged with wistfulness, unfulfillment, *frustration, unsatisfactoriness.*

> "Toward the midpoint of life's way," as Dante says, I reached what proved a crisis. Everything I had lived for—literature, music, writing, good friends, the joys of teaching—had ceased to satisfy. Not that my enjoyment of these things was less; in fact, I had every innocent source of joy the world offered. But I found myself thirsting for something more, much more, without knowing what or why.[17]

No recognition, experience, or object ultimately satisfies. Tugging at our coattails when we get what we crave is often the longing—as Rockefeller sighed—for "just a little more." Things could be better because things do not satisfy, and we wish they did. Things could be better because every day we experience painful sensations, separations, and associations. Not only do external earthquakes, wars, and injustice assail us, but also internal doubts, depression, and discontent.

This is not only how things are, but also perhaps the way they must be. Suffering/*duḥkha*/unsatisfactoriness may provide the necessary backdrop to peace/joy/contentment:

> We are all tempted to go to a place where there is no suffering, where there is only peace and happiness. You may be tempted to consider that the Kingdom of Heaven is such a place, that the Pure Land is such a place. We tend to believe that there is a place where we can go by abandoning, or leaving behind, this world full of suffering, confusion, and pollution. The pollutions that afflict us are anger and hatred, despair, sorrow and fear. When you suffer so much, the tendency to want to leave it behind becomes very strong. I don't want to be here any more, I want to get out. "Stop the world, I want to get off."
>
> Look deeply and you will touch the fact that happiness and well-being cannot be separated from suffering and ill-being. This is the interbeing nature of happiness and suffering. There

> is an illusion to be removed—that happiness can be without suffering, that well-being can be without ill-being, that right can be without left.
>
> If you don't know what hunger is, you would never know the pleasant feeling of having something to eat. Do you prefer not to have any moments of being hungry at all? Or, do you prefer sometimes to be hungry in order to be able to enjoy eating some bread, some butter, some muesli? Imagine someone who is never hungry; he or she has no desire to eat at all. Why do you eat when you are not hungry? I think you like to preserve the privilege of being hungry from time to time so you may enjoy the joy of eating. If you are not thirsty, then the drinks are not appealing to you, even Coca-Cola! If you don't suffer, you would not know what happiness is.
>
> I think we need some suffering, all of us, in order to appreciate the happiness that is available to us. You should know that breathing in and out, for many of us, is a wonderful thing. If you have an asthma crisis, if you have a stuffed-up nose, if you have a lung infection, if you are caught in a room with no fresh air, then you know the joy of being in the open air, with your lungs still in good condition, with your nose free. You enjoy walking then and breathing, in and out. Breathing in and out and walking can be very enjoyable.
>
> To have two feet strong enough to run and walk around is also a great joy. There are times when you have a broken leg, when you have a sprained ankle, or when you are very sick. The outside seems very tempting, but you cannot get up and go out. You cannot run or walk. In these moments of suffering, you know that walking is a joy, that breathing is a joy, and just looking at the blue sky is a joy. We all need some amount of suffering in order to be able to appreciate the well-being and happiness that are available to us. You need the darkness in order to appreciate the beautiful morning.[18]

To sum up, Theravāda urges that everything is either tinged or permeated with *duḥkha*. Nothing ultimately satisfies. Nothing has an independent self that lasts and does not change. Revered Thai monk Buddhadāsa Bhikkhu therefore concluded that "[t]here is nothing that we should want to get, to have, to be. In short: Nothing is worth getting. Nothing is worth being." Instead, we should develop an "indifference to all phenomena."[19]

Many Buddhists, to say nothing of outsiders, question Buddhadāsa's conclusion. They prefer pleasure to pain, the savory to the insipid, art over graffiti, action to indifference. But most will agree that alongside life's joys we often experience pain, injustice, and separation. Buddhism proposes one understanding of *duḥkha*'s cause and cure; other faiths suggest different ones. But in this at least the Theravādists are right—suffering infuses our lives. Things could be better.

The name Allah prominently adorns the wall of the Sheik Zayed Grand Mosque in Abu Dhabi.

2

WORTH KNOWING

(Islam)

Because things could be better, many disbelieve in God. After all, if God exists, and especially if he is powerful and loving, why so much suffering and death? Why tornados, AIDS, and injustice? The existence of God may seem a curious proposal to follow the notion that things could be better. Certainly the Theravāda that drew attention to *duḥkha* in chapter 1 denies the deity now proposed in chapter 2:

> What is the Buddhist answer to this question? Was the Buddha a Theist, an Atheist, an Agnostic or a Positivist? The answer is fairly clear. Given the above definition of God in its usual interpretation [a Personal Creator God, who is a Supreme being possessed of the characteristics of omniscience, omnipotence and infinite goodness], the Buddha is an atheist and Buddhism in both its Theravāda and Mahāyāna forms is atheism.[20]

The existence of evil and suffering is not the only reason people question God's existence. Many, particularly within the scientific community, urge that the universe is explicable without appealing to a transcendent deity and that no incontrovertible evidence proves he exists:

> I believe that a physical system is completely determined by the arrangement of its particles. Tell me how the particles making up the earth, the sun, the galaxy, and everything else are arranged, and you've fully articulated reality. This reductionist

> view is common among physicists, but there are certainly people who think otherwise. Especially when it comes to life, some believe that an essential non-physical aspect (spirit, soul, life force, chi, and so on) is required to animate the physical. Although I remain open to this possibility, I've never encountered any evidence to support it. The position that makes the most sense to me is that one's physical and mental characteristics are nothing but a manifestation of how the particles in one's body are arranged. Specify the particle arrangement and you've specified everything.[21]

So although most faiths would agree with chapter 1 that Things Could Be Better, some debate chapter 2's assertion that God Exists and Is Worth Knowing. Theravāda particularly demurs.

The West often distinguishes religious from scientific or historical assertions. Religion and science are said to operate in distinct spheres and employ diverse means of verification. Assertions from both can therefore be considered "true" even if they appear unrelated or contradictory. Such an approach produces problems. As already suggested, in matters of objective reality there can be only one correct answer to any given question. In objective issues, what is true for one person must be true for all. Certainly life asks many subjective questions whose answers vary from individual to individual ("How do you feel?" "What is the most exciting sport? the best music? the finest food?"). But in matters of objective reality ("How much is two plus two?" "By what process does the sun produce energy?" "Does the earth rest on the back of a great turtle?"), only one answer corresponds to the way things are. Even if no answer can be given that perfectly explains all details (e.g., to the question "How does the sun produce energy?"), some answers are right as far as they go, and others wrong ("By fusing hydrogen nuclei into helium nuclei" is right, though many more details could be given; "By oxidizing some combustible material" is wrong).

Of all the religions that urge God's existence, none does so at a more foundational level than does Islam. The first of Islam's five pillars is its *shahādah*—"I bear witness that there is no god but God, and Muḥammad is His Apostle." Non-Muslims may demur regarding the second phrase and question specifics the Qur'ān ascribes to The God (*al-Ilāh*, contracted to

Allāh) in the first. But setting aside whether Allah can be equated, for example, with Yahweh of the Tanakh or the Father of Jesus in the New Testament, we find at the core of the Qur'ān a single, unique, omnipotent, omniscient, righteous-yet-merciful creator God. God's oneness or uniqueness (*tawḥīd*) is particularly important in Islam; associating other deities or "partners" with him (*shirk*) is among the most grievous of errors. Repeatedly, then, the Qur'ān asserts the existence of the one God and proceeds to describe His attributes:[22]

> And your God is One God: there is no god but He,
> Most Gracious, Most Merciful 2.163
> the Living, the Self-subsisting, Eternal 2.255; 3.2
> the Exalted in Might, the Wise 3.6, 18, 62
> the Creator of all things 6.102
> who has produced you from the earth and settled you therein 11.61
> all things He comprehends in His knowledge 20.98
> the Lord of the Throne of Honor! 23.116
> Lord of the Throne Supreme! 27.26
> To Him be praise, at the first and at the last 28.70
> Everything (that exists) will perish except His own Face 28.88
> Supreme and Irresistible,—the Lord of the heavens and the earth, and all between,—exalted in Might, able to enforce His Will, forgiving again and again 38.65–66
> Who forgives Sin, accepts Repentance, is Strict in Punishment, and has a Long Reach (in all things). There is no god but He: to Him is the Final Goal 40.3
> Who gives life and gives death,—the Lord and Cherisher to you and your earliest ancestors 44.8.

God does more than exist. He created in the past, observes people's actions in the present, and will impartially recompense in the future. God's judgment will be based on his comprehensive vision and absolute justice, yet tempered by his mercy:

> God is never unjust in the least degree 4.40
> Verily God will not deal unjustly with man in anything 10.44

Not one will your Lord treat with injustice 18.49
God . . . brings to light what is hidden in the heavens and the earth, and knows what you hide and what you reveal 27.25
"O my son!" (said Luqmān), "If there be (but) the weight of a mustard seed and it were (hidden) in a rock, or (anywhere) in the heavens or on earth, God will bring it forth: for God understands the finest mysteries, (and) is well-acquainted (with them)." 31.16
To God belongs all that is in the heavens and on earth. Whether you show what is in your minds or conceal it, God calls you to account for it 2.284
He declares the Truth, and He is the best of judges 6.57
God takes careful account of all things 4.86
We shall set up scales of justice for the day of Judgment, so that not a soul will be dealt with unjustly in the least. And if there be (no more than) the weight of a mustard seed, we will bring it (to account): and enough are We to take account 21.47
God is Exalted in Power—the Lord of Retribution 14.47
Fear God, and know that God is strict in punishment 2.196, 211; 3.11; 5.2; 8.25
Those who believe and work righteous deeds,—from them shall We blot out all evil (that may be) in them, and We shall reward them according to the best of their deeds 29.7

As this last *āyah* suggests, God is merciful and forgiving as well as just. Repeatedly the Qur'ān describes God as "Most Merciful" (*Ar Raḥīm*) and "Oft-Forgiving" (*Al Ghafūr*). These traits must be included in any fair description of how the Qur'ān depicts God's justice.

A key Qur'ānic description of God may be found in *Āyat al Kursī*, the "Verse of the Throne" (2.255):

God! There is no god
But He,—the Living,
The Self-Subsisting, Eternal.
No slumber can seize Him

Nor sleep. His are all things
In the heavens and on earth.
Who is there who can intercede
In His presence except
As He permits? He knows
What (appears to His creatures
as) Before or After
Or Behind them.
Nor shall they compass
Aught of His knowledge
Except as He wills.
His Throne extends
Over the heavens
And the earth, and He feels
No fatigue in guarding
And preserving them,
For He is the Most High,
The Supreme (in glory).

Another may be found in 59.22–4:

God is He, than Whom
There is no other god;—
Who knows (all things)
Both secret and open;
He, Most Gracious,
Most Merciful.
God is he, than Whom
There is no other god;—
the Sovereign, the Holy One,
the Source of Peace (and Perfection),
the Guardian of Faith,
the Preserver of Safety,
the Exalted in Might,
the Irresistible, the Supreme:
Glory to God!

> (High is He)
> Above the partners
> They attribute to Him.
> He is God, the Creator,
> The Evolver,
> The Bestower of Forms
> (or Colors).
> To Him belong
> The Most Beautiful Names.
> Whatever is in
> The heavens and on earth
> Declares
> His Praises and Glory:
> and He is the Exalted
> In Might, the Wise.

One short *sūra* (112) devotes itself to God's unity:

> Say: He is God,
> The One and Only;
> God, the Eternal, Absolute;
> He does not beget,
> Nor is he begotten;
> And there is none
> Like unto Him.

God's nature has been discussed for centuries by Muslim theologians.[23] But perhaps God is more to be revered and obeyed than analyzed and defined. After all, *islām* means "peaceful surrender" or "submission" to the will of God; and a *muslim* is "one who submits."

As suggested in sūra 56 above, Islam ascribes to God ninety-nine "most beautiful names" (*al-asmā' al-ḥusnā*). In meditating on these, believers come to grasp who God is and so find comfort and strength: "[God] guides to himself those who turn to him in penitence, those who believe, and whose hearts find satisfaction in the remembrance of God, for without doubt in the remembrance of God do hearts find satisfaction" (13.27b–28). Those who memorize the names will enter paradise. Many of the faithful use a "rosary" of ninety-nine beads as an aid to repeating them. Although there is not strict uniformity on the identification (or even number) of these names, a typical list includes these:

Allāh	Allah; The Greatest Name
Ar-Raḥmān	The Compassionate, The Gracious
Ar-Raḥīm	The Merciful
Al-Malik	The King; The Absolute Ruler
Al-Quddūs	The Holy One
As-Salām	The Sound One; The Bestower of Peace
Al-Mu'min	The Granter of Security; The Inspirer of Faith
Al-Muhaymin	The Guardian
Al-'Aziz	The Mighty; The Victorious
Al-Jabbār	The Compeller
Al-Mutakabbir	The Greatest
Al-Khāliq	The Creator
Al-Bāri'	The Maker of Order
Al-Muṣawwir	The Bestower of Form; The Shaper of Beauty
Al-Ghaffār	The Forgiver
Al-Qahhār	The Subduer
Al-Wahhāb	The One Who Gives Freely
Ar-Razzāq	The Sustainer; The Provider
Al-Fattāh	The Opener
Al-'Alīm	The All-Knowing
Al-Qābiḍ	The Withholder
Al-Bāsiṭ	The Expender; The Reliever
Al-Khāfiḍ	The Abaser
Ar-Rāfi'	The Exalter
Al-Mu'izz	The Bestower of Honor
Al-Mudhill	The Humiliator
As-Samī'	The All-Hearing
Al-Basīr	The All-Seeing

Al-Ḥakam	The Judge
Al-'Adl	The Just; The Equitable
Al-Laṭīf	The Subtle One; The Gentle
Al-Khabīr	The All-Aware
Al-Ḥalīm	The Forbearing
Al-'Aẓīm	The Magnificent; The Incomparably Great
Al-Ghafūr	The Forgiving; The Hider of Faults
Ash-Shakūr	The Rewarder of Thankfulness
Al-'Alī	The Most High
Al-Kabīr	The Greatest; The Grand One
Al-Ḥafīz	The Preserver
Al-Muqīt	The Nourisher; The Sustainer
Al-Ḥasīb	The Accounter; He Who Satisfies Creation's Needs
Al-Jalīl	The Mighty; The Sublime
Al-Karīm	The Generous
Ar-Raqīb	The Watchful
Al-Mujīb	The Responsive
Al-Wāsi'	The All-Encompassing
Al-Ḥakīm	The Wise
Al-Wadūd	The Loving One
Al-Majīd	The Most Glorious
Al-Bā'ith	The Resurrector
Ash-Shahīd	The Witness
Al-Ḥaqq	The Truth; The Real One
Al-Wakīl	The Trustee; The Dispenser of Affairs
Al-Qawī	The Most Strong
Al-Matīn	The Forceful; The Firm; The Authoritative
Al-Walī	The Governor; The Protector; The Patron
Al-Ḥamīd	The Praised One; The Praiseworthy
Al-Muḥṣī	The Appraiser
Al-Mubdī'	The Originator

Al-Mu'īd	The Restorer (to Life)
Al-Muḥyī	The Giver of Life
Al-Mumīt	The Taker of Life
Al-Ḥayy	The Ever-Living One
Al-Qayyūm	The Self-Existing One
Al-Wājid	The Self-Sufficient; The All-Perceiving; The Finder
Al-Mājid	The Glorious
Al-Aḥad or Al-Wāḥid	The One
Aṣ-Ṣamad	The Satisfier of All Needs
Al-Qādir	The Omnipotent; He Who Does What He Wills
Al-Muqtadir	The Powerful
Al-Muqaddim	The Expediter; The One Who Causes to Be Near Him
Al-Mu'akhkhir	The Delayer; The One Who Causes to Be Far From Him
Al-Awwal	The First
Al-Ākhir	The Last
Aẓ-Ẓāhir	The Manifest One
Al-Bāṭin	The Hidden One
Al-Wālī	The Protector; The One Who Has Charge Over All
Al-Muta'ālī	The Most Exalted; The Supreme
Al-Barr	The Source and Doer of Good
At-Tawwāb	The Granter and Accepter of Repentance
Al-Muntaqim	The Avenger
Al-'Afū	The Forgiver
Ar-Ra'ūf	The Clement; The Most Kind
Mālik al-Mulk	The Owner of All
Dhū-l-Jalāl wa-l-Ikrām	The Lord of Majesty and Bounty
Al-Muqsiṭ	The Just; The Equitable
Al-Jāmi'	The Gatherer
Al-Ghanī	The Rich
Al-Mughnī	The Enricher

Al-Māni‘	The Preventer of Harm
Aḍ-Ḍārr	The Creator of the Harmful; The Afflicter
An-Nāfi‘	The Creator of Good; The Benefiter
An-Nūr	The Light
Al-Hādī	The Guide
Al-Badī‘	The Originator; The Matchless One
Al-Bāqī	The Everlasting One
Al-Wārith	The Inheritor of All
Ar-Rashīd	The Righteous Teacher; the Guide
Aṣ-Ṣabūr	The Patient One

The centrality of God for Muslims is evident in their recitation of the *basmala*[24] before doing or saying anything significant: "In the name of God, Most Gracious, Most Merciful." They often qualify assertions with *in shā'a Allāh,* "if God wills." Consequently

> it would be difficult to observe a more thorough manifestation of devotion to God than is evinced by the followers of Islam. No other religion appears to inculcate as much dependence on God in the trivia of daily life; nor does God figure so centrally among other religious groups in the ups and downs of ordinary living. Indeed, no task, commitment, performance, journey, or repose, however minute or momentous, pleasurable or unpleasurable, is undertaken without first invoking the name of Allah.[25]

Perhaps "over 90 percent of Muslim theology is concerned with Allah as the one real God who is indivisible in nature."[26] One can be a nontheistic Hindu; some Jews deny any deity; Thomas J. J. Altizer recently updated his 1966 *Gospel of Christian Atheism.* But it seems impossible to be a Muslim and not believe in God.

Some observers have thought that Muslims appear more occupied with law or what God commands than with God himself. To put it another way, such observers suggest that some Muslims have expended more intellectual energy on studying the *sunnah* of the Prophet than on understanding the nature of God.[27] But the Qur'ān and Ḥadīth are far more than legal codes.

God himself is central, not only as a theoretical underpinning for all Islam's laws and regulations, but as a personal entity whom people can to some degree know, with whom they can relate, and whom they can love. "[A]ny starting point for revitalizing the world of Islam must begin with Muslims' connection with the transcendent reality which lies at the heart of the message of Islam" since there is a deep-rooted "sense of the sacred which the allegiance to the religion of Islam implies."[28]

Abū Ḥāmid al-Ghazālī (1058–1111) was one of Islam's greatest philosophers, theologians, jurists, and mystics. He has been called the Proof of Islam (*ḥujjat al-Islām*), the Ornament of Faith (*zain al-dīn*), and the Renewer of Religion (*mujaddid*). Al-Ghazālī arguably has exerted on Islam an impact greater than any person other than Muḥammad, and is the only teacher Muslims have equated with the four great Imams.[29] His importance continues today—his *Iḥyā' 'ulūm al-din* (*The Revival of the Religious Sciences*), widely regarded as the greatest work of Muslim spirituality, is perhaps the most read work in the Muslim world after the Qur'ān,[30] "the most-quoted Muslim text after the Quran and the hadith,"[31] and still serves as a standard theological expression of Sunni Islam.

The opening lengthy chapter of *Revival*, "Acquisition of Knowledge," demonstrates that al-Ghazālī was not an irrationalist who denigrated thought, study, and learning.[32] By contrast, he criticized blind acceptance of authority and was willing to entertain doubt. Therefore his detailed discussion of love for God in Book IV of *Revival*, and the value he assigned to it, do not stem from mindless creedalism:

> Know, O dear readers, that love of God is the last stage and the highest in rank[.] There is no higher stage after acquisition of love of God. Before it, there are the stages of repentance, patience and renunciation. These are preliminaries to love of God. Though it is difficult to enter the region of love, it is possible for human mind to be filled up with God's love as a result of firm faith. To believe in God's love is difficult, even some learned men thought it impossible. They say that it means to be engaged in divine worship. They say that love grows for a being of equal status and hence God's love is impossible.
>
> Know O readers, that all the Ulema or learned men are unanimous that Love of God and His Apostle is compulsory.

If there [is] no existence of such love, how is it compulsory? To obey injunction, is the fruit of love but the birth of the tree of love is necessary before getting fruit . . .

Know, O readers, that pleasure comes out of appreciation. There are innumerable natures of man and every nature has got its own taste and pleasure. To get the object for which a nature has been created is the meaning of taste. These natures have been given to man with a set purpose and not in vain. For instance, the nature of anger is to take revenge. The greed for food has been created to earn food as it is food that preserves the body. Eyes get pleasure from beautiful sight, ear from sweet sound and nose from sweet scent. So there are different tastes and pleasures for different organs.

Similarly soul has got a nature which is termed divine light. God says: He whose breast God has expanded for Islam remains upon divine light. Some say that it is intellect, some say it is secret ins[i]ght, some say it is light of certainty of faith. There is no meaning of engagement with these names. Soul can be separated from its special attributes which is outside the five senses and unimaginable as the creation of the world is uniimaginable [sic]. The nature of that soul is termed by us as intellect by which man is differentiated from beasts and by which spiritual experience can be gained. So the nature of intellect is Marfat or spiritual knowledge of God. In this there lies its pleasure, just as good sight is the pleasure of eye and sweet sound is the pleasure of ear.

The pleasure which is found in spiritual knowledge is not found in the knowledge of other things . . . The more is the honour of the acquainted thing, the more is the taste and pleasure . . . God is the most high and the most honourable. So the pleasure gained by the pursuit of His attributes is the greatest. So divine knowledge is the best of all kinds of knowledge. It is thus proved that the best and highest pleasure can be obtained by the pursuit of knowledge relating to God and His attributies [sic]. It is many times more than the pleasure gained by satisfaction of lust or greed by the sense organs.

> Pleasure differs in respect of difference of objects. For instance there is difference in the pleasure of cohabitation and songs. Then again there is difference in the cohabitation of a young man and that of an old man. Again pleasure is of two kinds, external pleasure gained by five sense organs and internal pleasure as power, victory, honour which are outside the pleasure of the five sense organs. It is also true that one likes power of rule more than delicious foods, but a boy will certainly like delicious foods more than power of rule. Similarly the pleasure of spiritual knowledge of God and search of His attributes are more to some men than the pleasure of power of rule. God says: Nobody knows what pleasure pleasing to the eyes lies in store for him. The Prophet said: God prepared for the righteous servants such happiness as no eye has seen, no ear has heard and no heart of man has conceived. But now he will not understand it. He who has got this spiritual pleasure immerses himself in the sea of Marfat and gives up all earthly powers, name and fame, treasures and riches, as he knows that all these earthly things will vanish and He will ever remain. He will one day have to give up these earthly pleasures by the event of death. When his sight goes out of these things limited by space, his sight then knows no distance. At that time the agnostic [sic] searches such a paradise as covers the whole earth and heaven.[33]

Understanding God necessarily precedes loving him: "Without acquaintance and understanding, love does not take form . . ." People should worship God not because they fear hell or desire paradise, but because they recognize who he is and therefore love him. Spiritual pleasure is a sign of maturity, not of credulity or weakness. A boy takes pleasure in sports; a young man in cohabiting with women; the more mature in power, name, and fame; the most seasoned in spiritual pleasure. This last person will gladly abandon the earlier pursuits for spiritual pleasure, though the younger will laugh at him or her for doing so. The greater one's spiritual knowledge (*marfat*, or perhaps *ma'rifah*) of God in this world, the more he will appreciate the beauty of God in the next, and the more fortunate he will be there. Love for God can be stimulated by severing all worldly connections, removing from the mind love of things other than God, and increasing the power of *marfat* and extending it over the entire heart.

People often fail to see God not because he isn't there or because the evidence for his existence is weak, but because his light is too strong. There is in fact good evidence for God: "He who looks at the writing on a paper knows the existence of a writer. The heaven and earth and what is therein are the writings of that Great Writer with the pen of power. He loves God and knows Him through His works."

An early love for God may fade should one later mix with corrupt society. God loves the one who loves him. Love for God and love for the world cannot coexist. Signs that an individual loves God include: 1) delight in meeting with Him (and therefore welcoming death), 2) sacrificing dear things for God, 3) giving oneself to *zikr* (remembrance of God, often involving recalling his names), 4) serving God in solitude, 5) sorrow at the inability to remember God always, 6) feeling happiness and not tiredness in divine service, 7) loving all people who are obedient to God, 8) remaining fearful (i.e., remembering the nobility of God and revering him), 9) keeping love for God secret (i.e., neither flaunting nor taking pride in it), and 10) satisfaction and contentment.[34]

Love of God is thus the greatest good for al-Ghazālī. It grows out of a right knowledge of who he is, but even more out of personal experience of Him. Genuine love for God results in obedience.[35]

Belief in a single high God is not confined to Islam and other monotheistic religions such as Judaism, Christianity, and Sikhism. It occurs in altered form in Hinduism and traditional faiths. While *Nirguṇa Brahman* is not "God" in the traditional sense, it is nevertheless a unity that resembles deity in some ways. According to Sarvepalli Rādhakrishnan, president of India from 1962–1967, "To admit the various descriptions of God is not to lapse into polytheism." It is true that most Hindus hold to "unsatisfactory conceptions of God." But "[t]he cultivated tolerate popular notions as inadequate signs and shadows of the incomprehensible" and "the thinking Hindu desires to escape from the confusion of the gods into the silence of the Supreme."[36] Even traditional faiths in widely scattered villages throughout the world often embrace belief in a high (though distant and inaccessible) God. Thus what Islam asserts with particular vigor—that there is one God—is also held in various degrees by people throughout the world.

A belief's popularity, of course, does not make it true. The arguments theists adduce in support of God's existence include logical, philosophical, or scientific considerations (such as the order and complexity of the universe and its capacity to allow life, or the problem of the rise of consciousness and personality from the unconscious and impersonal), accounts of God's revealing himself in some objective manner, the human sense of morality, and experiences (such as answered prayer or a sense of peace, forgiveness, and acceptance). Clearly these do not *prove* God. Much has been written detailing such arguments; this book is not one of them. It will simply agree that the Muslims are right—there is a God, he can be known (truly, though not exhaustively) and is worth knowing, and loving him is humanity's highest good.

The Confucian theme of the older generation passing on its wisdom to the younger in the Singapore Botanic Gardens.

3

NOBODY'S PERFECT

(Confucianism)

"Why Can't We Be Good?" Can anyone explain "Why Evil Exists"?[37] Contemplated for centuries, such questions continue contemporary. Can we, like God, be noble? How high does humanity hope to soar; what altitude do we actually attain?

No ideology focuses more on human behavior than does Confucianism. Its thinkers mention the Lord of Heaven but scrutinize humanity on earth. "Chinese philosophy is distinguished in its commitment to and observation of the human condition."[38] Consequently, "neither ontology nor cognitive problems occupy as conspicuous a place in the speculations and reflections of Chinese thinkers as does the subject matter of the human being."[39] To this day Chinese religion remains "less about enlightenment and salvation in the world to come, and more about cultivating one's character and maintaining harmony in the natural and human worlds."[40] Confucianism consequently sometimes seems more a philosophy than a religion. As such it ponders ideal and actual human practice.

According to the *Analects*—the "Conversations" or "Selected Sayings" of Confucius—optimal human behavior is epitomized by *rén*. The ideogram for *rén* combines the radicals "human" and "two." *Rén* embraces a spectrum of nuances and is rendered variously "empathy, consideration for others, humaneness, benevolence, goodness, human-heartedness." As the virtue of the superior human (*jūnzī*, "gentleman"), *rén* refers to an inner orientation of loyalty and respectful reciprocity in contrast with *li*, external propriety or ritual.[41] Another *Analects* term, *dé*, when used of people, often means "character" or "moral force," in contrast with *li*, physical force.[42] Here is an olio of *Analects* sayings contemplating *rén, jūnzī,* and *dé*.[43]

To learn and then do, is not that a pleasure? When friends come from afar do we not rejoice? To live unknown and not fret, is not that to be a gentleman?

The superior man bends his attention to what is radical [or "what lies at the root" or "what is fundamental," rather than lesser pursuits].

When you have faults, do not fear to [admit and] abandon them.

When the noble man eats he does not try to stuff himself; at rest he does not seek perfect comfort; he is diligent in his work and careful in speech. He avails himself to people of the Way and thereby corrects himself.

In the Book of Poetry are three hundred pieces, but the design of them all may be embraced in that one sentence—"Have no depraved thoughts."

The nobler type of man is broad-minded and not partisan. The inferior man is partisan and not broad-minded.

A gentleman never contends in anything he does—except perhaps in archery. Even then, he bows to his rival and yields him the way as they ascend the pavilion; in like manner he descends and offers him the penalty cup—in his contentions he is still a gentleman.

Riches and honors are what men desire. If they cannot be obtained in [accordance with the Way], they should not be held. Poverty and meanness are what men dislike. If it cannot be obtained in [accordance with the Way], they should not be avoided.

The mind of the superior man is conversant with righteousness; the mind of the mean man is conversant with gain.

Meng Chih-fan never brags. He was covering the rear in a rout; but on coming to the gate he whipped his horse and cried, Not courage kept me behind; my horse won't go! [The gentleman often belittles his own accomplishments.]

If raw substance dominates refinement [i.e., if nature dominates culture], you will be coarse. If refinement dominates raw substance, you will be clerical [i.e., pedantic]. When refinement and raw qualities are well blended, you will be a noble man.

The noble man is always at ease with himself. The inferior man is always anxious.

A man to whom an orphan, a few feet high, or the fate of an hundred towns, may be entrusted, and whom no crisis can corrupt, is he not a gentleman, a gentleman indeed?

The scholar must not be without breadth of mind and vigorous endurance. His burden is heavy and his course is long. Perfect virtue is the burden which he considers it is his to sustain; is it not heavy? Only with death does his course stop; is it not long?

The Master was wishing to go and live among the nine wild tribes of the east. Someone said, "They are rude. How can you do such a thing?" The Master said, "If a superior man dwelt among them, what rudeness would there be?"

Confucius, in his village, looked simple and sincere, and as if he were one who was not able to speak. When he was in the prince's ancestral temple, or in the court, he spoke minutely on every point, but cautiously.

When you go out your front gate, continue to treat each person as though receiving an honored guest. When directing the actions of subordinates, do so as though officiating at a great ritual sacrifice. Do not do to others what you would not wish done to you.

The gentleman brings out what is most admirable in people; he does not bring out what is bad in them. The petty man does the opposite.

A superior man considers it necessary that the terms he uses be spoken appropriately, and that . . . in his words there be nothing incorrect [or indefinite, arbitrary, left to chance].

In private life be courteous, in handling public business be serious, with all men be conscientious. Even though you go among barbarians you may not relinquish these.

Tzŭ Kung asked: "What must an Officer be like to merit his name?" "If in his personal conduct," replied the Master, "he [is mindful of anything that might be dishonorable in his own behavior], and wherever sent will not disgrace his Prince's commission, he may be said to merit his title."

"I would venture to ask who may be ranked next," said Tzŭ Kung. "He whom his relatives commend as filial and whose neighbors commend as brotherly," was the answer.

"I would venture to ask the next," said Tzŭ Kung. "He is one who always stands by his word," was the answer, "and who persists in all he undertakes . . ."

A gentleman is easy to serve and hard to please. If we go from the Way to please him, he is not pleased; but his commands are measured to the [aptitude of each individual] man. A small man is hard to serve and easy to please. Though we go from the Way to please him, he is pleased; but he expects everything of his men [regardless of their individual abilities].

The well-bred are dignified but not pompous. The ill-bred are pompous, but not dignified.

Formerly people studied to improve themselves; now they do so to impress others.

The superior man may indeed have to endure want, but the mean man, when he is in want, gives way to unbridled license.

A gentleman asks of himself, the small man asks of others.

The gentleman is firm but not stubbornly unbending.

There are three things which the superior man guards against. In youth, when the physical powers are not yet settled, he guards against lust. When he is strong, and the physical powers are full of vigor, he guards against quarrelsomeness. When he is old, and the animal powers are decayed, he guards against covetousness.

The superior man, having obtained their confidence, may then impose labors on his people. If he have not gained their confidence, they will think that he is oppressing them. Having obtained the confidence of his prince, he may then remonstrate with him. If he have not gained his confidence, the prince will think that he is vilifying him.

Whether he has to do with many people or few, or with

> things great or small, he does not dare to indicate any disrespect; is not this to maintain a dignified ease without any pride? He adjusts his clothes and cap, and throws a dignity into his looks, so that, thus dignified, he is looked at with awe; is not this to be majestic without being fierce?
>
> Without recognizing the ordinances of Heaven, it is impossible to be a superior man.

Some today might object to Confucius' paternalism. Others may find Master Kung's rigorous ritualism stiflingly stuffy or his air elitist, as did the Daoists. Despite such objections there is much to admire in Confucius's Gentleman or Knight of the Way.

His ideal, unfortunately, remains an ideal. *Rén* is so lofty that it can be ascribed only to legendary heroes such as Po I, not to historical persons.[44] Though we describe it in detail and seek it assiduously, the perfect practice of Goodness eludes us. Even after decades of trying, all fall short. Were a true king to arise, *rén* might still require a generation to establish itself.[45]

The problem begins in the human heart. Despite all our talk, we really do not *want* to be Good:

> I have never seen one who loved Virtue, nor one who hated what was not Virtuous. He who loved Virtue would esteem nothing above it; and he who hated what is not Virtuous would himself be so Virtuous that he would allow nothing evil to adhere to him. Is there any one able for a single day to devote his strength to Virtue ? I have never seen such a one whose ability would be insufficient.
>
> Is virtue a thing remote? I wish to be virtuous, and lo! virtue is at hand.
>
> *The blossoms of the cherry,*
> *how they flutter and turn.*
> *It's not that I don't think of you,*
> *but your house is far away.*
>
> The Master said, He doesn't really think of her. If he did, why would he worry how far it was? [i.e., we fail to achieve *rén* not because it is "far away," but because we don't value it enough.]

Other desires often prove stronger:

> In vain have I looked for one whose desire to build up his moral power was as strong as sexual desire.

Our understanding too often is deficient:

> Those who know virtue are few.
>
> It is all over! I have not yet seen one who could perceive his faults, and inwardly accuse himself.
>
> He who day by day finds out where he is deficient, and who month by month never forgets that in which he has become proficient, may truly be called a lover of learning.

Consequently, Confucius hesitates to describe *anyone* as Good, including himself:

> Măng Woo asked about Tsze-loo, whether he was perfectly virtuous. The Master said, "I do not know." He asked again, when the Master replied, "In a kingdom of a thousand chariots, Yew might be employed to manage the military levies, but I do not know whether he is perfectly virtuous." "And what do you say of K'ew?" The Master replied, "In a city of a thousand families, or a House of a hundred chariots, K'ew might be employed as governor, but I do not know whether he is perfectly virtuous." "What do you say of Ch'ih?" The Master replied, "With his sash girt and standing in a court, Ch'ih might be employed to converse with the visitors and guests, but I do not know whether he is perfectly virtuous."
>
> How can we call even Wei-shêng Kao [the legendary paragon of truthfulness] upright? When someone asked him for vinegar he went and begged it from the people next door, and then gave it as though it were his own gift.
>
> As to being a Sage, or a man of Virtue, how dare I presume to such a claim!
>
> The Master seldom spoke on profit, on the orderings of

Providence, and on perfection [i.e., perfect virtue, refusing to either define it or attribute it to anyone then living].

The way of the superior man is threefold, but I am not equal to it. Virtuous, he is free from anxieties; wise, he is free from perplexities; bold, he is free from fear.

Tzu-kung was always criticizing other people. The Master said, It is fortunate for Ssu that he is so perfect himself as to have time to spare for this. I myself have none.

(A wise man) is not distressed that people do not know him, he is distressed at his own lack of ability.[46]

The nature of a wise man includes four achievements, none of which I have attained: 1) To appreciate my father as I wish my son to appreciate me. This I have not been able to do. 2) To serve my superior officers as I desire my subordinate officials to serve me. This I have not been able to do. 3) To treat my elder brother in the same way I would expect my younger brother to treat me. This I have not been able to do. 4) To be as considerate of friends as I would like to have my friends be considerate of me. This I have not been able to do.[47]

It is better to talk only of what is "near" or "lies in the direction of" Goodness:

As for Goodness—you yourself desire rank and standing; then help others to get rank and standing. You want to turn your own merits to account; then help others to turn theirs to account—in fact, the ability to take one's own feelings as a guide—that is the sort of thing that lies in the direction of Goodness.

The firm, the bold, the simple, the slow in speech are near to humaneness.

Even should someone strongly crave Goodness, he will inevitably find himself short of the strength or endurance to attain it:

Yen K'ew said, "It is not that I do not delight in your doctrines, but my strength is insufficient."

> Yen Yüan heaved a deep sigh and said: "The more I look up at it the higher it rises. The more I probe it the more impenetrable it becomes. I catch a glimpse of it in front, and it is instantly behind. But our Master step by step skillfully lures men on. He has broadened me by culture, and restrained me by reverence. If I wished to stop I could not, and when at times I have exhausted all my powers, something seems to stand majestically before me, yet though I seek to pursue my path towards it, I find never a way."

We can only lament our weakness and content ourselves with lesser attainments:

> A sage I have never managed to see. If I could see a true gentleman, that would be enough . . . A truly good person I have never managed to see. If I could see a person of constancy, that would be enough. With nothingness pretending to possession, emptiness pretending to fullness, want pretending to affluence, true constancy is hard to find.[48]

Some may object that Confucius did acknowledge his own significant progress in the Way toward Goodness:

> At fifteen, I had my mind bent on learning. At thirty, I stood firm. At forty, I had no doubts. At fifty, I knew the decrees of heaven. At sixty, my ear was an obedient organ for the reception of truth. At seventy, I could follow what my heart desired, without transgressing what was right.
>
> Given a few more years of life to finish my study of the Book of Changes and I may be free from great errors.[49]

Or perhaps with Zhū Xī (1130–1200 CE) we need to look beneath a superficial reading, and understand that Confucius's disclaimers of knowledge or attainment are "only ritual modesty; 'How could a Sage really err, how could a Sage truly not know?'" Perhaps in 5.8 when Confucius says to Tzu-kung of Hui, "[Y]ou and I are not equal to him," we should understand him to mean, "I grant you are not equal to him."[50] Nevertheless, a straightforward reading of the *Analects* suggests that all people are imperfect. This assessment is buttressed in the Master's *Genuine Living*:

> Nature, which the wise man [*jūnzī*] emulates, is apparent everywhere but also hidden in each thing.
>
> The most ignorant people have some knowledge of it, yet even the wisest of men cannot comprehend it fully. The most degenerate people embody it somewhat, but even the wisest of men cannot emulate it perfectly. [For] magnificent as the universe is, man still wants it to be different.
>
> So, when the learned man expresses his ideals of greatness, the actual world does not fully exemplify them. And when he expresses his ideals of minute distinctions, nothing in the actual world can embody them.[51]

On the question of human nature, Hsün Tzu is more suspicious than Confucius, Mencius more sanguine. The *Three-Character Classic*, a Confucian primer for children, begins by asserting, "People at birth are naturally good. Their natures are similar; their habits become different." Though written more than a millennium after Mencius, these lines epitomize a cornerstone of his thought. Hsün Tsu disagrees and writes that "the nature of man is evil; his goodness is acquired training."[52] The *Analects* asserts neither claim unambiguously. Rather, Tzu-kung lamented, "To hear the Master on his art and precepts is granted us; but to hear him on man's nature and the Way of Heaven is not."[53] It is significant then that this foundational document of a faith that focuses upon human conduct declines to characterize human nature. It does conclude, however, that try as we might, no one succeeds in being perfectly good.

One later Confucian attempt distinguishes between abstract human nature, which invariably is good, and individual persons endowed with that nature, who inevitably are not:

> [W]hen an individual thing comes into existence, a certain *Li* is inherent in it, which makes it what it is and constitutes its nature. And a man, like other things, is a concrete particular

produced in the concrete world. Hence what we call human nature is simply the *Li* of humanity that is inherent in the individual . . .

A man, in order to have concrete existence, must be the embodiment of *Ch'i*. The *Li* for all men is the same, and it is the *Ch'i* that makes them different . . . Thus any individual, besides what he receives from *Li*, also has what he receives from *Ch'i*, and this is what Chu Hsi calls the physical endowment.

Such is Chu Hsi's theory of the origin of evil. As pointed out by Plato long ago, every individual, in order to have concreteness, must be an embodiment of matter, by which, consequently, he is implicated, so that he necessarily falls short of the ideal. A concrete circle, for example, can only be relatively and not absolutely round. That is the irony of the concrete world, in which man is no exception. Chu Hsi says: "Everything depends on its physical endowment. *Li*, on the other hand, is nothing but good, for since it is *Li*, how can it be evil? What is evil lies in the physical endowment. Mencius' doctrine assents absolutely that the nature is good. In this he apparently takes account only of the nature *per se* but not of the *Ch'i*, and thus in this respect his statement is incomplete. The Ch'eng school, however, supplements this with the doctrine of the physical nature, and so in it we get a complete and all-round view of the problem."

The term "physical nature" here means the nature as it is found actually inherent in the physical endowment of an individual. As thus found, it always strives for the ideal, as Plato would say, but always falls short of it and cannot attain it. *Li* in its originally universal form, however, Chu Hsi calls "the nature of Heaven and Earth," by way of distinction. This distinction was already made by Chang Tsai and is followed by Ch'eng Yi and Chu Hsi. According to them, the use of this distinction completely solves the old controversy as to whether human nature is good and [sic] bad.[54]

Regardless of whether or not one adopts this solution, the Master's belief in the ubiquity of wrong in the human heart was echoed centuries after his passing:

> If only it were all so simple! If only there were evil people somewhere insidiously committing evil deeds, and it were necessary only to separate them from the rest of us and destroy them. But the line dividing good and evil cuts through the heart of every human being. And who is willing to destroy a piece of his own heart?[55]

Howard Bloom concurs with Solzhenitsyn's assessment and argues engagingly and articulately, even if not always convincingly, that evil is an integral element of human nature.[56]

If this is so, then it will be necessary to acknowledge our innate evil if we are to engineer a better human future, or any future at all. Within the context of the spread of nuclear weapons, in whose development he played no small part, J. Robert Oppenheimer spoke of a

> trait of European society which seems to me rather missing in our secularised age . . . It is the knowledge of the inwardness of evil . . . [W]e tend to see all devils as foreigners . . . we reflect and project and externalise what we cannot bear to see within us. When we are blind to the evil in ourselves, we de-humanise ourselves, and we deprive ourselves not only of our own destiny, but of any possibility of dealing with the evil in others . . . By taking thought of our often grim responsibility, by knowing something of our profound and omnipresent imperfection, we may help our children's children to a world less cruel, perhaps less unjust, less likely to end in catastrophe beyond words.[57]

A year later he added,

> We most of all should try to be experts in the worst about ourselves; we should not be astonished to find some evil there, that

> we find so very readily abroad and in all others; nor should we, as Rousseau tried to, comfort ourselves that it is the responsibility and the fault of others, that we are just naturally good; nor should we let Calvin persuade us that despite our obvious duty we are without any power, however small and limited, to deal with what we find of evil in ourselves. In this knowledge . . . there is scope for what we most need: self-knowledge, courage, humour, and some charity.[58]

Solzhenitsyn and Oppenheimer are urging nothing new. Thirteenth-century Zen master Dōgen expressed the fact of human imperfection simply:

> One day Zhuyi said, "What is the essential meaning of buddha dharma?"
>
> Daolin said, "Refrain from unwholesome action, do wholesome action." Zhuyi said, "If that is so, a three-year-old child could say it."
>
> Daolin said, "A three-year-old child may say this, but even an eighty-year-old person cannot practice it."
>
> Zhuyi bowed in gratitude and left.[59]

Dōgen was unconsciously expanding upon Confucius. And Confucius was right—we envision high ideals for ourselves. Humanity can and should be something great. Some of us manage to make significant strides in that direction. But try as hard as we like, evil still lurks within: "The heart of the sons of men is full of evil, and madness is in their heart while they live, and after that they go to the dead."[60] "It is ever so with the things that Men begin: there is a frost in Spring, or a blight in Summer, and they fail of their promise."[61] No one is perfect.

A Buffalo Nat in Myanmar.

4

DISTANCE

(*Primal Religions*)

Most concur with Confucius that people aren't perfect. To err is human, so why the surprise when someone slips? We do not demand flawlessness from our children; why should we expect it from others or God require it of us? In fact, evil is perhaps not only universal but necessary—an evolutionary stratagem assisting our species' survival.[62]

Two varieties of imperfection should be distinguished. The first is natural, creaturely limitation. No one can run a one-minute mile. Most of us cannot instantly reel off the cube root of 473,618. We cannot stay alert for seventeen days with no sleep. No shame accompanies such incapacities—they are part of being human. Developmental immaturity is a subset of this creaturely limitation. Infants soil their diapers, cry rather than articulate their needs, and regurgitate on those who hold them. None of this shocks us, and we continue to love and nurture our newborns.

The second type of imperfection is willful, culpable choice. It is knowing the truth but embracing a lie. It is oppressing others to amass excess for oneself. It is hubris and condescension; murder and rape; vandalism and neglect. These are not amoral creaturely limitations, but immoral conscious choices. To a philosopher such actions are evil; to a theologian they are sin. The word *sin* implies a god against whom offense is made, whose character and will have been despised. All sin is evil. But without a god evil is not sin.[63] Whatever we call it, at the heart of vice lies culpable moral failure and therefore guilt.

Many of the world's traditional religions (formerly called primal or primitive religions) include stories of a high god. When we first encounter them traditional religions appear either animistic or polytheistic. They pre-occupy themselves either with spirits that putatively inhabit physical objects such as trees, boulders, or streams, or with multiple deities. But closer investigation often unveils belief in a single high creator God above these.

> With only a few exceptions, the creation myths describe a "beginningless God" whose wish summons the universe into being. The myths tell how this was accomplished, by what magic, and what has happened to people in the world since then. But the first storytellers seldom ask whence came the Creator Himself. God, regardless of the name or form given him, already rules the void. He broods over the stormy darkness.[64]

"High Gods were and seem always to have been pre-eminent figures both among low races and in the higher civilizations." Researchers used to think that they were not original components of traditional religions but "survivals borrowed from Christian and Muslim monotheistic teaching." However, we can no longer attribute all high gods to borrowing, but should defer to "evidence produced by the most reliable trained anthropologists who have testified to the belief [in high gods] as genuinely primitive all over the world." Consequently, "beneficent and ethical transcendental if somewhat otiose Sky-gods are and have been genuine indigenous figures in rudimentary society independent of missionary or other extraneous influences."[65]

Often this god formerly fraternized with humanity. "In those days, when the world was young, heaven and earth were hardly apart from each other as they are now."[66] But because of human misbehavior he has withdrawn and hidden. Thai rice myths provide examples:

> Long time ago, people did not have to grow rice, rice grew by itself in the field. The rice grain was as big as a boat. It took a whole month to eat up a single rice grain. A widow said the rice grain was too big to pound she therefore beat the rice grain with a heavy stick. *Mae Khao* (Rice goddess) felt humiliated and resentful so she went back to the rice field and since then people had to go to invite her from the field to their houses (*su khwan khao*).[67]

Reminiscent of Eden, this myth evokes an earlier idyllic era when food was easier to obtain than now. But unfortunately the "rice goddess was angry because she was beaten thus she flew away."[68]

The Yao of northern Mozambique describe the fear of the animals and the departure of Mulungu because of human cruelty:

> At first there were no people. Only Mulungu and the decent peaceful beasts were in the world.
>
> One day Chameleon sat weaving a fish-trap, and when he had finished he set it in the river. In the morning he pulled the trap and it was full of fish, which he took home and ate.
>
> He set the trap again. In the morning he pulled it out and it was empty: no fish.
>
> "Bad luck," he said, and set the trap again.
>
> The next morning when he pulled the trap he found a little man and woman in it. He had never seen any creatures like this.
>
> "What can they be?" he said. "Today I behold the unknown." And he picked up the fish-trap and took the two creatures to Mulungu.
>
> "Father," said Chameleon, "see what I have brought."
>
> Mulungu looked. "Take them out of the trap," he said. "Put them down on the earth and they will grow."
>
> Chameleon did this. And the man and woman grew. They grew until they became as tall as men and women are today.
>
> All the animals watched to see what the people would do. They made fire. They rubbed two sticks together in a special way and thus made fire. The fire caught in the bush and roared through the forest and the animals had to run to escape the flames.
>
> The people caught a buffalo and killed it and roasted it in the fire and ate it. Then next day they did the same thing. Every day they set fires and killed some animal and ate it.
>
> "They are burning up everything!" said Mulungu. "They are killing my people!"
>
> All the beasts ran into the forest as far away from mankind as they could get. Chameleon went into the high trees.

> "I'm leaving!" said Mulungu.
>
> He called to Spider. "How do you climb on high?" he said.
>
> "Very nicely," said Spider. And Spider spun a rope for Mulungu and Mulungu climbed the rope and went to live in the sky.
>
> Thus the gods were driven off the face of the earth by the cruelty of man.[69]

Another story suggests that the problem was quarrelsomeness more than cruelty.

> Akongo [the supreme Ngombe god] was not always as he is now. In the beginning the creator lived among men; but men were quarrelsome. One day they had a big quarrel and Akongo left them to themselves. He went and hid in the forest and nobody has seen him since. People today can't tell what he is like.[70]

Other myths repeat the Edenic motif that disobedience to a dietary decree distanced humanity from its creator and its own true self.

> In the beginning the earth was burned by fire, including rocky mountains. The fire kept burning for millions of years, and was followed by heavy rains for millions of years. When the rains stopped, the fragrance of the burned soil evaporated, ascending to heaven. It reached the head of heaven, named Khun Sig Cha, and proceeded to the realm of celestial beings. The celestial beings smelled the fragrance of the burned soil. Eight of these beings, four male and four female, went to Khun Sig Cha and made a plea to go down to earth.
>
> Khun Sig Cha gave permission, but with a serious warning: "You may go down to earth, but I warn you: absolutely do not eat the cream of the soil. If you eat it, you will lose your might and will not be able to return to your realm." They promised to strictly obey his warning.
>
> They came down to earth and roamed around. They walked on the creamy soil, felt its softness, and smelled its fragrance.

> They could not resist the temptation. One of them ate and was impressed with its sweetness. Others were also persuaded to eat the creamy soil. After have eaten it, they wanted to return to heaven, but could not fly back. So ever since they have stayed on earth.
>
> All eight celestial beings married. Time passed and they had nothing to eat. Khun Sig Cha came down and, knowing they lacked food, he gave them eight pumpkins. They ate, but kept the seeds for future reproduction. The four couples had children. They multiplied rapidly to a total of eight million within a short time. They were crowded and scattered to the four corners of the earth. Every group grew rapidly.[71]

In this instance humanity's loss of its own former status is primary; increased distance from the high god secondary. Despite the separation, Khun Sig Cha did not completely withdraw and ignore these fallen beings; he still took the initiative to provide for them.

The Nuer, a cattle-herding Sudanese people, speak of God as *kwoth nhial* or *kwoth a nhial*, Spirit of the sky or Spirit who is in the sky.

> God, Spirit in the heavens who is like wind and air, is the creator and mover of all things. Since he made the world he is addressed in prayers as *kwoth ghaua*, Spirit of the universe, with the sense of creator of the universe . . .
>
> Whether they are speaking about events which happened *ne walka*, in the beginning or long ago, or about happenings of yesterday or today, God, Creative Spirit, is the final Nuer explanation of everything. When asked how things began or how they have come to be what they are they answer that God made them or that it was his will that they have come to be what they are. The heavens and the earth and the waters on the earth, and the beasts and birds and reptiles and fish were made by him, and he is the author of custom and tradition . . . Above all else God is thought of as the giver and sustainer of life. He also brings death. It is true that Nuer seldom attribute death—in such cases as death by lightning or following the breach of

> a divinely sanctioned interdiction—to the direct intervention of God, but rather to natural circumstances or to the action of a lesser spirit, but they nevertheless regard the natural circumstances or the spirits as instruments or agents of God, and the final appeal in sickness is made to him. Nuer have often told me that it is God who takes the life, whether a man dies from spear, wild beast, or sickness, for these are all *nyin kwoth*, instruments of God.
>
> In the Nuer conception of God he is thus creative Spirit. He is also a *ran*, a living person, whose *yiegh*, breath or life, sustains man. I have never heard Nuer suggest that he has human form, but though he is himself ubiquitous and invisible, he sees and hears all that happens and he can be angry and can love (the Nuer word is *nkok*, and if we here translate it 'to love' it must be understood in the preferential sense of *agapō* or *diligo*: when Nuer say that God loves something they mean that he is partial to it).[72]

In Nuer thought, God is closer and more accessible through prayer and sacrifice than are the high gods of many other traditional peoples. But even for them he was once closer still:

> The myth relates that there was once a rope from heaven to earth and how anyone who became old climbed up by it to God in heaven and after being rejuvenated there returned to earth. One day a hyena—an appropriate figure in a myth relating to the origin of death—and what is known in the Sudan as a durra-bird, most likely a weaver-bird, entered heaven by this means. God gave instructions that the two guests were to be well watched and not allowed to return to earth where they would certainly cause trouble. One night they escaped and climbed down the rope, and when they were near the earth the hyena cut the rope and the part above the cut was drawn upwards towards heaven. So the connection between heaven and earth was cut and those who grow old must now die, for what had happened could not be made not to have happened.[73]

Though not the dénouement of man's defiance against a divine decree, the divide between God and humanity still devolves from disregard of his directive: "Indeed the whole human race suffers death on account of what was no more than a trivial oversight. If man had prevented the hyena and the durra-bird from escaping from heaven there would have been no death."[74]

These stories may suggest neither the depth of sin and culpability urged by other faiths nor the sword of Damocles that therefore dangles. But they do at least recognize that humanity has erred and incurred unnatural distance from its Creator. This theme not only comprises "perhaps the most persistent in African mythology,"[75] it also echoes around the world. Even the Greek gods were once closer and kinder to humanity than later myths suggest:

> In the days of old the gods had the whole earth distributed among them by allotment. There was no quarrelling; for you cannot rightly suppose that the gods did not know what was proper for each of them to have, or, knowing this, that they would seek to procure for themselves by contention that which more properly belonged to others. They all of them by just apportionment obtained what they wanted, and peopled their own districts; and when they had peopled them they tended us, their nurselings and possessions, as shepherds tend their flocks, excepting only that they did not use blows or bodily force, as shepherds do, but governed us like pilots from the stern of the vessel, which is an easy way of guiding animals, holding our souls by the rudder of persuasion according to their own pleasure;—thus did they guide all mortal creatures.

The fabled Atlantis belonged to Poseidon, who with his consort Cleito populated the island. It was a realm of fertility, culture, peace, and virtue peopled by a virtuous race until eventually they turned from their simple morality to greed and thirst for power.

> For many generations, as long as the divine nature lasted in them, they were obedient to the laws, and well-affectioned towards the god [Poseidon], whose seed they were; for they possessed true and in every way great spirits, uniting gentleness with wisdom

> in the various chances of life, and in their intercourse with one another. They despised everything but virtue, caring little for their present state of life, and thinking lightly of the possession of gold and other property, which seemed only a burden to them; neither were they intoxicated by luxury; nor did wealth deprive them of their self-control; but they were sober, and saw clearly that all these goods are increased by virtue and friendship with one another, whereas by too great regard and respect for them, they are lost and friendship with them. By such reflections and by the continuance in them of a divine nature, the qualities which we have described grew and increased among them; but when the divine portion began to fade away, and became diluted too often and too much with the mortal admixture, and the human nature got the upper hand, they then, being unable to bear their fortune, behaved unseemly, and to him who had an eye to see grew visibly debased, for they were losing the fairest of their precious gifts; but to those who had no eye to see the true happiness, they appeared glorious and blessed at the very time when they were full of avarice and unrighteous power. Zeus, the god of gods, who rules according to law, and is able to see into such things, perceiving that an honorable race was in a woeful plight, and wanting to inflict punishment on them, that they might be chastened and improve, collected all the gods into their most holy habitation, which, being placed in the center of the world, beholds all created things.[76]

Because they turned against the gods and morality, the Atlanteans and their idyllic island perished.

Eliminating God from our ideology reduces the concepts of sin and guilt to those of ignorance and immaturity. "With sin regarded as ignorance rather than disobedience to divine command, man is relieved of the guilt complex which so bedevils the Western mind."[77] Calling a tumor benign rather than malignant may similarly relieve a patient of fears that bedevil his soul, but such a misdiagnosis does not cure his cancer. It helps no one to imagine problems where none exist, but neither should we understate a serious situation. If human evil does go beyond ignorance to arrogance, and offends not only people but God, then that problem needs to be acknowledged and alleviated. We must be certain our problem is not just a guilt complex but guilt.

Even those who hold to nontheistic ideologies urge us to acknowledge the reality and depth of human evil:

> One of the chief characteristics of the emerging Buddhism in America has been the avoidance of the problem of evil. As one observer remarked, people in the West become absorbed in "therapeutic Buddhism," while in Asia it is "faith Buddhism." The goal of therapy is a healthy, happy, and productive life. That is fine, but that is only one half of the story of our life. Unless we grapple with the other half—evil, sin, suffering, and death—our story remains incomplete. We all need to seriously consider the words of the noted Jewish scholar Gershom Scholem: "To the intellect the problem [of evil] is no real problem at all. All that is needed is to understand that evil is relative, more, that it does not really exist . . . [but] the power of evil is real, and the mind which is conscious of this fact refuses to content itself with intellectual tours de force, however brilliant, which try to explain away the existence of something it knows to be there."[78]

The power of evil can neither be ignored nor demoted to something less. Evil separates people from their own truest humanity, from each other, and from God. Primal religionists are right in this much—humanity has done worse than just act immaturely, we have sinned. And sin separates us from the high God.

> God's plan made a hopeful beginning,
> But Man spoiled his chances by sinning;
> We trust that the story
> Will end in great glory,
> But at present the other side's winning.
>
> —Oliver Wendell Holmes

בַּמָּה֙ אֲקַדֵּ֣ם יְהוָ֔ה
אִכַּ֖ף לֵאלֹהֵ֣י מָר֑וֹם
הַאֲקַדְּמֶ֣נּוּ בְעוֹל֔וֹת
בַּעֲגָלִ֖ים בְּנֵ֥י שָׁנָֽה׃
הֲיִרְצֶ֤ה יְהוָה֙ בְּאַלְפֵ֣י אֵילִ֔ים
בְּרִֽבְב֖וֹת נַֽחֲלֵי־שָׁ֑מֶן
הַאֶתֵּ֤ן בְּכוֹרִי֙ פִּשְׁעִ֔י
פְּרִ֥י בִטְנִ֖י חַטַּ֥את נַפְשִֽׁי׃
הִגִּ֥יד לְךָ֛ אָדָ֖ם מַה־טּ֑וֹב
וּמָֽה־יְהוָ֞ה דּוֹרֵ֣שׁ מִמְּךָ֗
כִּ֣י אִם־עֲשׂ֤וֹת מִשְׁפָּט֙
וְאַ֣הֲבַת חֶ֔סֶד
וְהַצְנֵ֥עַ לֶ֖כֶת עִם־אֱלֹהֶֽיךָ׃

The Jewish faith is tied to its texts. Here is a passage from Micah.

5

PREFERENCE

(*Judaism*)

In Hunan, China, a tunnel peers from a mountain face. At a distance of 1,146 meters, its twin stares out of a facing cliff. Dehang Canyon, dropping 350 meters down, separates the two. For centuries there was no way between them except for birds. Then in 2012 the gap was spanned by Aizhai, the world's highest and longest tunnel-to-tunnel bridge.

Can the gulf separating God and humanity, gouged by sin, be spanned? Would God want it to be? If he has determined to wash his hands of further relationship with recalcitrant humanity, does it make any sense to sidle up and try to change his mind?

Marcion came to Rome around 138 CE. Though raised as a Christian, he proposed ideas that led to his excommunication. Marcion taught that the church had erred in tying its gospel to Judaism. The god of the Jewish scriptures, whom he called the *Dēmiourgos* ("Craftsman" or "Creator"), is not the Father of whom Jesus spoke. Since his creation is beset by suffering, and since he acted in bloody, vindictive ways, the Old Testament god is not good. A second god, previously hidden, took pity on humanity and sent Christ to rescue us from the Dēmiourgos.

Marcion's view has been rejected by all three Abrahamic faiths. Nevertheless the notion still circulates in academe and elsewhere that the Jews' Yahweh is wrathful, quick to judge, unloving, and perhaps petulant—in stark contrast with the New Testament God of Jesus. But this is not so. Though Yahweh (traditionally translated "[the] Lord") is indeed righteous and will judge—indeed *must* judge if he is to remain righteous—he loves people and would prefer that they repent so he can pardon.

In Psalm 103 Yahweh is a loving, forgiving father:

> Yahweh is merciful and gracious,
> slow to anger, and plenteous in mercy.
> He will not always chide,
> nor will he keep his anger for ever.
> He has not dealt with us after our sins,
> nor rewarded us according to our iniquities.
> For as the heaven is high above the earth,
> so great is his mercy toward those who fear him.
> As far as the east is from the west,
> so far has he removed our transgressions from us.
> As a father pities his children,
> so Yahweh pities those who fear him.
> For he knows our frame;
> he remembers that we are dust.
> As for man, his days are as grass:
> as a flower of the field, so he flourishes.
> For the wind passes over it, and it is gone;
> and its place shall remember it no more.
> But Yahweh's mercy is from everlasting to everlasting
> on those who fear him,
> and his righteousness unto children's children;
> To those who keep his covenant,
> and who remember his commandments to do them.[79]

A Marcionite sympathizer might object that even this text cites Yahweh's anger. But God as the Great Father disciplines only out of love and for his children's good:

> My son, do not despise the chastening of Yahweh;
> or be weary of his correction:
> For whom Yahweh loves he corrects;
> even as a father the son in whom he delights.[80]

Underneath even calamitous judgment, imposed not as instructive discipline but punishment, lies God's love, mercy, and grace:

> He has also broken my teeth with gravel stones;
>   he has covered me with ashes.
> You have removed my soul far off from peace:
>   I forgot prosperity.
> And I said, My strength and my hope
>   are perished from Yahweh:
> Remembering my affliction and my misery,
>   the wormwood and the gall.
> My soul has them still in remembrance,
>   and is humbled in me.
> This I recall to my mind,
>   therefore have I hope.
> It is of Yahweh's mercies that we are not consumed,
>   because his compassions fail not.
> They are new every morning:
>   great is your faithfulness.
> Yahweh is my portion, says my soul;
>   therefore will I hope in him.
> Yahweh is good unto those who wait for him,
>   to the soul that seeks him.
> It is good that a man should both hope
>   and quietly wait for the salvation of Yahweh.
> It is good for a man
>   that he bear the yoke in his youth.
> He sits alone and keeps silence,
>   because he has borne it upon him.
> He puts his mouth in the dust—
>   there may yet be hope.
> He gives his cheek to the one who smites him—
>   he is filled full with reproach.
> For the Lord will not cast off for ever:

But though he cause grief,
yet will he have compassion
according to the multitude of his mercies.
For he does not afflict willingly
or grieve the children of men.[81]

Thus, when Yahweh decreed disaster for his people, he did not delight in punishment and in fact often relented:

[I]t was I who taught Ephraim to walk;
I took them up by their arms,
but they did not know that I healed them.
I led them with cords of kindness,
with the bands of love,
and I became to them
as one who eases the yoke on their jaws,
and I bent down to them and fed them.
They shall not return to the land of Egypt,
but Assyria shall be their king,
because they have refused to return to me.
The sword shall rage against their cities,
consume the bars of their gates,
and devour them because of their own counsels.
My people are bent on turning away from me,
and though they call out to the Most High,
he shall not raise them up at all.
How can I give you up, O Ephraim?
How can I hand you over, O Israel?
How can I make you like Admah?
How can I treat you like Zeboiim?
My heart recoils within me;
my compassion grows warm and tender.
I will not execute my burning anger;
I will not again destroy Ephraim;

> for I am God and not a man,
> the Holy One in your midst,
> and I will not come in wrath.[82]

Objections that these gracious promises apply only to Israel, a small slice of humanity, are answered by the story of Jonah. Yahweh sent his prophet to warn the Assyrian city Nineveh that doom threatened because of her wickedness. It was Jonah, not Yahweh, who resented extending grace to the Ninevites. The story's climax consists of a question left dangling in the air, in which Yahweh expresses compassion for all humanity—in fact for all sentient life:

> And God said to Jonah, "Are you doing well to be angry about the gourd?" And he said, "I do well to be angry, even unto death."
>
> Then Yahweh said, "You have had pity on the gourd, for which you have not labored, neither made it grow; which came up in a night, and perished in a night. And should not I spare Nineveh, that great city, in which are more than 120,000 persons that cannot discern between their right hand and their left hand, and also many cattle?"[83]

Not only Tanakh, but Talmud too tempers justice and judgment with a preference for pardon.

> The first Hebrew patriarch addressed the Deity as "the Judge of the whole earth" (Gen. xviii. 25), and the Talmud regards Him in the same light. As the Creator of the world and of the human race, He holds His creatures to account for the manner of their living.
>
> His judgments are always just. "With Him there is no unrighteousness, nor forgetfulness, nor respect of persons, nor taking of bribes" (Aboth IV. 29). R. Jochannan b. Zakkai, on his deathbed, told his disciples that he was about to be judged

by One "Whom I cannot appease with (flattering) words nor bribe with money" (Ber. 28*b*).

Nor is there anything arbitrary about His decisions. A Roman matron said to a Rabbi: "Your God draws near to Himself whomever he likes, without regard to justice!" He set before her a basket of figs, from which she kept picking and eating the choicest. He said to her: "You know how to make a wise selection, and would you assert that the Holy One, blessed be He, does not? He chooses and draws near unto Himself the person whose acts are good" (Num. R. III. 2).

In the Rabbinic literature an eternal conflict is represented as being waged between God's justice and mercy. There is scarcely a passage which refers to His capacity as Judge which does not also allude to His attribute of compassion.

The divine appellation *Elohim*, translated "God," was understood to denote His aspect of judgment and JHVH, translated "Lord," His aspect of mercy (Gen. R. XXXIII. 3), and the combination of the two names in the verse, "These are the generations of the heaven and earth when they were created, in the day that the Lord God (JHVH *Elohim*) made earth and heaven" (Gen. ii. 4) is explained as follows: "It may be likened to a king who had empty vessels. The king said, 'If I put hot water into them they will crack; if I put icy cold water into them they will contract.' What did the king do? He mixed the hot with the cold and poured the mixture into the vessels, and they endured. Similarly said the Holy One, blessed be He, 'If I create the world only with the attribute of mercy, sins will multiply beyond all bounds; if I create it only with the attribute of justice, how can the world last? Behold, I will create it with both attributes; would that it might endure!'" (Gen. R. XII. 15).

Indeed, it was only because the quality of mercy prevailed at Creation that the human race was allowed to come into being . . . [Compassion's] victory over stern justice is the reason of the world's continuance in the face of wickedness . . . God is not long-suffering with the righteous only but equally with the wicked . . . "The attribute of grace," it

> was taught, "exceeds that of punishment (i.e. justice) by five-hundredfold." . . .
>
> The divine compassion is evidenced by extreme eagerness to save man from condemnation. "Though nine hundred and ninety-nine angels attest for a man's conviction and only one angel attests for his defence, the Holy One, blessed by He, inclines the scales in his favour" (p. Kid. 61*d*). When, however, He is compelled by justice to exact punishment from evil-doers, he does so with regret and pain. Noble expression is given to this thought in the legend that at the overthrow of the Egyptians by the Red Sea, the ministering angels wished to offer a song of triumph to God; but He checked them, saying: "The work of My hands is drowned in the sea, and you would offer Me a song!" (Sanh. 39*b*).
>
> While believing, therefore that He is the Judge of the Universe, the Rabbis delighted in calling Him *Rachmana* (the Merciful), and taught that "the world is judged by grace" (Aboth III. 19).[84]

Thus, the truth that sin separates humanity from God is sustained but tempered with hope since God longs to end the estrangement. This is true not just for a select few but for all humanity, as Jonah implies. A final prophetic passage again weaves the themes of sin, judgment, God's preference for repentance and forgiveness, and warnings:

> Yet you say, "The way of the Lord is not just." Hear now, O house of Israel: Is my way not just? Is it not your ways that are not just? When a righteous person turns away from his righteousness and does injustice, he shall die for it; for the injustice that he has done he shall die. Again, when a wicked person turns away from the wickedness he has committed and does what is just and right, he shall save his life. Because he considered and turned away from all the transgressions that he had committed, he shall surely live; he shall not die. Yet the house of Israel says, "The way of the Lord is not just." O house of Israel, are my ways not just? Is it not your ways that are not just?

> Therefore I will judge you, O house of Israel, every one according to his ways, declares the Lord Yahweh. Repent and turn from all your transgressions, lest iniquity be your ruin. Cast away from you all the transgressions that you have committed, and make yourselves a new heart and a new spirit! Why will you die, O house of Israel? For *I have no pleasure in the death of anyone*, declares the Lord Yahweh; so turn, and live.[85]

The Jews are right—God differentiates between good and evil and does not pretend they are the same. Since he is just he will judge. But he would rather forgive.

בַּמָּה אֲקַדֵּם יְהוָה

אִכַּף לֵאלֹהֵי מָרוֹם

הַאֲקַדְּמֶנּוּ בְעוֹלוֹת

בַּעֲגָלִים בְּנֵי שָׁנָה׃

הֲיִרְצֶה יְהוָה בְּאַלְפֵי אֵילִים

בְּרִבְבוֹת נַחֲלֵי־שָׁמֶן

הַאֶתֵּן בְּכוֹרִי פִּשְׁעִי

פְּרִי בִטְנִי חַטַּאת נַפְשִׁי׃

הִגִּיד לְךָ אָדָם מַה־טּוֹב

וּמָה־יְהוָה דּוֹרֵשׁ מִמְּךָ

כִּי אִם־עֲשׂוֹת מִשְׁפָּט

וְאַהֲבַת חֶסֶד

וְהַצְנֵעַ לֶכֶת עִם־אֱלֹהֶיךָ׃

Sri Harmandir Sahib, or the Golden Temple in Amritsar at nighttime.

6

GOOD

(*Theravāda, Jainism, Sikhism*)

Many religions agree: God is good; we only wish we were. How can God and humanity be reconciled? Perhaps renouncing sin and practicing justice would help. Replace evil and folly with virtue and wisdom. Stop exploiting people; nourish them instead. Seek and honor God rather than ignoring and blaspheming him.

Both theists and atheists value grooming character and caring for people; axiology and ethics preoccupy both faith and nonfaith communities. So nontheists might recast the first paragraph by saying, "Life is at times unsatisfying. Humans often do not achieve their potential. How can we make our lives as noble and significant as possible?" Their answers would ignore theology. This chapter will start with two nontheistic religions in exploring the goodness of being good and conclude with input from one theistic faith.

Although Theravāda Buddhism speaks of gods, it disallows any transcendent creator. These Theravādan devas simply occupy strata of existence higher than the human, where they exercise greater powers and enjoy profounder ease. They are subject to *karma, saṃsāra,* and rebecoming just as we are. Humans can become such gods, but our ultimate goal should supersede that. We should labor instead to escape entirely the wearisome cycle of birth-and-death by extinguishing desire and achieving nirvāṇa. Nirvāṇa can be won through right understanding and following the Eightfold Noble Path.

Understanding and the effort required to attain it are discussed in *The Foundations of Mindfulness:*

> Bhikkhus, this is the direct path for the purification of beings, for the surmounting of sorrow and lamentation, for the disappearance of pain and grief, for the attainment of the true way, for the realisation of Nibbāna—namely, the four foundations of mindfulness.
>
> What are the four? Here, bhikkhus, a bhikkhu[86] abides contemplating the body as a body, ardent, fully aware, and mindful, having put away covetousness and grief for the world. He abides contemplating feelings as feelings, ardent, fully aware, and mindful, having put away covetousness and grief for the world. He abides contemplating mind as mind, ardent, fully aware, and mindful, having put away covetousness and grief for the world. He abides contemplating mind-objects as mind-objects, ardent, fully aware, and mindful, having put away covetousness and grief for the world.
>
> And how, bhikkhus, does a bhikkhu abide contemplating the body as a body? Here a bhikkhu, gone to the forest or to the root of a tree or to an empty hut, sits down; having folded his legs crosswise, set his body erect, and established mindfulness in front of him, ever mindful he breathes in, mindful he breathes out. Breathing in long, he understands: "I breathe in long"; or breathing out long he understands: "I breathe out long." Breathing in short, he understands: "I breathe out short."[87]

The sūtra specifies the disciplines necessary to achieve mindfulness. Included are contemplation of what the Buddha considers the present impurity and the eventual dissolution of the body:

> Again, bhikkhus, a bhikkhu reviews this same body up from the soles of the feet and down from the top of the hair, bounded by skin, as full of many kinds of impurity thus: "In this body there are head-hairs, body-hairs, nails, teeth, skin, flesh, sinews, bones, bone-marrow, kidneys, heart, liver, diaphragm, spleen, lungs, intestines, mesentery, contents of the stomach, feces, bile, phlegm, pus, blood, sweat, fat, tears, grease, spittle, snot, oil of the joints, and urine" . . .

> In this way he abides contemplating the body as a body internally, externally, and both internally and externally . . . And he abides independent, not clinging to anything in the world. That too is how a bhikkhu abides contemplating the body as a body . . .
>
> Again, bhikkhus, as though he were to see a corpse thrown aside in a charnel ground, one, two, or three days dead, bloated, livid, and oozing matter, a bhikkhu compares this same body with it thus: "This body too is of the same nature, it will be like that, it is not exempt from that fate."[88]

Thus in Theravāda, escaping saṃsāra for nirvāṇa requires mindfulness and the disciplined effort to achieve it. Right living is also necessary. Steps three to five of Buddhism's Eightfold Noble Path outline its understanding of morality (*śīla*) or right living. The middle of these specifies Five Precepts:

> Here, a noble disciple, having abandoned the destruction of life, abstains from the destruction of life. By abstaining from the destruction of life, the noble disciple gives to an immeasurable number of beings freedom from fear, enmity, and affliction. He himself in turn enjoys immeasurable freedom from fear, enmity, and affliction. This is the first gift . . . This is the fourth stream of merit . . . that leads to what is wished for, desired, and agreeable, to one's welfare and happiness.
>
> Again, a noble disciple, having abandoned the taking of what is not given, abstains from taking what is not given . . . abstains from sexual misconduct . . . abstains from false speech . . . abstains from liquor, wine, and intoxicants, the basis for heedlessness. By abstaining from liquor, wine, and intoxicants, the basis for heedlessness, the noble disciple gives to an immeasurable number of beings freedom from fear, enmity, and affliction. He himself in turn enjoys immeasurable freedom from fear, enmity, and affliction.[89]

The days preceding the first, eighth, fifteenth, and twenty-third nights of the lunar month are *uposatha*, days of special observance to cleanse the mind and generate tranquility. On *uposatha* devout lay Buddhists, following the example of the arahants or "worthy ones," strengthen the third precept from avoiding sexual misconduct to shunning sex altogether and add three more:

> As long as they live the arahants abandon sexual activity and observe celibacy, living apart, abstaining from sexual intercourse, the common person's practice . . .
>
> As long as they live the arahants eat once a day, abstaining from eating at night and from food outside the proper time [i.e., from dawn until noon] . . .
>
> As long as they live the arahants abstain from dancing, singing, instrumental music, and unsuitable shows, and from adorning and beautifying themselves by wearing garlands and applying scents and unguents . . .
>
> As long as they live the arahants abandon and abstain from the use of high and luxurious beds; they lie down on a low resting place, either a small bed or a straw mat . . .
>
> It is in this way, bhikkhus, that the uposatha is observed complete in eight factors, so that it is of great fruit and benefit, extraordinarily brilliant and pervasive.[90]

The *Dhammapada,* probably the most widely read Theravāda document, extols discipline and self-reliance. Chapter 2 (or verses 21–32) bears the title "Appamāda" (Pāli [P.]; in Sanskrit [S.] "Apramāda"), variously translated as Earnestness, Vigilance, Diligence, Conscientiousness, or Non-heedlessness. It is "the absence of that giddiness or thoughtlessness which characterizes the state of mind of worldly people"[91] or "diligence in all one's activities . . . the foundation of all virtuous qualities."[92]

21. Earnestness is the path of immortality (Nirvâ*n*a), thoughtlessness the path of death. Those who are in earnest do not die, those who are thoughtless are as if dead already.
22. Those who are advanced in earnestness, having understood this clearly, delight in earnestness, and rejoice in the knowledge of the elect.

23. These wise people, meditative, steady, always possessed of strong powers, attain to Nirvâ*n*a, the highest happiness.
24. If an earnest person has roused himself, if he is not forgetful, if his deeds are pure, if he acts with consideration, if he restrains himself, and lives according to law—then his glory will increase.
25. By rousing himself, by earnestness, by restraint and control, the wise man may make for himself an island which no flood can overwhelm.
26. Fools follow after vanity, men of evil wisdom. The wise man keeps earnestness as his best jewel.
27. Follow not after vanity, nor after the enjoyment of love and lust! He who is earnest and meditative, obtains ample joy.
28. When the learned man drives away vanity by earnestness, he, the wise, climbing the terraced heights of wisdom, looks down upon the fools, serene he looks upon the toiling crowd, as one that stands on a mountain looks down upon them that stand upon the plain.
29. Earnest among the thoughtless, awake among the sleepers, the wise man advances like a racer, leaving behind the hack.
30. By earnestness did Indra rise to the lordship of the gods. People praise earnestness; thoughtlessness is always blamed.
31. A Bhikshu (mendicant) who delights in earnestness, who looks with fear on thoughtlessness, moves about like fire, burning all his fetters, small or large.
32. A Bhikshu who delights in reflection, who looks with fear on thoughtlessness, cannot fall away from his perfect state—he is close upon Nirvâ*n*a.

These themes of attentiveness, effort, and self-reliance recur throughout the *Dhammapada:*

33. As a fletcher makes straight his arrow, a wise man makes straight his trembling and unsteady thought, which is difficult to guard, difficult to hold back.

34. As a fish taken from his watery home and thrown on the dry ground, our thought trembles all over in order to escape the dominion of Mâra (the tempter).
35. It is good to tame the mind, which is difficult to hold in and flighty, rushing wherever it lists; a tamed mind brings happiness.
103. If one man conquer in battle a thousand times thousand men, and if another conquer himself, he is the greatest of conquerors.
104, 105. One's own self conquered is better than all other people; not even a god, a Gandharva, not Mâra with Brahman could change into defeat the victory of a man who has vanquished himself, and always lives under restraint.
145. Well-makers lead the water wherever they like; fletchers bend the arrow; carpenters bend a log of wood; good people fashion themselves.
159. If a man make himself as he teaches others to be, then, being himself well subdued, he may subdue others; one's own self is indeed difficult to subdue.
160. Self is the lord of self, who else could be the lord? With self well subdued, a man finds a lord such as few can find.
161. The evil done by oneself, self-begotten, self-bred, crushes the foolish, as a diamond breaks a precious stone.
165. By oneself the evil is done, by oneself one suffers; by oneself evil is left undone, by oneself one is purified. Purity and impurity belong to oneself, no one can purify another.
182. Difficult to obtain is the conception of men, difficult is the life of mortals, difficult is the hearing of the True Law, difficult is the attainment of Buddhahood.
183. Not to commit any sin, to do good, and to purify one's mind, that is the teaching of all the Awakened.
184. The Awakened call patience the highest penance, long-suffering the highest Nirvâ*n*a; for he is not an anchorite who strikes others, he is not an ascetic who insults others.
185. Not to blame, not to strike, to live restrained under the law, to be moderate in eating, to sleep and sit alone, and to dwell on the highest thoughts—this is the teaching of the Awakened.
209. He who gives himself to vanity, and does not give himself

to meditation, forgetting the real aim of life and grasping at pleasure, will in time envy him who has exerted himself in meditation.

217. He who possesses virtue and intelligence, who is just, speaks the truth, and does what is his own business, him the world will hold dear.

219. Kinsmen, friends, and lovers salute a man who has been long away, and returns safe from afar.

220. In like manner his good works receive him who has done good, and has gone from this world to the other—as kinsmen receive a friend on his return.

231. Beware of bodily anger, and control your body! Leave the sins of the body, and with your body practise virtue!

232. Beware of the anger of the tongue, and control your tongue! Leave the sins of the tongue, and practise virtue with your tongue!

233. Beware of the anger of the mind, and control your mind! Leave the sins of the mind, and practise virtue with your mind!

234. The wise who control their body, who control their tongue, the wise who control their mind, are indeed well controlled.

239. Let a wise man blow off the impurities of his self, as a smith blows off the impurities of silver, one by one, little by little, and from time to time.

240. As rust corrodes the very iron that formed it, thus do a transgressor's own works lead him to the evil path.

276. You yourself must make an effort. The Buddhas are only preachers. The thoughtful who enter the way are freed from the bondage of Mâra.

280. He who does not rouse himself when it is time to rise, who, though young and strong, is full of sloth, whose will and thought are weak, that lazy and idle man will never find the way to knowledge.

281. Watching his speech, well restrained in mind, let a man never commit any wrong with his body! Let a man but keep these three roads of action clear, and he will achieve the way which is taught by the wise.

282. Through zeal knowledge is gotten, through lack of zeal knowledge is lost; let a man who knows this double path of gain and loss thus place himself that knowledge may grow.
288. Sons are no help, nor a father, nor relations; there is no help from kinsfolk for one whom death has seized.
289. A wise and good man who knows the meaning of this, should quickly clear the way that leads to Nirvâ*n*a.
322. Mules are good, if tamed, and noble Sindhu horses, and elephants with large tusks; but he who tames himself is better still.
323. For with these animals does no man reach the untrodden country (Nirvâ*n*a), where a tamed man goes on a tamed animal, viz. on his own well-tamed self.
326. This mind of mine went formerly wandering about as it liked, as it listed, as it pleased; but I shall now hold it in thoroughly, as the rider who holds the hook holds in the furious elephant.
379. Rouse yourself by yourself, examine yourself by yourself, thus self-protected and attentive you will live happily, O Bhikshu!
380. For self is the lord of self, self is the refuge of self; therefore curb yourself as the merchant curbs a good horse.[93]

Right thinking and living are foundational to the Buddhist Way. Pursuing them should characterize daily life. The Buddha underscored the need for enlightened thought and action—and the individual effort to attain them—in his farewell address:

> Therefore, Ānanda, you should live as islands unto yourselves, being your own refuge, with no on[e] else as your refuge, with the Dhamma as an island, with the Dhamma as your refuge, with no other refuge. And how does a monk live as an island unto himself, . . . with no other refuge? Here, Ānanda, a monk abides contemplating the body as body, earnestly, clearly aware, mindful and having put away all hankering and fretting for the world, and likewise with regard to feelings,

> mind and mind-objects. That, Ānanda, is how a monk lives as an island unto himself, . . . with no other refuge. And those who now in my time or afterwards live thus, they will become the highest, if they are desirous of learning.[94]

In addition to Siddhārtha Gautama, who became the Buddha or Enlightened One sometime in the fourth to sixth century BCE, others about this time were also breaking away from Brahmanism with its rituals and hierarchy. Nataputta Vardhamana, for example, was given the title Mahāvīra or Great Hero. He was also called a *jina* or conqueror, from which his followers, the Jains, take their name. There were other buddhas before Siddhārtha, and at least twenty-three *tirthankaras* or ford finders preceded Nataputta Vardhamana.

Both Siddhārtha and Mahāvīra were born into high social standing but renounced their assets and families at age thirty. Both practiced asceticism in their search for meaning, but after nearly starving himself, Siddhārtha realized that spiritual reality was not found there any more than in indulgence. Thus after enlightenment he urged a Middle Way between the two. Mahāvīra, by contrast, persisted in and intensified his asceticism. Upon leaving home at age thirty he pulled out his hair; Siddhārtha only cut his. Mahāvīra wandered naked; Siddhārtha wore a robe. Mahāvīra starved himself to death; Siddhārtha regularly ate, though not after midday. If, then, we seek an example of extreme discipline and self-reliance, Mahāvīra and the Jains provide one.

Jain monks and nuns commit themselves to follow the Five Mahavratas or Great Vows. Two terms need explaining. *Nirgrantha* (P. *nigaṇṭha*) means "free from all ties." Early Buddhist literature used *nirgraṇṭha* to refer to Jains in general and Mahāvīra in particular, since the latter claimed that their practices liberated them from all bonds. The passage below uses "Jain" instead of "Nirgrantha" for ease of reading. The Sanskrit *kevala jñāna* means "perfect, absolute knowledge." Kevala is "the highest knowledge and intuition . . . infinite, supreme, unobstructed, unimpeded, complete, and perfect."[95] One who attains such knowledge is a *Kevalin*. The *Kalpa Sutra* describes the struggle by which Mahāvīra won kevala:

> The Venerable One lived, except in the rainy season, all the eight months of summer and winter, in villages only a single night, in towns only five nights; he was indifferent alike

to the smell of ordure and of sandal, to straw and jewels, dirt and gold, pleasure and pain, attached neither to this world nor to that beyond, desiring neither life nor death, arrived at the other shore of the sa*m*sâra, and he exerted himself for the suppression of the defilement of Karman.

With supreme knowledge, with supreme intuition, with supreme conduct, in blameless lodgings, in blameless wandering, with supreme valor, with supreme uprightness, with supreme mildness, with supreme dexterity, with supreme patience, with supreme freedom from passions, with supreme control, with supreme contentment, with supreme understanding, on the supreme path to final liberation, which is the fruit of veracity, control, penance, and good conduct, the Venerable One meditated on himself for twelve years.

During the thirteenth year, in the second month of summer, in the fourth fortnight, the light (fortnight) of Vai*s*âkha, on its tenth day, when the shadow had turned towards the east and the first wake was over, on the day called Suvrata, in the Muhûrta called Vigaya, outside of the town *Gri*mbhikagrâma on the bank of the river Rigupâlika, not far from an old temple, in the field of the householder Sâmâga, under a Sal tree, when the moon was in conjunction with the asterism Uttaraphalgunî, (the Venerable One) in a squatting position with joined heels, exposing himself to the heat of the sun, after fasting two and a half days without drinking water, being engaged in deep meditation, reached the highest knowledge and intuition, called Kevala, which is infinite, supreme, unobstructed, unimpeded, complete, and full.

When the Venerable Ascetic Mahâvîra had become a *Gin*a and Arhat, he was a Kevalin, omniscient and comprehending all objects; he knew and saw all conditions of the world, of gods, men, and demons: whence they come, whither they go, whether they are born as men or animals (*k*yavana) or become gods or hell-beings (upapâda), the ideas, the thoughts of their minds, the food, doings, desires, the open and secret deeds of all the living beings in the whole world; he the Arhat,

> for whom there is no secret, knew and saw all conditions of all living beings in the world, what they thought, spoke, or did at any moment.[96]

In what follows, then, the title *Kevalin* should be understood as a fully enlightened, omniscient *jina* or *tīrthaṅkara* such as Mahāvīra.

1. The first great vow, Sir, runs thus: I renounce all killing of living beings, whether subtle or gross, whether movable or immovable. Nor shall I myself kill living beings, nor cause others to do it, nor consent to it. As long as I live, I confess and blame, repent and exempt myself of these sins, in the thrice threefold way, in mind, speech, and body. There are five clauses:
   a. A Jain is careful in his walk, not careless. The Kevalin assigns as the reason, that a Jain, careless in his walk, might with his feet hurt or displace or injure or kill living beings. Hence a Jain is careful in his walk, not careless in his walk.
   b. A Jain searches into his mind (i.e., his thoughts and intentions). If his mind is sinful, blamable, intent on works, acting on impulses, produces division and dissension, quarrels, faults, and pains, injures living beings, or kills creatures, he should not employ such a mind in action; but if, on the contrary, it is not sinful,[97] then he may put it in action.
   c. A Jain searches into his speech; if his speech is sinful, he should not utter that speech. But if, on the contrary, it is not sinful, then he may utter it.
   d. A Jain is careful in laying down his utensils of begging, he is not careless in it. The Kevalin says: A Jain who is careless in laying down his utensils of begging, might hurt or displace or injure or kill all sorts of living beings. Hence a Jain is careful in laying down his utensils of begging, he is not careless in it.
   e. A Jain eats and drinks after inspecting his food and drink; he does not eat and drink without inspecting his food and drink. The Kevalin says: If a Jain would eat and drink

without inspecting his food and drink, he might hurt and displace or injure or kill all sorts of living beings. Hence a Jain eats and drinks after inspecting his food and drink, not without doing so.

In this way the great vow is correctly practiced, followed, executed, explained, established, effected according to the precept. This is, Sir, the first great vow: Abstinence from killing any living beings.

2. The second great vow runs thus: I renounce all vices of lying speech arising from anger or greed or fear or mirth. I shall neither myself speak lies, nor cause others to speak lies, nor consent to the speaking of lies by others. I confess and blame, repent and exempt myself of these sins in the thrice threefold way, in mind, speech, and body. There are five clauses:
    a. A Jain speaks after deliberation, not without deliberation. The Kevalin says: Without deliberation a Jain might utter a falsehood in his speech. A Jain speaks after deliberation, not without deliberation.
    b. A Jain comprehends (and renounces) anger, he is not angry. The Kevalin says: A Jain who is moved by anger, and is angry, might utter a falsehood.
    c. A Jain comprehends (and renounces) greed, he is not greedy.
    d. A Jain comprehends (and renounces) fear, he is not afraid.
    e. A Jain comprehends (and renounces) mirth, he is not mirthful.
3. The third great vow runs thus: I renounce all taking of anything not given, either in a village or a town or a wood, either of little or much, of small or great, of living or lifeless things. I shall neither take myself what is not given, nor cause others to take it, nor consent to their taking it. As long as I live, I confess and blame, repent and exempt myself of these sins in the thrice threefold way, in mind, speech, and body. There are five clauses:
    a. A Jain begs after deliberation, for a limited ground, not without deliberation. The Kevalin says: If a Jain begs

without deliberation for a limited ground, he might take what is not given.

b. A Jain consumes his food and drink with permission (of his superior), not without his permission. The Kevalin says: If a Jain consumes his food and drink without the superior's permission, he might . . .

c. A Jain who has taken possession of some ground, should always take possession of a limited part of it and for a fixed time . . .

d. A Jain who has taken possession of some ground, should constantly have his grant renewed . . .

e. A Jain begs for a limited ground for his co-religionists after deliberation, not without deliberation . . .

4. The fourth great vow runs thus: I renounce all sexual pleasures, either with gods or men or animals. I shall not give way to sensuality [etc.]. There are five clauses:

   a. A Jain does not continually discuss topics relating to women. The Kevalin says: If a Jain discusses such topics, he might fall from the law declared by the Kevalin, because of the destruction or disturbance of his peace.

   b. A Jain does not regard and contemplate the lovely forms of women.

   c. A Jain does not recall to his mind the pleasures and amusements he formerly had with women.

   d. A Jain does not eat and drink too much, nor does he drink liquors or eat highly-seasoned dishes.

   e. A Jain does not occupy a bed or couch affected by women, animals, or eunuchs.

5. The fifth great vow runs thus: I renounce all attachments, whether little or much, small or great, living or lifeless; neither shall I myself form such attachments, nor cause others to do so, nor consent to their doing so. There are five clauses:

   a. If a creature with ears hears agreeable and disagreeable sounds, it should not be attached to, nor delighted with, nor desiring of, nor infatuated by, nor covetous of, nor disturbed by the agreeable or disagreeable sounds. The

> Kevalin says: If a Jain is thus affected by the pleasant or unpleasant sounds, he might fall. If it is impossible not to hear sounds, which reach the ear, the mendicant should avoid love or hate, originated by them. A creature with ears hears agreeable and disagreeable sounds.
>
> b. If a creature with eyes sees agreeable and disagreeable forms or colors, it should not be attached to them.
>
> c. If a creature with an organ of smell smells agreeable or disagreeable smells, it should not be attached to them.
>
> d. If a creature with a tongue tastes agreeable or disagreeable tastes, it should not be attached to them.
>
> e. If a creature with an organ of feeling feels agreeable or disagreeable touches, it should not be attached to them.
>
> He who is well provided with these great vows and their twenty-five clauses is really Houseless, if he, according to the sacred lore, the precepts, and the way correctly practices, follows, executes, explains, establishes, and, according to the precept, effects them.[98]

Another sūtra specifies safeguards to assist the seeker to shun sexual stimulation (vow 4):

> Here, indeed, the venerable Sthaviras have declared ten conditions for the realisation of celibacy, by hearing and understanding which the monks will reach a high degree of self-dịscipline, of Sa*m*vara, and of contemplation, will be well protected (by the three Guptis), will guard their senses, guard their chastity, and will thus never be remiss (in the attendance on their religious duties) . . .
>
> 1. A Jain may occupy various places for sleep or rest; but a Jain should not occupy places, for sleep or rest, frequented by women, cattle, or eunuchs. The preceptor has explained the reason for this. If a Jain occupies places for sleep or rest, frequented by women, cattle, or eunuchs, then, though he be chaste, there may arise a doubt with regard to his chastity, or a sensual desire, or a feeling of remorse, or he will break the

> rules, or he will become a slave to passion, or he will acquire a dangerous illness of long duration, or he will desert the faith which the Kêvalin has proclaimed. Therefore a Jain should not occupy places, for sleep or rest, frequented by women, cattle, or eunuchs.
>
> 2. A Jain should not converse with women.
> 3. A Jain should not sit together with women on the same seat.
> 4. A Jain should not look at, or contemplate, the charms and beauties of women.
> 5. A Jain should not, behind a screen, or curtain, or wall, listen to the screeching or screaming or singing or laughing or giggling or crying of women.
> 6. A Jain should not recall to his memory the pleasure and amusements which in the past he enjoyed together with women.
> 7. A Jain should not eat well-dressed food.
> 8. A Jain should not eat or drink to excess.
> 9. A Jain should not wear ornaments. The preceptor has explained the reason for this. If he wears ornaments, or adorns his body, he might become an object of desire to women. When he is an object of desire to women, then . . .
> 10. A Jain should not care for sounds, colors, tastes, smells, and feelings.[99]

Jainism obviously values its vision of virtue and the uncompromising discipline necessary to achieve it. But its agenda carries three costs. First, Jains acknowledge no difference between good and bad. Mahāvīra was commended for being "indifferent alike to the smell of ordure and of sandal, to straw and jewels, dirt and gold, pleasure and pain." He achieved what the Jains call *kevala* only after submitting to great hardship—posing "in a squatting position with joined heels, exposing himself to the heat of the sun, after fasting two and a half days without drinking water, being engaged in deep meditation." A Jain disciple renounces mirth and does not prefer some sounds, sights, smells, tastes, and feelings above others. A male renounces all contact with women, as well as memories of past pleasant contacts.

Second, the Jain faces a conundrum. *Ahiṃsā* or non-injury to any life is the primary Jain value. Hence the holy wear gauze masks, refuse to kindle fires, and sweep the path before themselves to avoid harming any insect. But modern microbiology warns that such precautions do not prevent our harming or killing innumerable life-forms of which Mahāvīra was unaware. Further, the noblest way to die in Jainism is to purposely starve, thereby killing not only oneself but the microbes that live in and on one's person. Eating entails killing life; not eating does the same. If *ahiṃsā* is the highest good, it seems impossible to achieve.

Third, it confuses biology with evil. In Jainism sexual abstinence is somehow holier than sexual enjoyment. Those who profess to value life forget how life comes to be. Biology is not evil—far from it—though sex can certainly be misused.

Siddhārtha Gautama had practiced asceticism in his pursuit of enlightenment and discovered it to be a dead end. So it is no surprise that the Pāli sūtras reject Mahāvīra as one of the Six Sectarian Teachers[100] and a heretic:

> Even by howling along the wretched jackal
> Remains a vile beast, never the lion's peer.
> So though he be the teacher of a group,
> The naked ascetic, speaker of falsehood,
> Arousing suspicion by his conduct,
> Bears no resemblance to superior men.[101]

Buddhism and Jainism are atheistic and address only personal and interhuman ethics. Theistic religions also espouse ethical values and define what is good, but they discuss as well relating to God.

Sikhism, founded by Gurū Nānak in the early sixteenth century, is a relatively recent monotheism. Its Scripture is the Ādi Granth ("Original Book") or, since it has taken the place of living gurūs, the Śrī Gurū Granth Sāhib ("Honorable Gurū in Book Form"). The Ādi Granth's opening poem, the Japjī Sāhib, is key to all that follows and epitomizes Sikh doctrine. The Japjī speaks much of the greatness of God and appropriate worship, as would be expected of any monotheistic religion, but also urges that piety and righteous behavior are means to secure God's blessing:

> How shall *man* become true before God? How shall the veil of falsehood be rent?

By walking, O Nanak, according to the will of the Commander as preordained . . .

If I please Him, that is my place of pilgrimage to bathe in; if I please Him not, what ablutions shall I make?

What can all the created beings I behold obtain without *previous* good acts?

Precious stones, jewels, and gems *shall be treasured up* in your heart if you hearken to even one word of the Guru . . .

The condition of him who obeys God cannot be described.

Whoever tries to describe it, shall afterward repent.

There is no paper, or pen, or writer

To describe *the condition* of him who obeys God.

So pure is His name—

Whoever obeys God knows *the pleasure of it* in his own heart.

By obeying Him wisdom and understanding *enter* the mind;

By obeying Him man knows all worlds;

By obeying Him man suffers not punishment;

By obeying Him man shall not depart with Jam [the god of death]—

So pure is God's name—

Whoever obeys God knows the pleasure of it in his own heart.

By obeying Him man's path is not obstructed;

By obeying Him man departs with honor and distinction;

By obeying Him man proceeds in ecstasy on his way;

By obeying Him man forms an alliance with virtue—

So pure is God's name—

Whoever obeys God knows the pleasure of it in his own heart.

By obeying Him man attains the gate of salvation;

By obeying Him man is saved with his family;

By obeying Him the Guru is saved, and saves his disciples;

By obeying Him, O Nanak, man wanders not *in quest* of alms—

So pure is God's name—

Whoever obeys God knows the pleasure of it in his own heart. . . .

When the hands, feet, and *other members of* the body are covered with filth,

It is removed by washing with water.

When your clothes are polluted,

Apply soap, and the impurity shall be washed away.

So when the mind is defiled by sin,

It is cleansed by the love of the Name.

Men do not become saints or sinners by merely calling themselves so.

The recording angels take with them a record of *man's* acts.

It is he himself sows, and he himself eats.

Nanak, man suffers transmigration by God's order.

Pilgrimage, austerities, mercy, and almsgiving on general and special occasions

Whosoever performs, *may obtain* some little honor;

But he who hears and obeys and loves *God* in his heart,

Shall wash off his *impurity* in the place of pilgrimage within him . . .

Make contentment and modesty your earrings, self-respect your wallet, meditation the ashes to *smear on your body*;

Make your body, which is only a morsel for death, your beggar's coat, and faith your rule of life and your staff.

Make association with men your Ai Panth [a sect of Yogis], and the conquest of your heart the conquest of the world . . .

Were one tongue to become a hundred thousand, and a hundred thousand to become twentyfold more,

I would utter the name of the one Lord of the world hundreds of thousands of times *with all my tongues.*

In this way I should ascend the stairs of the Lord, and become one with Him.

On hearing of the exaltation of the religious the vile become jealous.

Nanak, *the former* have found the Kind One, while false is the boasting of the false . . .

The Merciful One marks them according to their acts,

The bad and the good shall there be distinguished.

> Nanak, on arrival there, this shall be seen . . .
> Make continence your furnace, resignation your goldsmith,
> Understanding your anvil, divine knowledge your tools,
> The fear *of God* your bellows, austerities your fire,
> Divine love your crucible, and melt God's name therein,
> In such a true mint the Word shall be coined.
> This is the practice of those on whom God looks with an eye of favor.
> Nanak, the Kind One by a glance makes them happy . . .
> Merits and demerits shall be read out in the presence of the Judge.
> According to men's acts, some shall be near, and others distant *from God*.[102]

Theravāda Buddhists, Jains, and Sikhs agree: discipline and self-responsibility are good. Theists must not invoke orthodox thoughts about God as a justification for injustice among people. The Tanakh ascribes Nineveh's impending judgment not to bad theology but to wicked practice. The New Testament finds Paul discoursing to Felix on "righteousness, self-control and the judgment to come" and frequently warns that judgment will be based on deeds. The Qur'ān urges its readers to restrain from evil and do good in view of coming judgment.[103]

However, amid all this talk about judgment to come and the virtues of self-control, a cloud as small as a man's hand rises from the sea. Can any of us ever exercise perfect self-discipline? Confucius doubted whether anyone truly wanted Goodness. Jainism suggests the conundra that emerge from pushing our attempts to their logical conclusions, to say nothing of the danger of misdefining righteousness to begin with. Then too, can any amount of repentance cancel the debt incurred from years of subpar performance? So while discipline and self-reliance are indeed good, a question lingers: Are even our best efforts good enough?

Avalokiteśvara Bodhisattva in Hanoi's One Pillar Pagoda

7

BUT GOOD ENOUGH?

(*Mahāyāna, Jōdo Shinshū*)

The Buddha's dying counsel was "Rely on yourself."[104] However, perfect practice proved impossible for hoi polloi outside the *Saṅgha*. Fortunately for the laity, subsequent sūtras suggested saviors to aid the weak. The original Buddhist ideal had been the *arhat* (P. *arahant*), a "worthy one" who through individual effort "eradicated the outflows, destroyed the defilements, freed himself from fetters, and attained awakening." But becoming an arhat and thereby achieving individual liberation not only proved beyond the ken of the commoner, but to some seemed selfish.[105]

A new ideal thus emerged—that of the *bodhisattva* (P. *bodhisatta*) or "enlightenment being" who out of compassion delays his (and later her) enlightenment to first help others achieve theirs. The original Theravāda ("way of the elders") was consequently derisively dubbed *Hīnayāna* ("lesser vehicle") in contrast to this broader *Mahāyāna* ("great vehicle"). The lesser vehicle could carry only the few and hardy to nirvāṇa, the great had room for many; the lesser led only to arhatship, the great all the way to becoming a buddha. The ideal for the still-later *Vajrayāna* ("diamond vehicle") would be the *siddha*, guru, lama, "one who is accomplished" in tantric powers and could help others use these to attain enlightenment.

Mahāyāna Buddhists insist that their doctrines had always been part of the Buddha's original teaching but were left undisclosed to the masses until his followers were mature enough to receive them. At any rate, Mahāyāna proposes multiple bodhisattvas who can clear the path for easier passage through life's problems. The most popular, especially in China, assumes various names and forms. In Sanskrit he is Avalokiteśvara, in Chinese Guanyin, in

Japanese Kannon, in Tibetan Spyan-ras-gzigs—the "Lord who looks down" and observes the suffering in this world. He represents infinite compassion. In order to aid as many as possible, Avalokiteśvara appears in thirty-three different ways, originally male, but later often female or androgynous. One popular image has eleven heads and a thousand arms fanned out like a peacock's tail. From the palm of each hand gazes an eye to see all; the thousand arms equip him to help all. The *Lotus Sūtra* describes some of the ways Avalokiteśvara can help:

> All the myriads of creatures who in this world are suffering troubles will, if they hear the name of the Bodhisattva Mahâsattva Avalokite*s*vara, be released from that mass of troubles. Those who shall keep the name of Avalokite*s*vara, if they fall into a great mass of fire, be delivered therefrom by virtue of the lustre of the Bodhisattva Mahâsattva. In case creatures, carried off by the current of rivers, should implore Avalokite*s*vara, all rivers will afford them a ford. In case many hundred thousand myriads of creatures, sailing in a ship on the ocean, should see their bullion, gold, gems, pearls, lapis lazuli, conch shells, stones, corals, emeralds, Maŝragalvas, read pearls, and other goods lost, and the ship by a vehement untimely gale cast on the island of Giantesses, and, if in that ship a single being implores Avalokite*s*vara, all will be saved from that island of Giantesses.
>
> If a man given up to capital punishment implores Avalokite*s*vara, the swords of the executioners shall snap asunder. Further, if the whole triple chiliocosm were teeming with goblins and giants, they would by virtue of the name of Avalokite*s*vara being pronounced lose the faculty of sight in their wicked designs. If some creature shall be bound in wooden or iron manacles, chains or fetters, be he guilty or innocent, then those manacles, chains or fetters shall give way as soon as the name of Avalokite*s*vara is pronounced. Such is the power of the Bodhisattva Mahâsattva Avalokite*s*vara. If this whole triple chiliocosm were teeming with knaves, enemies, and robbers armed

> with swords, and if a merchant leader of a caravan marched with a caravan rich in jewels; if then they perceived those robbers, knaves, and enemies armed with swords, and in their anxiety and fright thought themselves helpless; if, further, that leading merchant spoke to the caravan in this strain: Be not afraid, young gentlemen, be not frightened; invoke, all of you, with one voice Avalokite*s*vara, the giver of safety; then you shall be delivered from this danger by which you are threatened. If a woman, desirous of male offspring, adores Avalokite*s*vara, she shall get a son, nice, handsome, and beautiful; one possessed of the characteristics of a male child, generally beloved and winning, who has planted good roots. If a woman is desirous of getting a daughter, a nice, handsome, beautiful girl shall be born to her.[106]

Obviously Avalokiteśvara can deliver from daily life's diverse difficulties. Infertile women continue to beseech this bodhisattva, under various names, for conception. The informed follower of Siddhārtha Gautama, however, does not pursue solving present problems as much as escaping the perennial parade of birth-and-death. Is there anyone who can assist the seeker to escape saṃsāra for nirvāṇa?

Another Mahāyāna text, *The Larger Sutra on Amitāyus,* describes numerous buddhas who lived eons before Siddhārtha Gautama. One so impressed a king that he abandoned his throne and vowed to himself become a buddha, no matter how long and difficult the process. (For definitions of some unfamiliar terms, see note 107.)

> The Buddha [Siddhārtha Gautama] said to Ananda, "In the distant past—innumerable, incalculable and inconceivable kalpas[107] ago—a Tathagata named Dipankara appeared in the world. Having taught and freed innumerable beings and led them all along the path of Enlightenment, he passed into Nirvana. [Then follows a list of dozens of other buddhas who succeeded him.] All these Buddhas have already passed into Nirvana.

"Then appeared a Buddha named Lokeshvararaja, the Tathagata, Arhat, Perfectly Enlightened One, Possessed of Wisdom and Practice, Perfected One, Knower of the World, Unsurpassed One, Tamer of Men, Master of Gods and Men, Buddha and World-Honored One.

"At that time there was a king, who, having heard the Buddha's exposition of the Dharma, rejoiced in his heart and awakened aspiration for the highest, perfect Enlightenment. He renounced his kingdom and the throne, and became a monk named Dharmakara. Having superior intelligence, courage and wisdom, he distinguished himself in the world. He went to see the Tathagata Lokeshvararaja, knelt down at his feet, walked round him three times keeping him always on his right, prostrated himself on the ground, and putting his palms together in worship, praised the Buddha . . .

"Having spoken [verses in praise], the Bhiksu Dharmakara said to the Buddha Lokeshvararaja, 'Respectfully, World-Honored One, I announce that I have awakened aspiration for the highest, perfect Enlightenment. I beseech you to explain the Dharma to me fully, so that I can perform practices for the establishment of a pure Buddha-land adorned with infinite excellent qualities. So please teach me how to attain Enlightenment quickly and to remove the roots of afflictions of birth-and-death for all.' . . .

"At that time the Buddha Lokeshvararaja recognized the Bhiksu Dharmakara's noble and high aspirations, and taught him as follows: 'If, for example, one keeps on bailing water out of a great ocean with a pint-measure, one will be able to reach the bottom after many kalpas and then obtain rare treasures. Likewise, if one sincerely, diligently and unceasingly seeks the Way, one will be able to reach one's destination. What vow is there which cannot be fulfilled?'

"Then the Buddha Lokeshvararaja explained in detail the greater and lesser aspects of two hundred and ten kotis of Buddha-lands, together with the good and evil natures of heavenly and human beings living there. He revealed them all to the Bhiksu just as he had requested. Then the Bhiksu, having heard the Buddha's exposition of the glorious pure land and also having seen all of them, resolved upon his supreme, unsurpassed vows. His mind being serene and his aspirations free of attachment, he was unexcelled throughout the world. For five full kalpas he contemplated the vows, and then chose the pure practices for the establishment of his Buddha-land."

Ananda asked the Buddha, "How long was the life-span of beings in the land of the Buddha Lokeshvararaja?"

The Buddha replied, "The length of life of that Buddha was forty-two kalpas."

He continued, "After that Dharmakara Bodhisattva adopted the pure practices which had led to the establishment of the excellent lands of two hundred and ten kotis of Buddhas. When he had finished this task, he went to the Buddha, knelt down at his feet, walked round him three times, joined his palms in worship and sat down. He then said to the Buddha, 'I have adopted the pure practices for the establishment of a glorious Buddha-land.' The Buddha said to him, 'You should proclaim this. Know that now is the right time. Encourage and delight the entire assembly. Hearing this, other bodhisattvas will practice this Dharma and so fulfill their innumerable great vows.' The Bhiksu replied, 'I beg you to grant me your attention. Now I will fully proclaim my vows.

'If, when I attain Buddhahood,

1) there should be in my land a hell, a realm of hungry spirits, or a realm of animals
2) humans and devas in my land should after death fall again into the three evil realms
3) humans and devas in my land should not all be the color of pure gold
4) humans and devas in my land should not all be of one appearance
5) humans and devas in my land should not remember all their previous lives
6) humans and devas in my land should not possess the divine eye

7) humans and devas in my land should not possess the divine ear
8) humans and devas in my land should not possess the faculty of knowing the thoughts of others
9) humans and devas in my land should not possess the supernatural power of travelling anywhere in one instant
10) humans and devas in my land should give rise to thoughts of self-attachment
11) humans and devas in my land should not unfailingly reach Nirvana
12) my light should be limited
13) my life-span should be limited
14) the number of the *shravakas* in my land could be known
15) humans and devas in my land should have limited life-spans
16) humans and devas in my land should even hear of any wrongdoing
17) innumerable Buddhas in the land of the ten quarters should not all praise and glorify my Name
18) sentient beings in the lands of the ten quarters who sincerely and joyfully entrust themselves to me, desire to be born in my land, and call my Name, even ten times, should not be born there (except for those who commit the five gravest offenses and abuse the right Dharma) . . .

Thirty provisos follow that further specify glories that Dharmakara will require in his Buddha-land, excellencies of the myriads who attain it, and worship that is therefore due him. Interesting among these are:

35) women who, having heard my Name, rejoice in faith, awaken aspiration for Enlightenment and wish to renounce womanhood, should after death be reborn again as women
38) humans and devas in my land should not obtain clothing, as soon as such a desire arises in their minds, and if the fine robes as prescribed and praised by the Buddhas should not be spontaneously provided for them to wear, and if these clothes should need sewing, bleaching, dyeing or washing

44) bodhisattvas who hear my Name should not rejoice so greatly as to dance and perform the bodhisattva practices and should not acquire stores of merit[,]
may I not attain perfect Enlightenment.'"[108]

This sūtra proposes the saga of a man who labors through eons to groom the requisite perfections to become a buddha, but forgoes his own enlightenment unless he can first create a land of ease to which all who call on him go when they die. From there they inevitably attain nirvāṇa. Although he specifies forty-eight criteria that must be met before he accepts buddhahood, the eighteenth is fundamental. In it Dharmākara refuses enlightenment unless all who invoke his name are born in his Pure Land. In this arrangement, people attain nirvāṇa not through individual effort to follow the Path but through Dharmākara's aid. Apparently bad karma need not hinder them either (except for those who commit the five gravest offenses and abuse the right Dharma). Dharmākara's agenda differs from Siddhārtha's counsel to "live as islands unto yourselves, being your own refuge, with no one else as your refuge, with the Dhamma as an island, with the Dhamma as your refuge, with no other refuge."

Pure Land Buddhists believe that Dharmākara did attain enlightenment; hence his vow must have been fulfilled. They thus confidently assert that he has succeeded in creating Sukhāvatī, the Western Paradise or Pure Land, filled with ease and delights. All who call on him will enter his Pure Land upon death, and from there without fail will attain nirvāṇa. He has become the Buddha Amitābha (Sanskrit for "Infinite Light"; in Japanese Amida and in Chinese O-mi-t'o). Since he grants long life he is also called Amitāyus (Sanskrit for "Infinite Life").

The Amitābha cult arose around 100 CE, came to the forefront in China some five hundred years later, and from there traveled to Japan. A key developer of Japanese Amitābha devotion was Hōnen (1133–1212). He rejected his era's predisposition toward difficult monastic practice, urging instead that all can attain enlightenment just as they are. Being a woman, a layperson, or a commoner poses no impediment. Important to Hōnen's thinking was belief in Buddhism's three stages—the period of the True Dharma (*shōbō*) immediately following the Buddha's lifetime, in which for centuries his teachings would be transmitted accurately and his followers able to achieve enlightenment through their own efforts; the period of the Counterfeit or

Simulated Dharma (*zōbō*), in which for further centuries the substance of his teachings would be gone but the trappings remain; and finally the period of the Corrupt Dharma or End of the Dharma (*mappō*), in which even the trappings would disappear.[109] Achieving enlightenment during mappō would be all but impossible. In Japan many agreed that mappō had begun in 1052, a belief confirmed by the fiery destruction in that year of the Hasedera temple.

Thus, of the two channels of deliverance—*jiriki* (self-power) and *tariki* (other-power)—only tariki remained a viable option. During mappō one could not hope to personally achieve enlightenment. How then might one escape saṃsāra? For Hōnen, the myth of the king who became Dharmākara Bodhisattva (Hōzō Bosatsu in Japanese) who became Amida Buddha meant that in the present evil age, calling upon Amida was the only way. Hōnen therefore made the practice of *nembutsu*, chanting *namu Amida Butsu* ("Hail to" or "I entrust myself to Amitābha Buddha"), central to his Jōdo Shū or "Pure Land School" of Buddhism. He explains why:

> [S]ince the nembutsu is easy, it is open to everyone, while the various other practices are not open to people of all capacities because they are difficult. Was it not in order to bring all sentient beings without exception to birth that he [Dharmākara] in his original vow cast aside the difficult practice and selected the easy one?
>
> If the original vow required us to make images of the Buddha and to build stūpas, the poor and destitute would surely have no hope of birth [in the Pure Land], but the fact is that the rich and highborn are few, while the poor and lowborn are exceedingly many. If the original vow required us to have wisdom and intelligence, the dull and foolish would surely have no hope of birth, but the fact is that the wise are few and the foolish are very numerous. Again, if the original vow required us to hear and understand many teachings, those who have heard and understood little would surely have no hope of birth, but the fact is that those who have heard much are few and those who have heard little are very many. Further, if the original vow required us to observe the precepts and abide by the monastic rules, those who have broken the precepts and those

> who have never undertaken them would surely have no hope of birth, but the fact is that those who observe the precepts are few, while those who have broken them are exceedingly many. As for the other various practices, they should be understood in the same way.
>
> We should know that if the original vow required us to perform the manifold practices mentioned above, then those who are able to attain birth would be few, while those unable to do so would be very many. For this reason the Tathāgata Amida, in the distant past when he was the *bhikṣu* Dharmākara, moved by impartial compassion and wishing to save all beings universally, did not select the manifold practices, such as making images of the Buddha and building stūpas, as corresponding to his original vow concerning birth. Instead he selected the single practice of reciting the nembutsu.[110]

For Hōnen reciting the nembutsu was *the* way of salvation, the practice Amida himself selected. Reciting it excels understanding all Buddha Gautama's dharma: "Even if you study Śākyamuni's whole teaching, you should still become an ignorant man who doesn't know a word and regards himself as ignorant as a nun or a layman. Never behave as a wise man, but single-mindedly recite the nembutsu."[111] One of his early biographies claims he chanted seventy thousand times per day,[112] as did Tao-ch'o (562–645) before him.[113] Observing the Buddhist precepts was at best "an auxiliary practice to be taken up after first establishing faith in Amida."[114] The wife of his disciple Shinran recalls that her husband "heard the Master [i.e., Hōnen] teach that when it comes to the matter of salvation in the afterlife, there was no difference between a good person or evil person, for *only* the single-hearted Nembutsu was necessary in order to become liberated from the suffering of birth-and-death."[115] Recitation is so important that people should attend to their daily needs simply so that they can continue to chant:

> How should we spend this life? We should spend our life so that we can recite the nembutsu. If something hinders our practice of the nembutsu, it should be abandoned and stopped . . . Clothing, food, and shelter: these three are the auxiliary acts of the

> nembutsu; that is to say that anything that can enable a secure life is an auxiliary act of the nembutsu. People who do not recite the nembutsu and love and care about their bodies will surely fall into the three evil realms [hell, hungry ghosts, animals] after death. Yet why should people who recite the nembutsu not care about their bodies, which will be born in the Pure Land? You should care for yourself as much as possible. If you think such acts are not auxiliary acts of the nembutsu and become attached to them, they will become the karma for falling into the three evil realms. If you care for yourself in order to recite the nembutsu and attain birth in the Pure Land, such a secure life will become an auxiliary act of the nembutsu. Everything is like this.[116]
>
> . . . People should always live by creating the proper condition for being able to say the nembutsu. If you cannot say the nembutsu as a celibate, say it by getting married. If you cannot say it by being married, say it as a celibate. If you cannot say it while remaining at one place, say it as you wander on your travels. If you cannot say it on your travels, say it at home. If you cannot say it while securing your daily necessities, say it by having others obtain them for you. If you cannot say it by others obtaining the necessities for you, say it by securing them yourself. If you cannot say it by yourself, say it with together with friends and comrades. If you cannot say it with other people, say it by yourself confined at home. Food, clothing, and shelter are necessary only in so far as they create the proper condition for people to say the nembutsu.[117]

In summary, "one thing is clear, [Hōnen] believed that birth in Amida Buddha's Sukhāvatī was essential to the realization of enlightenment and that the sole practice to be recommended in reaching this goal was the recitation of Amida Buddha's name."[118]

Hōnen's disciple Shinran (1173–1263) advanced his sensei's agenda and established the Jōdo Shinshū or "True Pure Land School," Japan's largest Buddhist sect today. Shinran feared that reciting the nembutsu itself could be considered a good work performed to earn one's deliverance. But in Shinran's view humans are so depraved that they cannot generate the requisite humble state of mind that would allow a proper, selfless, believing invocation of the name. Hence, it must be Amida himself who generates faith within the believer. It is the working of the original vow that evokes an entrusting response (*shinjin*), not the striving of aspirants to themselves generate faith.[119] Shinran put it this way:

> [S]ince the beginningless past, the multitudes of beings have been transmigrating in the ocean of ignorance, sinking aimlessly in the cycle of all forms of existence and bound to the cycle of all forms of pain; accordingly, they lack the entrusting that is pure. In the manner of their existence, they have no entrusting that is true and real. Hence, it is difficult for them to encounter the unexcelled virtues, difficult to realize the supreme, pure shinjin. In all small foolish beings, at all times, thoughts of greed and desire incessantly defile any goodness of heart; thoughts of anger and hatred constantly consume the dharma-treasure. Even if one urgently acts and urgently practices as though sweeping fire from one's head, all these acts must be called "poisoned and sundry good," and "false and deceitful practice." They cannot be called "true and real action." To seek to be born in the land of immeasurable light through such false and poisoned good is completely wrong. Why? Because when the Tathagata was performing bodhisattva practices, there was not a moment—not an instant—when his practice in the three modes of action was tainted by the hindrance of doubt. Because this mind is the Tathagata's mind of great compassion, it necessarily becomes the truly decisive cause of attaining the fulfilled land. The Tathagata, turning with compassion toward the ocean of living beings in pain and affliction, has given unhindered and vast pure shinjin to the ocean of sentient beings. This is called the "true and real shinjin that is [Amida's] benefiting of others."[120]

Recent Jōdo Shinshū literature reiterates that entrusting is not something we do, but something that Amida does in and for us:

> Amida Buddha does not state that he will liberate us if we entrust ourselves to him. What he does state is that we should rest assured of his absolute guarantee for our liberation.
>
> In other words, Amida Buddha's aspiration or vow to "liberate" exists first, and our experiencing that calling voice is what *shinjin* is. There is no prior condition placed on that vow.[121]

> The Primal Vow of salvation is likened to a powerful magnet that draws all beings to itself. Even if one is unaware of it or resists it, its power of attraction will eventually prevail.[122]

Because for Shinran faith is not generated by people but granted by Amida, "a qualitative difference [exists] between Shinran's understanding of faith and that found in the Buddhist tradition before him."[123] Whereas Hōnen and Jōdo Shū promote repeated repetition of the nembutsu, Shinran and Jōdo Shinshū reply that one sincere invocation is enough.[124] Gone is any inclination to count one's iterations of the nembutsu and take spiritual solace or pride in the number. Salvation arises through Amida's ancient, prevenient, and effective vow that calls, arouses entrusting, and evokes invocation of the name. It is not achieved through any seeker's repeated chanting. Subsequent repetitions of the nembutsu may be done in gratitude for what Amida has accomplished but do not constitute a means to gain his favor. Because birth in the Pure Land is the work of Amida Buddha from first to last, "all the sentient beings throughout the ten quarters, without a single exception, will be born in the Pure Land,"[125] apparently even those whom the pivotal eighteenth vow excludes.[126]

Tannishō, or *A Record in Lament of Divergences*, was probably written by Yuien-bō, one of Shinran's disciples, within three decades of the master's death. It attempts to clarify Jōdo Shinshū doctrines vis-à-vis other views. Numbers in parentheses indicate the sections from which the below paragraphs may be found.

> "Saved by the inconceivable working of Amida's Vow, I shall realize birth in the Pure Land": the moment you entrust yourself thus to the Vow, so that the mind set upon saying the nembutsu arises within you, you are immediately brought to share in the benefit of being grasped by Amida, never to be abandoned.

Know that the Primal Vow of Amida makes no distinction between people young and old, good and evil; only shinjin is essential. For it is the Vow to save the person whose karmic evil is deep and grave and whose blind passions abound.

Thus, for those who entrust themselves to the Primal Vow, no good acts are required, because no good surpasses the nembutsu. Nor need they despair of the evil they commit, for no evil can obstruct the working of Amida's Primal Vow. (1)

As for me, I simply accept and entrust myself to what my revered teacher told me, "Just say the nembutsu and be saved by Amida"; nothing else is involved.

I have no idea whether the nembutsu is truly the seed for my being born in the Pure Land or whether it is the karmic act for which I must fall into hell. Should I have been deceived by Master Hōnen and saying the nembutsu, were to fall into hell, even then I would have no regrets.

The reason is, if I could attain Buddhahood by endeavoring in other practices, but said the nembutsu and so fell into hell, then I would feel regret at having been deceived. But I am incapable of any other practice, so hell is decidedly my abode whatever I do. (2)

It is impossible for us, who are possessed of blind passions, to free ourselves from birth-and-death through any practice whatever. Sorrowing at this, Amida made the Vow, the essential intent of which is the evil person's attainment of Buddhahood. Hence, evil persons who entrust themselves to Other Power are precisely the ones who possess the true cause of birth. (3)

The nembutsu, for its practicers, is not a practice or a good act. Since it is not performed out of one's own designs, it is not a practice. Since it is not good done through one's own calculation, it is not a good act. Because it arises wholly from Other Power and is free of self-power, for the practicer, it is not a practice or a good act. (8)

"Although I say the nembutsu, the feeling of dancing with joy is faint within me, and I have no thought of wanting to go to the Pure Land quickly. How should it be [for a person of nembutsu]?"

When I asked the Master this, he answered, "I, too, have had this question, and the same thought occurs to you, Yuien-bō!

"When I reflect deeply on it, by the very fact that I do not rejoice at what should fill me with such joy that I dance in the air and dance on earth, I realize all the more that my birth is completely settled. What suppresses the heart that should rejoice and keeps one from rejoicing is the action of blind passions. Nevertheless, the Buddha, knowing this beforehand, called us 'foolish beings possessed of blind passions'; thus, becoming aware that the compassionate Vow of Other Power is indeed for the sake of ourselves, who are such beings, we find it all the more trustworthy . . .

"Amida pities especially the person who has no thought of wanting to go to the Pure Land quickly. Reflecting on this, we feel the great Vow of great compassion to be all the more trustworthy and realize that our birth is settled." (9)

There was, in these days, a person who had fallen into wrong views. He asserted that since the Vow was made to save the person who had committed evil, one should purposely do evil as an act for attaining birth. As rumors of misdeeds gradually spread, Shinran wrote in a letter, "Do not take a liking to poison just because there is an antidote." This was in order to put an end to that wrong understanding. It by no means implies that evil can obstruct one's attainment of birth. (13)

To believe that each time you say the Name your karmic evil is eradicated is nothing but to strive to attain birth by eliminating your karmic evil through your own efforts. In that case, you can attain birth only by being diligent in the nembutsu to the very point of death . . .

If we entrust ourselves to Amida's Vow that grasps and never abandons us, then even though, through unforeseen circumstances, we commit an evil act and die without saying the nembutsu at the very end, we will immediately realize birth in the Pure Land. Moreover, even if we do say the Name at the point of death, it will be nothing other than our expression of gratitude for Amida's benevolence, entrusting ourselves to the Buddha more

> and more as the very time of enlightenment draws near. (14)
>
> For the person of wholehearted single practice of the nembutsu, change of heart occurs only once . . .
>
> If shinjin has become settled, birth will be brought about by Amida's design, so there must be no calculating on our part. (16)
>
> The Master [Shinran] would often say, When I consider deeply the Vow of Amida, which arose from five kalpas of profound thought, I realize that it was entirely for the sake of myself alone! Then how I am filled with gratitude for the Primal Vow, in which Amida resolved to save me, though I am burdened with such heavy karma . . .
>
> "I know nothing at all of good or evil. For if I could know thoroughly, as Amida Tathagata knows, that an act was good, then I would know good. If I could know thoroughly, as the Tathagata knows, that an act was evil, then I would know evil. But with a foolish being full of blind passions, in this fleeting world—this burning house—all matters without exception are empty and false, totally without truth and sincerity. The nembutsu alone is true and real" [Postscript].[127]

Traditional Buddhism has no place for God. "[T]he Buddha is an atheist and Buddhism in both its Theravāda and Mahāyāna forms is atheism." The world is "without a refuge and without God"[128] because "God is really a superstition."[129] Thomas J.J. Altizer was therefore correct when he said that "Buddhism is that horizon most innocent of God, most free of any sense or awareness of an absolute sovereignty and transcendence" and that "Godhead has been more deeply and more comprehensively dissolved in the Buddhist tradition than in any other tradition."[130]

Yet in the person of the king who became Dharmākara Bodhisattva who became Amida Buddha, we find a being[131] who is:

- a creator (of the Pure Land Sukhāvatī)
- eternal or immortal (his vow is "prior to the beginningless beginning of time"[132])
- morally perfect ("for inconceivable millions of measureless kalpas, there was not a moment, not an instant, when his practice in the three modes of action was not pure, or lacked this true mind . . . [H]e never

harbored a single thought of greed, anger, or folly, nor any impulse of desire, harmfulness, or wrath; he cherished no thought of form, sound, smell, taste or tangible thing. The constant warmth of affection and respect he felt for all sentient beings was like that for close relatives . . . His nature was harmonious and adaptable, without any violence or ill will. He always embraced a heart of compassion and patience for all sentient beings, and was never deceptive or flattering, never slothful . . . [H]e was stalwart and fearless and never retreated."[133])

- essentially omniscient (his vow takes in "all beings unconditionally. It foresees all the wishes, desires, and aspirations, as well as the failures and dejections, experienced by humanity."[134])
- infinite (the name *Amida* means "'immeasurable,' that which is not measurable and beyond conceptual understanding."[135])
- essentially omnipotent (as evidenced not only in his ability to create, but also because his vow "has prepared answers and solutions for the needs of every human being" with the result that "the depth and scope of the working of the Primal Vow is beyond our imagination."[136])
- unique, or qualitatively different from all human beings (his morally perfect practice as noted above contrasts with the fact that "all beings, an ocean of multitudes, have since the beginningless past down to this day, this very moment, been evil and defiled, completely lacking the mind of purity. They have been false and deceitful, completely lacking the mind of truth and reality." Apparently apart from Amida Buddha "[t]here is not one living being in this world" who eludes the description of being an "evil person." He exercised "suprahuman resolve, reflection, and praxis."[137])

Rejecting any Creator and Sustainer of the physical universe that we see, sense, and inhabit, Shin Buddhists instead place their confidence in an undocumented human-turned-creator and ruler of a land that no one has ever seen, with qualities hard to imagine, lying an incalculable distance to the west, wherever "west" may be in a multidimensional universe. Jōdo Shinshū is part of the Buddhist fold, but it is not immediately clear to many non-Buddhists how Amida differs from God and how a system that urges abandonment of self for faith in Amida fits within that originally atheistic, self-reliant ideology.

Nevertheless the Pure Land schools illustrate the fact that many people who aspire to such virtues as tranquility, morality, and non-injury find themselves only imperfectly practicing them and thus find themselves in need of one to save them. They, to say nothing of others, fall short of their ideals. And so arises a search for forgiveness and help.

Multitudes of Shin Buddhists find solace in this buddha who vows to save all. Shinran spoke of his own contentment in this faith to the extent that even had Hōnen deceived him he would have no regrets. More recently, Taitetsu Unno describes a housewife who, before dying from cancer at the age of forty-six, found consolation in entrusting herself to the compassion of Amida Buddha. His own grandmother was a "simple and unaffected woman" who lived a difficult life but "could not contain the joy she felt of having been embraced by Immeasurable Light and Immeasurable Life." Unno, a former professor at Smith College, concludes by describing how he himself has benefitted from nembutsu practice:

> As a closure, I return to the three questions with which my journey began in the order of their significance. First, who am I? Whence do I come? Wither [sic] do I go? The answer is simple. I am a limited karmic being, full of ignorance and forever wandering, who has been endowed with a gift, the single thread of nembutsu. Guided by the single thread of nembutsu, I emerge from the darkness of countless past lives and see the light of day that enables me to become truly and really myself. I have arrived, I have come home. The agitations and chaos in my life are part of my reality, knowing full well that my ultimate destiny is the Pure Land of Immeasurable Light and Life.
>
> Second, what is the one word of compassion? I realize now that it's not so much the word but the source that is crucial. No matter how articulate a person may be, if the word comes from a limited intellect and calculating mind, it will be mere word play (*prapanca*), covering up one's ignorance and never reaching the depth of human feeling. But this awareness enables me to give up discursive strategies as an answer and to entrust myself to the reality of great compassion. From its depth, then, emerges the genuine word (*desana*) that uplifts all of life as

> is. It may appear as a single word, or an eloquent silence, or namu-amida-butsu itself.
>
> Finally, is my friend who took his own life happy now? Who is to say? As far as I am concerned, I have no choice but to entrust myself to the working of great compassion that vowed to work ceaselessly until all beings, even a single blade of grass, are liberated into the universe of boundless light. I need no convincing that my friend now lives in the heart of great compassion, beyond any measure of happiness or unhappiness. He joins the chorus of countless enlightened beings in the universe all praising the Name of Amida, and whenever I hear namu-amida-butsu being intoned, I hear his reassuring voice that all is well.[138]

Testimonies abound that people have experienced peace upon entrusting themselves to Amida. Non-Shin Buddhists might urge that outsiders leave well enough alone, be glad for those who have found meaning, and ask no questions. But questions arise anyway. Why reject a God who created and sustains the world we *can* see in order to embrace a demigod over one we cannot, lying distantly in an undefinable direction? How wise is trusting this king-turned-buddha unknown in history, whose story only emerges in Mahāyāna sūtras and so is best described as "the most widely venerated of the *nonhistorical* (that is, Dhyani) Buddhas"[139] (emphasis added)? Why chant when no one hears?

Such questions gain importance since the sūtras that describe Amida laud the practice of upāya. *Upāya-kauśalya*, "expedient means" or "skillful means," describes the Buddha's telling untrue tales to impel the ignorant toward enlightenment. He is a kindly father laboring to rescue his foolish children who would otherwise ignore him. He spins stories to seduce them into the path. Though fabrications, his fables were intended for good, so he remains guiltless in telling them. The tale of the Phantom City illustrates:

> Monks, you must understand this. The Thus Come One in his use of expedient means penetrates deeply into the nature of living beings. He knows how their minds delight in petty doctrines and how deeply they are attached to the five desires. And because they are like this, when he expounds nirvana, he

does so in such a way that these persons, hearing it, can readily believe and accept it.

Let us suppose there is a stretch of bad road five hundred yojanas long, steep and difficult, wild and deserted, with no inhabitants around, a truly fearful place. And suppose there are a number of people who want to pass over this road so they can reach a place where there are rare treasures. They have a leader, of comprehensive wisdom and keen understanding, who is thoroughly acquainted with this steep road, knows the layout of its passes and defiles, and is prepared to guide the group of people and go with them over this difficult terrain.

The group he is leading, after going part way on the road, become disheartened and say to the leader, "We are utterly exhausted and fearful as well. We cannot go any farther. Since there is still such a long distance ahead, we would like now to turn around and go back."

The leader, a man of many expedients, thinks to himself, What a pity that they should abandon the many rare treasures they are seeking and want to turn around and go back! Having had this thought, he resorts to the power of expedient means and, when they have gone three hundred yojanas along the steep road, conjures up a city. He says to the group, "Don't be afraid! You must not turn back, for now here is a great city where you can stop, rest, and do just as you please. If you enter this city you will be completely at ease and tranquil. Then later, if you feel you can go on to the place where the treasure is, you can leave the city."

At that time the members of the group, being utterly exhausted, are overjoyed in mind, exclaiming over such an unprecedented event, "Now we can escape from this dreadful road and find ease and tranquility!" The people in the group thereupon press forward and enter the city where, feeling that they have been saved from their difficulties, they have a sense of complete ease and tranquility.

At that time the leader, knowing that the people have become rested and are no longer fearful or weary, wipes out the phantom city and says to the group, "You must go now.

> The place where the treasure is is close by. That great city of a while ago was a mere phantom that I conjured up so that you could rest." . . .
>
> The Buddha is like that leader who, in order to provide a place to rest, conjured up a great city and then, when he knew that the travelers were already rested, said to them, "The place where the treasure is is nearby. This city is not real. It is merely something I conjured up."[140]

From within Mahāyāna itself then, let alone assessment by dispassionate historians, the saga of Dharmākara Bodhisattva and Amida Buddha is historically questionable. Even if a vestige of fact underlies it, why should anyone believe that simply because Dharmākara vowed to create a pure land he was actually able to do so? Altruism and well-wishing are fine, but demonstrated ability to accomplish is better. If we are intent on finding home, we want to arrive at an actual abode, not a fleeting phantom. This is particularly so if one's life is at stake, and perhaps one's eternity.

Mahāyāna in general and Jōdo Shinshū in particular have erected a cairn urging that though discipline and self-control are good, they are not good enough. Even our best falls short; we must look for help beyond ourselves. But their myth does not reassure. It is told by those who endorse fables presented as truths as long as they lead to putatively noble ends. Amida's story may comfort those who choose to believe it, but believing does not make it true. Such comfort may prove fleeting in the end, just as the temporary (yet real) comfort from a placebo does not cure a disease. Would it not be nice if there were a better way, a surer way, a more historically plausible way, to lead us from our weakness and waywardness to a home of eternal light and life?

Nam Mô

Christian church near the foot of Mt. Snowdon, Wales.

8

WHAT WORKS

(*Christianity*)

When you hear the word *lamb,* what comes to mind? A white, fluffy quadruped frolicking on a grassy hillock? The poem about Mary and her little one? A favorite Mideastern entrée?

To ancient Jews, *lamb* meant "sacrifice." When John the Baptizer introduced Jesus as "the Lamb of God, who takes away the sin of the world," his metaphor clicked. Long before Israel emerged as a nation, a sacrificial lamb effected acceptance with God. A ram took Isaac's (or, for Muslims, Ishmael's) place when God tested Abraham to see whom he prized more. Enslaved Israel averted the death of her firstborn by daubing a lamb's blood on the door and devouring its meat. John's hearers knew the function of a lamb to promote peace with God.[141]

Western sensitivities and Eastern *ahiṃsā* may cause people today to recoil at the idea of sacrifice or dismiss it as primitive and unrelated to true spirituality. Sacrifice, however, continues to be crucial for several faiths. If we allow the possibility that animal offerings were God's idea rather than Moses's, then sacrifice may be necessary despite educated objections.

After Orual, heroine queen of *Till We Have Faces*, makes her under world complaint before the gods, the shade of the Fox rises to defend her. The Fox Lysias, her educated Greek slave and counselor, had in life labored to dissuade Orual from credence in the local goddess Ungit, both the ancient and updated versions. The Fox had urged reliance on human wisdom instead, but beyond death he knows better:

> Oh, Minos, or Rhadamanthus, or Persephone, or by whatever name you are called, I am to blame for most of this, and I should bear the punishment. I taught her, as men teach a parrot, to say, "Lies of poets," and "Ungit's a false image." I made her think that ended the question. I never said, Too true an image of the demon within. And then the other face of Ungit (she has a thousand) . . . something live anyway. And the real gods more alive. Neither they nor Ungit mere thoughts or words. I never told her why the old Priest got something from the dark House that I never got from my trim sentences. She never asked me (I was content she shouldn't ask) why the people got something from the shapeless stone which no one ever got from that painted doll of Arnom's. Of course, I didn't know; but I never told her I didn't know. I don't know now. Only that the way to the true gods is more like the house of Ungit . . . oh, it's unlike too, more unlike than we yet dream, but that's the easy knowledge, the first lesson; only a fool would stay there, posturing and repeating it. The Priest knew at least that there must be sacrifices. They will have sacrifices—will have man. Yes, and the very heart, center, ground, roots of a man; dark and strong and costly as blood. Send me away, Minos, even to Tartarus, if Tartarus can cure glibness. I made her think that a prattle of maxims would do, all thin and clear as water. For of course water's good; and it didn't cost much, not where I grew up. So I fed her on words.[142]

Philosophy is not enough; God exists (though, as with Ungit, often grossly misrepresented in human religions); sacrifice is essential in approaching him.

Thus, primal religions may be correct when they claim that sacrifice plays a role in approaching the divine. For example, certain remote upland regions still practice varieties of the "Southeast Asian Megalithic Complex." Central to these are "communal feasts in which cattle, water buffalo or *mithan* (Asiatic bison) are slaughtered and offered to the inhabitants of the sky world."[143] Nuances of exactly why such sacrifices are made vary around the world, but generating some benefit to those who offer is the common thread. "Spiritual potency is obtained by establishing and renewing relationship with the skypeople. Sacrifices of cattle, water buffalo or *mithan* are the primary means through which this is accomplished."[144] Though sacrifices may have been unrelated to atonement in ancient China (eighth through fifth centuries BCE), according to the Confucian classic *Li Chi* or *Book of Rites*, "Of all elements in ritual 'none is more important than sacrifice.'"[145]

But a question remains, both for the sacrifices prescribed by the primal religions and those mandated by Moses: How can the blood of an *animal* atone before *God* for the sins of a *human*?

They can't. The New Testament book of Hebrews explains:

> [T]he gifts and sacrifices that are being offered can't perfect the conscience of the one who is serving. These are superficial regulations . . . that have been imposed until the time of the new order . . .
>
> The Law is a shadow of the good things that are coming, not the real things themselves. It never can perfect the ones who are trying to draw near to God through the same sacrifices that are offered continually every year. Otherwise, wouldn't they have stopped being offered? If the people carrying out their religious duties had been completely cleansed once, no one would have been aware of sin anymore. Instead, these sacrifices are a reminder of sin every year, because it's impossible for the blood of bulls and goats to take away sins.[146]

Although God mandates sacrifice, animals cannot ultimately qualify. Only human sacrifice can atone for human sin. Thus the need for the crucifixion of Jesus. Foreseeing his impending execution Jesus prayed, "Abba, Father, for you all things are possible. Take this cup of suffering away from me. However—not what I want but what you want."[147] Since God did not remove that cup he evidently did require the crucifixion, and the rest is history.

Until Jesus no acceptable offering had arisen. He was uniquely qualified to serve as the Lamb of God. He alone was morally spotless, just as the Levitical animal sacrifices that foreshadowed him had to be physically spotless. Jesus was also willing: "I am the good shepherd. The good shepherd lays down his life for the sheep. . . . No one takes it from me, but I give it up because I want to. I have the right to give it up, and I have the right to take it up again."[148]

In what ways does Christ's sacrifice benefit the believer?

(1) He delivers from God's wrath. Love is central to God's character. His wrath, which is "not so much an emotion or an angry frame of mind as it is the settled opposition of his holiness to evil,"[149] is aroused by sin. God will judge but prefers to forgive. His foundational love for humanity and goodwill toward all creation form the backdrop for his real and terrifying judgments. These are intended to evoke change and punish recalcitrance. *The Jewish Study Bible* comments on the promise of reward and the threat of punishment:

> [T]he disasters threatened here are not punishments. Rather they are warnings arranged as a series of successive attempts to discipline the Israelites, that is, to force them into obedience. Each stage demonstrates an example of the sort of deadly disaster God may let loose upon them if they persist in their refusal to obey. Even the final stage, though it includes the element of vengeance and seems at first to be aimed at bringing Israel's national existence to an end (as in Deuteronomy), is finally revealed to be yet another attempt at making Israel walk the straight and narrow. This stage, entailing destruction and exile, will culminate in Israel's remorse; when this occurs God will remember his covenant and try once again to implement His plan of abiding in their midst and ruling over them. The effect of this diatribe is complex. On the one hand, it rains down upon the listener an unending barrage of fire and brimstone. The very contemplation of the horrors described forces the individual to consider the consequences of acting against the will of a God so uncompromising and so powerful. On the other hand, it casts God not in the role of the petty tyrant exacting retaliation for each infringement but rather as the undeterred ruler, patient but far from passive, who realizes that he may not achieve his end immediately and that severe measures may be necessary. God is pictured here as compelled to give repeated second chances, since he is bound and determined to have his way and cannot simply give up. In Priestly thought, the covenant cannot ever become null and void.[150]

The God who is love will nevertheless judge—first to turn people away from sin, then to punish those who refuse. The New Testament says the same:

> [D]o you have contempt for the riches of God's generosity, tolerance, and patience? Don't you realize that God's kindness is supposed to lead you to change your heart and life? You are storing up wrath for yourself because of your stubbornness and your heart that refuses to change. God's just judgment will be revealed on the day of wrath. God will repay everyone based on their works. On the one hand, he will give eternal life to those who look for glory, honor, and immortality based on their patient good work. But on the other hand, there will be wrath and anger for those who obey wickedness instead of the truth because they are acting out of selfishness and disobedience. There will be trouble and distress for every human being who does evil, for the Jew first and also for the Greek. But there will be glory, honor, and peace for everyone who does what is good, for the Jew first and also for the Greek. God does not have favorites.[151]

God's wrath or "settled opposition to evil" targets not only sinful deeds but also culpable disbelief: "Whoever does not believe stands condemned already because he has not believed in the name of God's one and only Son . . . whoever rejects the Son will not see life, for God's wrath remains on him." God says all need a deliverer; in Jesus he has provided one; refusal to believe constitutes calling God mistaken or misleading. Such disbelief elicits wrath: some people will "perish because they refused to love the truth and so be saved."[152] But God first disciplines in an attempt to transform doubters into believers. For those who do turn, Jesus, by his sacrificial death, "saves" and "rescues" from God's wrath.[153]

(2) He serves as substitute. Justice demands punishment for sin. A just God cannot simply dismiss sin as if it hadn't happened. He can only justly pardon because Christ has paid the penalty:

> God presented Christ as a sacrifice of atonement, through the shedding of his blood . . . to demonstrate his righteousness,

> because in his forbearance he had left the sins committed beforehand unpunished—he did it to demonstrate his righteousness at the present time, so as to be just and the one who justifies those who have faith in Jesus.[154]

God can simultaneously be just and justifier because Jesus served as a "sacrifice of atonement." The penalty has been paid. God is not overlooking sin—an innocent victim took the place of the guilty sinner.

Other New Testament texts reiterate this theme of substitution. "[T]he man Christ Jesus . . . gave himself up as a ransom for all people."[155] "Christ redeemed us from the curse of the law by becoming a curse for us."[156] Though Jewish exegesis disagrees, the New Testament understands the Suffering Servant of Isaiah 53 to be the Messiah Jesus:

> He is despised and rejected by men;
>   a man of sorrows, and acquainted with grief:
> and we hid as it were our faces from him;
>   he was despised, and we esteemed him not.
> Surely he has borne our griefs,
>   and carried our sorrows:
> yet we esteemed him stricken,
>   smitten of God, and afflicted.
> But he was wounded for our transgressions,
>   he was bruised for our iniquities:
> the chastisement that brought us peace was upon him;
>   and with his stripes we are healed.
> All we like sheep have gone astray;
>   we have turned every one to his own way;
> and Yahweh has laid on him the iniquity of us all.
> He was oppressed, and he was afflicted,
>   yet he opened not his mouth:
> he is brought as a lamb to the slaughter,
>   and as a sheep before her shearers is dumb,
>   so he did not open his mouth.
> He was taken from prison and from judgment:
>   and who shall declare his generation?

> for he was cut off out of the land of the living:
> for the transgression of my people was he stricken.
> And he made his grave with the wicked,
> and with the rich in his death;
> although he had done no violence,
> neither was any deceit in his mouth.
> Yet it pleased Yahweh to bruise him;
> he has put him to grief:
> when you make his soul an offering for sin,
> he shall see his seed,
> he shall prolong his days,
> and the pleasure of Yahweh shall prosper in his hand.
> He shall see of the travail of his soul,
> and shall be satisfied:
> by his knowledge shall my righteous servant justify many;
> for he shall bear their iniquities.
> Therefore will I divide him a portion with the great,
> and he shall divide the spoil with the strong;
> because he has poured out his soul unto death:
> and he was numbered with the transgressors;
> and he bore the sin of many,
> and made intercession for the transgressors.[157]

Asked to whom this passage referred, the evangelist Philip replied with "the good news about Jesus."[158] Although the crucifixion of Christ provides many benefits, the foundational one is substitution.

(3) He reconciles believers with God.

> [A]ll the fullness of God
> was pleased to live in him,
> and he reconciled all things to
> himself through him—
> whether things on earth
> or in the heavens.
> He brought peace
> through the blood of his cross.

> Once you were alienated from God and you were enemies with him in your minds, which was shown by your evil actions. But now he has reconciled you by his physical body through death, to present you before God as a people who are holy, faultless, and without blame.[159]

> [I]f, while we were God's enemies, we were reconciled to him through the death of his Son, how much more, having been reconciled, shall we be saved through his life! Not only is this so, but we also boast in God through our Lord Jesus Christ, through whom we have now received reconciliation.[160]

These passages weave together the themes of rescue from wrath, substitution, and reconciliation. Christianity both echoes other religions and then goes further: God is worth knowing, sin separates, but the substitutionary sacrifice of the Lamb of God reconciles the estranged.

(4) He grants assurance of acceptance. As an historical person who offered an objective sacrifice, Jesus gives a more reasonable hope for acceptance than does Amida Buddha. The historicity of Jesus's crucifixion, which is the antitype of the Levitical sacrifices, is acknowledged even by contemporaries who reject his claims.[161] Hence the Christian's peace is less likely to devolve from wishful thinking:

> So what are we going to say about these things? If God is for us, who is against us? He didn't spare his own Son but gave him up for us all. Won't he also freely give us all things with him? Who will bring a charge against God's elect people? It is God who acquits them. Who is going to convict them? It is Christ Jesus who died, even more, who was raised, and who also is at God's right side. It is Christ Jesus who also pleads our case for us. Who will separate us from Christ's love? Will we be separated by trouble, or distress, or harassment, or famine, or nakedness, or danger, or sword? As it is written,
>
> *We are being put to death all day long for your sake.*
> *We are treated like sheep for slaughter.*
>
> But in all these things we win a sweeping victory through

> the one who loved us. I'm convinced that nothing can separate us from God's love in Christ Jesus our Lord: not death or life, not angels or rulers, not present things or future things, not powers or height or depth, or any other thing that is created.[162]

> Therefore, since the children share in flesh and blood, he also shared the same things in the same way. He did this to destroy the one who holds the power over death—the devil—by dying. He set free those who were held in slavery their entire lives by their fear of death.[163]

"It would be so wonderful to feel good about ourselves again . . . and feel we are people to be loved and admired. Religion properly understood can give us that feeling. It is perhaps the best and most valuable thing that religion ever does."[164] Properly understood, the crucifixion of Jesus does just this.

Christianity is many things: loving God and neighbor, practicing the Sermon on the Mount, caring for orphan and widow, and providing for the needs of self and others. But all are meaningless without Calvary and the empty tomb. The cross is therefore the symbol of Christianity, the glory of Christianity, the sine qua non of Christianity. Not because it is pretty but because it is powerful; not because it is popular but despite its propensity to polarize; not because it is the Christian's prejudice but because it is God's plan. It is through the cross of Jesus and his sacrificial blood that the Christian finds an objective basis to believe that God's wrath is appeased, the yawning chasm between God and himself or herself is bridged, the guilty conscience is legitimately stilled, and a final welcome home is assured.

The non-Christian, by contrast, may see the cross as scandalous,[165] unremarkable, or unnecessary. Many Buddhists cannot understand the choice of such a bloody, violent symbol and prefer instead to picture the Buddha peacefully pondering.[166] A Hindu, recalling Kālī swinging a severed head and dancing on Śiva's body, may not find a slain savior extraordinary. The Muslim, who honors Jesus as a prophet, believes neither that sacrifice is necessary nor that God would allow his servant to suffer so ignominiously:

> . . . they said (in boast),
> "We killed Christ Jesus

The son of Mary,
The Messenger of Allah"—
But they killed him not,
Nor crucified him,
But so it was made
To appear to them.
And those who differ
Therein are full of doubts,
With no (certain) knowledge,
But only conjecture to follow,
For of a surety
They killed him not—
Nay, Allah raised him up
Unto Himself; and Allah
Is Exalted in Power, Wise—[167]

Mystics who often think exclusively of love prefer "a God that would never cripple us with guilt or control us with fear."[168] The secular humanist may find the story of Jesus's crucifixion a rehash of primitive attempts to appease an angry deity. Such understandings and rejections have accompanied the gospel story from its early days:

> The message of the cross is foolishness to those who are being destroyed. But it is the power of God for those of us who are being saved. It is written in scripture: *I will destroy the wisdom of the wise, and I will reject the intelligence of the intelligent.* Where are the wise? Where are the legal experts? Where are today's debaters? Hasn't God made the wisdom of the world foolish? In God's wisdom, he determined that the world wouldn't come to know him through its wisdom. Instead, God was pleased to save those who believe through the foolishness of preaching. Jews ask for signs, and Greeks look for wisdom, but we preach Christ crucified, which is a scandal to Jews and foolishness to Gentiles. But to those who are called—both Jews and Greeks—Christ is God's power and God's wisdom. This is because the foolishness of God is

> wiser than human wisdom, and the weakness of God is stronger than human strength.[169]

Discipline and self-reliance are good. God is righteous, so upright motives and actions please him. But change cannot cancel culpability for crimes already committed. No one perfectly pursues or practices righteousness anyway. Self-power cannot restore relationship with God because change does not eradicate past debt and because our nature (as Confucius and Shinran observed) does not incline us toward flawless motives and actions. We need forgiveness and empowerment, both of which require Other-power.

The Shin Buddhist relies on the nonhistorical Amida and his vow. In the cross of Christ the Christian finds a more objective and powerful cure for human weakness. The crucifixion of the Lamb of God unveils the awfulness of human sin. We are guilty of more than creaturely immaturity and error. But the cross speaks just as strongly of God's love and grace. If God's Son died in my place and pronounces me forgiven, then forgiven I am. The human conscience can be cleansed because sin has not been reduced to something less; it has been fully faced and then paid for. The cross takes human sin and responsibility seriously. It takes the wrath of God seriously. It takes human inability seriously. It cleanses the conscience completely.

No wonder the Christian sings,

> In the cross of Christ I glory,
> Towering o'er the wrecks of time.
> All the light of sacred story
> Gathers round its head sublime.[170]

And,

> My sin—O the bliss of this glorious thought!—
> My sin, not in part but the whole
> Is nailed to the cross, and I bear it no more.
> Praise the Lord! Praise the Lord, O my soul!
> It is well with my soul.
> It is well, it is well, with my soul.[171]

Or in the words of one writer weaving the interworkings of faith, forgiveness, and a fulfilling life:

> [T]he appeal to any sort of good works can never be the basis of being a Christian and the criterion for justification in the sight of God. All that counts is to cling to God absolutely firmly through Jesus the Christ in a believing trust, against which neither human failures nor any good works can prevail, but from which works of love obviously follow. This is an extraordinarily consoling message which provides a solid basis for a man's life through all the inevitable failures, errors and despair. And it frees that life also from the pressure to produce pious works, sustaining it through even the worst situations in freedom, wisdom, love and hope . . .
>
> We began this book with the direct question: *Why should one be a Christian?* And the answer is equally direct: *In order to be truly human. . . .*
>
> *By following Jesus Christ*
> *man in the world of today*
> *can truly humanly live, act, suffer and die:*
> *in happiness and unhappiness, life and death,*
> *sustained by God and helpful to men.*[172]

The Christians are right: the crucifixion of Jesus exposes and expunges human sin in a way that nothing else can. It thus relieves "the guilt complex which so bedevils the Western mind" more completely than does the expedient of reducing guilt to a guilt complex. As the willing death of a qualified substitute, Christ's crucifixion provides the way for God to remain righteous yet remit the penalty due the sinner. It frees from liability before and estrangement from the holy God. Sacrifice satisfies. At least this one does. It satisfies first divine displeasure with sin and then the human conscience, which craves forgiveness, acceptance, and assurance.

Daoist worship in Vietnam. Such practices differ from the more philosophical Daoism of Lao Tzu and Chuang Tzu.

9

THE WISDOM OF FOLLY

(Daoism)

For centuries, people believed that the world sat, steady and secure, at the center of the spheres. Perhaps it rested on the shoulders of Atlas or the back of a turtle. Fewer imagine so today. Of course, since absolute space does not exist and all motion is relative, the world *can* be conceived as stationary. But the math to explain the motions of stars and galaxies vis-à-vis a static earth grows complex indeed.

The Way of the universe—what it is and how it works—is what Daoists strive to find and follow. This goal of harmony with nature induces in them a noncombative, live-and-let-live attitude, a stark contrast with Nietzsche's Übermensch and Will to Power. Humanity in Daoism is but one part of nature, neither its *telos* nor its *summum bonum* nor its lofty lord.[173] A basic text is the *Daodejing*, the *Classic of the Way and Its Power*.[174] The Way posited by this and other Daoist (or Taoist) texts turns out to be indescribable. (Parenthetical numbers refer to chapters in the *Daodejing*.)

> Tao that can be spoken of,
> Is not the Everlasting Tao.
> Name that can be named,
> Is not the Everlasting name. (1)
> Tao as a thing,
> Is entirely illusive and evasive. (21)
> There was something nebulous existing,
> Born before heaven and earth.
> Silent, empty,

> Standing alone, altering not,
> Moving cyclically without becoming exhausted,
> Which may be called the mother of all under heaven.
> I know not its name,
> I give its alias, Tao.
> If forced to picture it,
> I say it is "great."
> To say it is "great" is to say it is "moving away."
> To say it is "moving away" is to say it is "far away."
> To say it is "far away" is to say it is "returning." (25)

> This is the Tao: there is in It emotion and sincerity, but It does nothing and has no bodily form. It may be handed down by the teacher, but may not be received by his scholars. It may be apprehended by the mind, but It cannot be seen. It has Its root and ground of existence in Itself. Before there were heaven and earth, from of old, there It was, securely existing. From It came the mysterious existences of spirits, from It the mysterious existence of God. It produced heaven; It produced earth. It was before the Thâi-kî [the primal ether out of which all things were fashioned by the interaction of the Yin and Yang, imagined to be in the higher regions of space], and yet could not be considered high; It was below all space, and yet could not be considered deep. It was produced before heaven and earth, and yet could not be considered to have existed long; It was older than the highest antiquity, and yet could not be considered old.[175]

Though we can neither name nor articulate the Dao, it is the ancient source of all else, and it resembles a process or principle more than an entity:

> Tao is a whirling emptiness,
> Yet in use is inexhaustible.
> Fathomless,
> It seems to be the ancestor of ten thousand beings.
> It blunts the sharp,
> Unties the entangled,

Harmonizes the bright,
Mixes the dust.
Dark,
It seems perhaps to exist.
I do not know whose child it is,
It is an image of what precedes God. (4)

As a non-entity (or near non-entity) Tao is easily overlooked, but its workings are powerful:

Tao, when it is uttered by the mouth,
Is so bland it has no flavor.
When looked at, it is not enough to be seen.
When listened to, it is not enough to be heard,
When used, it is inexhaustible. (35)
When a superior person hears Tao,
He diligently practices it.
When a middling person hears Tao,
He hears it, he doesn't hear it.
When the inferior person hears Tao, he roars.
If Tao were not laughed at,
It would not be Tao . . .
Yet it is Tao alone,
That is good in lending help and fulfilling all. (41)

Tao, as non-being, functions by giving birth first to being (one); then to pairs of opposites—earth and heaven, *yin* and *yang*, dark and light, etc. (two); then to combinations of these opposites in varying proportions (three); and finally to the myriad of existing entities (ten thousand things):

Ten thousand things under heaven are born of being.
Being is born of non-being. (40)
Tao gives birth to one,
One gives birth to two,
Two gives birth to three,
Three gives birth to ten thousand beings.

> Ten thousand beings carry *yin* on their backs and embrace
> *yang* in their front,
> Blending these two vital breaths to attain harmony. (42)

The Way of things, then, is that they arise within the empty yet pregnant womb of the Tao, exist for a time, unravel, reenter the Tao's undifferentiated unity, and reemerge as something new. The process is inexorable and eternal. The wise understand and do not resist the process, and thus can enjoy a long, peaceful life.

> We are taught that to be truly free we must be able to work with change rather than against it—we must be able to dance gracefully with the ever-unfolding panorama of change that constitutes life. We are also taught that to remain simple, even if it appears to the outside world that we are simpletons, is the best way to align ourselves with the ever-unfolding Way. In addition we must be humble, flexible and detached from outward form.[176]

It is futile and impoverishing to seek to circumvent the way things are.

Several corollaries devolve from such a desire "to dance gracefully with the ever-unfolding panorama of change that constitutes life." The first is *wu wei* or "no action." By "no action" Daoism does not imply that people should be indifferent, practice *laissez faire* or Stoic apathy, and do nothing at all. What it means is that we should not take any conscious action against nature. Wu wei is "acting with, not against, the inner rhythms of things" in contrast with *wei*, imposing "an order on things alien to their inner rhythm."[177] Human action, *wei*, imposes an order on nature, and in so doing disrupts and destroys. By contrast, natural transformation, *hua*, "is the process by which natural beings unfold according to their inner rhythm."[178] Life is to be lived, to be loved, but this is possible only through cooperation with the way things are, not by fighting it. Wu wei does not imply, for example, that lying down is better than walking. Walking is how to get somewhere on land. For crossing a river, a boat is better. But how foolish to attempt land travel by rowing: "If you are travelling by water, your best plan is to use a boat; if by land, a carriage.

Take a boat, which will go easily along on the water, and try to push it along on the land, and all your lifetime it will not go so much as a fathom or two."[179]

Why try to push a leaf upriver? It would not be surprising to hear a Daoist ask, Why insist on rebuilding a city destroyed by a hurricane when it lies below sea level and continues to subside, when ocean levels are rising and storm strength increasing, and when even greater disasters threaten in the future? Why not recognize the nature of things and build somewhere else? Daoism displays little sense of "fighting nature" or "conquering mountains," as if nature were a foe that had to be shown who is boss.

> The true character of wu wei is not mere inactivity but *perfect action*—because it is act without activity. In other words, it is action not carried out independently of Heaven and earth and in conflict with the dynamism of the whole, but in perfect harmony with the whole. It is not mere passivity, but it is action that seems both effortless and spontaneous because performed "rightly," in perfect accordance with out nature and with our place in the scheme of things. It is completely free because there is in it no force and no violence . . .[180]

Le Guin's *Lathe of Heaven*[181] explores the disastrous nature of wei in contrast with wu wei.

Such noninterference applies to politics as well. In Daoism, as throughout most of human history, religious beliefs are not artificially bracketed off from social and political values. To suggest otherwise, as the West often does, is inexplicable to most of the world's people. What we think *of course* influences what we do. At any rate, wu wei means that the ideal ruler is one who governs as one would cook a small fish—with little labor, great care, and a light touch (60).

> The highest rulers, people do not know they have them
> The next level, people love them and praise them
> The next level, people fear them
> The next level, people despise them

If the rulers' trust is insufficient
Have no trust in them
Proceeding calmly, valuing their words
Task accomplished, matter settled
The people all say, "We did it naturally." (17 Lin)

Here the *Daodejing* suggests that the best government "is so inobtrusive its people barely know it exists . . . Government blends so well with the natural environment that its actions are indistinguishable from those of nature."[182] The latter part of this chapter concludes that

> The ideal way is to govern in an unhurried manner, where rulers are bound by their words, and therefore never speak lightly. Such rulers tend to do more and talk less. This, in turn, means the affairs of the state are conducted in a nondisruptive way. The people, unaware of all the work that goes into governing, assume that they did it themselves.[183]

A second corollary is humility. Humanity should not sit spiderlike at the center of a cosmic web, poised to snare and engorge itself on all that happens by. We are neither the apex up to which evolution has painfully struggled nor the reason for which all else exists. We are rather one small part of the natural world and need to fit harmoniously, not imperially, within it. To illustrate the value and power of humility, Daoists frequently cite water:

Best to be like water,
Which benefits the ten thousand things
And does not contend.
It pools where humans disdain to dwell,
Close to the Tao.
    Live in a good place.
    Keep your mind deep.
    Treat others well.
    Stand by your word.
    Keep good order.
    Do the right thing.

> Work when it's time.
> Only do not contend,
> And you will not go wrong. (8 Addiss)
>
> Nothing under heaven
> Is softer and weaker than water,
> Yet nothing can compare with it
> In attacking the hard and strong.
> Nothing can changc place with it.
> That the weak overcomes the strong,
> And the soft overcomes the hard,
> No one under heaven does not know,
> Though none can put it into practice. (78)
>
> If the body be overworked, and does not rest, it becomes worn out; if the spirit be used without cessation, it becomes overworked; and when that happens, it becomes exhausted. It is the nature of water, when free from admixture, to be clear, and, when not agitated, to be level; while if obstructed and not allowed to flow, it cannot preserve its clearness—being an image of the virtue of Heaven. Hence it is said, "To be guileless and pure, and free from all admixture; to be still and uniform, without undergoing any change; to be indifferent and do nothing; to move in the manner of Heaven—this is the way to nourish the spirit."[184]

Water is humble in that it always flows downhill and seeks the lowest place, the place nothing else wants:

> A large kingdom must be like the low ground towards which all streams flow down. It must be a point towards which all things under heaven converge. Its part must be that of the female in its dealings with all things under heaven. The female by quiescence conquers the male; by quiescence gets underneath. If a large kingdom can in the same way succeed in getting underneath a small kingdom then it will win the adherence of

the small kingdom; and it is because small kingdoms are by nature in this way underneath large kingdoms that they win the adherence of large kingdoms. The one must get underneath in order to do it; the other is underneath and therefore does it. What large countries really need is more inhabitants; and what small countries need is some place where their surplus inhabitants can go and get employment. Thus each gets what it needs. That is why I say the large kingdom must 'get underneath.' (61 Waley)

How does the sea
become the queen of all rivers and streams?
By lying lower than they do!
Hence, it is the queen of all rivers and streams.
One who humbles himself, therefore,
    can serve all people.
By putting himself last, he comes to be their leader.
Thus, when one of subtle virtue is set above people,
    they do not feel that he is their burden.
And, when he stands in front of people,
    they do not feel that he is an obstruction to them.
Therefore, the world follows one of subtle virtue joyfully,
    and never tires of doing so.
He does not compete with anyone,
    thus he is above all competition. (66 Hua-Ching Ni)

When a body is alive, it is soft and supple
—it is cold and rigid when it dies.
When plants are alive, they are tender and trailing
—and burnt and brittle when they're dead.
What's iron hard is what is dead, then
And what is fluid and sensuous and rippling is alive . . .
And that is why a huge army
With all its strength and complacency will be defeated:
Like a great tree
    axed down.

> Everything hard and strong will come down,
> And everything soft
> shall rise, shall overcome. (76 Man-Ho Kwok)
>
> Heaven and earth
> are enduring.
> The universe can live for ever,
> because it does not live for itself.
> And so both last—outliving themselves.
> The sage guides his people
> by putting himself last.
> Desiring nothing for himself,
> he knows how to channel desires.
> And is it not because he wants nothing
> that he is able to achieve everything? (7 Man-Ho Kwok)
>
> Like Lao Tzu, Master Chuang preaches an essential humility: not the humility of virtuousness and conscious self-abasement, which in the end is never entirely free from the unctuousness of Uriah Heep, but the basic, one might say, "ontological," or "cosmic" humility of the man who fully realizes his own nothingness and becomes totally forgetful of himself, "like a dry tree stump . . . like dead ashes."
>
> One may call this humility "cosmic," not only because it is rooted in the true nature of things, but also because it is full of life and awareness, responding with boundless vitality and joy to all living beings. It manifests itself everywhere by a Franciscan simplicity and connaturality with all living creatures. Half the "characters" who are brought before us to speak the mind of Chuang Tzu are animals—birds, fishes, frogs, and so on. Chuang Tzu's Taoism is nostalgic for the primordial climate of paradise . . .[185]

If humility is wisdom, simplicity of lifestyle follows as a third corollary. Thomas Merton redraws two familiar sketches from the *Chuang Tzu* [*Zhuangzi*].[186] One features a turtle, the second an owl and a phoenix:

Chuang Tzu with his bamboo pole
Was fishing in Pu river.
The Prince of Chu
Sent two vice-chancellors
With a formal document:
"We hereby appoint you
Prime Minister."
Chuang Tzu held his bamboo pole.
Still watching Pu river,
He said:
"I am told there is a sacred tortoise,
Offered and canonized
Three thousand years ago,
Venerated by the prince,
Wrapped in silk,
In a precious shrine
On an altar
in the Temple.
"What do you think:
Is it better to give up one's life
And leave a sacred shell
As an object of cult
In a cloud of incense
Three thousand years,
Or better to live
As a plain turtle
Dragging its tail in the mud?"
"For the turtle," said the Vice-Chancellor,
"Better to live
And drag its tail in the mud!"
"Go home!" said Chuang Tzu.
"Leave me here
To drag my tail in the mud!"

Hui Tzu was Prime Minister of Liang. He had what he believed to be inside information that Chuang Tzu coveted his post and was intriguing to supplant him. In fact, when Chuang Tzu came to visit Liang, the Prime Minister sent out the police to apprehend him. The police searched for him three days and three nights, but meanwhile Chuang presented himself before Hui Tzu of his own accord, and said:

"Have you heard about the bird
That lives in the south
The Phoenix that never grows old?
This undying Phoenix
Rises out of the South Sea
And flies to the Sea of the North,
Never alighting
Except on certain sacred trees.
He will touch no food
But the most exquisite
Rare fruit.
Drinks only
From clearest springs.
Once an owl
Chewing a dead rat
Already half-decayed,
Saw the Phoenix fly over,
Looked up,
And screeched with alarm,
Clutching the rat to himself
In fear and dismay.
Why are you so frantic
Clinging to your ministry
And screeching at me
In dismay?"[187]

Clearly Chuang Tzu preferred the simple pleasures of an ordinary turtle dragging its tail in the mud to the pomp of prime ministership—a position that would kill his freedom-loving spirit. That post so enviable to others seemed to him a half-decayed rat corpse compared to his everyday enjoyment of the Dao. Indeed, grasping and corrupt government can destroy the simple pleasures of life:

The people's hunger
Is due to the excess of their ruler's taxation
So they starve
The people's difficulty in being governed
Is due to the meddling of their ruler
So they are difficult to govern
The people's disregard for death
Is due to the glut in their ruler's pursuit of life
So they disregard death
Therefore those who do not strive for living
Are better than those who value living. (75 Lin)

The government is divided,
Fields are overgrown,
Granaries are empty,
But the nobles' clothes are gorgeous,
Their belts show off swords,
And they are glutted with food and drink.
Personal wealth is excessive.
This is called thieves' endowment,
 But it is not Tao. (53 Addiss)

For Daoists, simplicity surpasses power, pomp, position, and possessions. A sense of humor and not taking oneself too seriously naturally emerge from such simplicity, and these shine through the *Daodejing* and the *Zhuangzi*.

A fourth corollary is peace.

Military weapons are implements of ill omen,
Avoided even by natural creatures.
Hence the Taoist does not indulge in them.
The princely person in dwelling honors the left,
In military campaigns honors the right.
Hence military weapons are not implements of a princely
 person.
Military weapons, being implements of ill omen,
Are to be employed only in dire necessity.

Better to regard them with lack of interest.
Do not admire them.
If one admires them,
One would be rejoicing in the killing of people.
But whoever rejoices in the killing of people,
Will not be successful in the world.
Therefore in joyful affairs the left is honored,
In mournful affairs the right is honored.
The Second-in-Command takes the place of the left,
The Commander-in-Chief takes the place of the right,
Meaning that this is his place in the funeral rite.
When many people have been killed,
Wail them with sorrow and lamentations.
When victorious in battle,
Mark the occasion with the rite of funeral. (31)
In engaging in warfare it is said:
I dare not be the host but be the guest,
I dare not advance an inch but retreat a foot.
This is called to march without advancing,
To roll up one's sleeves without baring one's arms,
To throw a rope without an enemy,
To carry without a weapon.
Of all calamities,
None is greater than underestimating one's enemy.
In underestimating my enemy,
I risk losing my treasure.
Therefore when opposing armies are engaged in battle,
The sorrowful party will win. (69)
When the world practices Tao,
Fast horses are used for their dung.
When the world does not practice Tao,
War horses give birth at the borders.
Among offenses, none is greater than having what is desirable.
Among calamities, none is greater than not knowing contentment.
Among blames, none is greater than the desire for gain.

> Therefore the contentment that comes from knowing
> contentment
> Is a long lasting contentment. (46)
> The great generals are not warlike
> The great warriors do not get angry
> Those who are good at defeating enemies do not engage them
> Those who are good at managing people lower themselves
> It is called the virtue of non-contention
> It is called the power of managing people
> It is called being harmonious with Heaven
> The ultimate principle of the ancients. (68 Lin)

Peace, in fact, may be said to be the central message of the *Daodejing*—"the peace of all in the bosom of Tao from which all beings issue and in which all conflicts and struggles dissolve (ch 4.2). Its vision of peace is grounded in a vision of the ultimate reality as non-being whose passivity and self-abnegation allow all beings to be."[188] "Peace between humans and nature, and among nations and states, comes from the realization that we all have the same origin, live in one common environment, and share the same destiny."[189]

The Daoism described in this chapter is that of its classic texts, not the variants—some would say corruptions—that have arisen since. One commentator contemplates Lao Tzu's despondency

> could he have foreseen how his pure and idealistic teaching was destined to be dragged in the mire of degrading superstition, which for centuries has made Taoism a byword of reproach. Though frequently described as one of the "three religions of China," this cult is really little more than an inextricable mass of jugglery and fraud, absorbed from various popular belief and other sources, including even the rival creed of Buddhism, and conducted by a body of priests recruited from the very dregs of the Empire.[190]

It is not surprising that Lin Yutang (1895–1976), who migrated twice between Christianity and Daoism, "criticizes Taoism as a religion but appreciates the Taoism of Laozi and Zhuangzi."[191]

The original Daoist aspiration to embrace reality rather than fantasy appears so axiomatic that it should require no urging. But it does. A life well lived builds upon what is. It is insufficient—and can be catastrophic—to concoct a worldview that, though cohering internally, skews the universe externally.

So the Daoists are right. Insistence on truth is part of the path home. Only folly, waste, and ruin result from resisting reality and imposing upon it an alien agenda. Confucius agrees: "The wise man accepts his genuine nature. Even though he may be completely unknown, ignored by everyone, he lives without remorse."[192] When we contemplate our place in the grand scheme of things, Daoist values of humility, harmony, humor, and peace also commend themselves. But still we may ask, does traditional Daoism consider all the relevant facts about our universe before compiling its system? Has anything of substance escaped its attention? Is it possible to apply to overlooked truths and history this valid Daoist insistence upon living in accordance with what *is?*

If, for example, Muslims are right when they acknowledge a transcendent yet personal God, primal religionists are onto something when they suggest that human sin has carved a cavern distancing God from humanity, and Christians correctly confess that Christ's crucifixion closes the gap, then why not incorporate these truths into our worldview? If that is how things are, why fight them? If God exists, why ignore him? If not, why invoke him? Why follow theistic fictions if we wish, now and in the future, to embrace reality and arrive home? But if God *does* exist, then there is no sense fighting him, pretending that we can make it on our own, and charging solo down the road. A Daoist-type response would be to accept reality with humility rather than vaunt ourselves as stronger or nobler than we are. Better like the grass to bend in the breeze than with the tree stubbornly resist and fall; wiser with water to welcome the weaker rather than the worthier place.

Durga at the Sri Durgiana or Silver Temple in Amritsar.

10

RESPONDING TO GRACE

(*Hinduism*)

An epic battle looms. Duryodhana and the Kauravas have no intention of returning the kingdom they have finagled from their cousins the Pāṇḍavas. So on the fields of Kurukṣetra two armies gird for war. Before the clash commences Pāṇḍava champion Arjuna urges his charioteer Kṛṣṇa to drive him through no-man's-land between the two armies so he can eye his enemy:

> ARJUNA: O Krishna, drive my chariot between the two armies. I want to see those who desire to fight with me. With whom will this battle be fought? I want to see those assembled to fight for Duryodhana, those who seek to please the evil-minded son of Dhritarashtra by engaging in war . . .
>
> SANJAYA: And Arjuna, standing between the two armies, saw fathers and grandfathers, teachers, uncles, and brothers, sons and grandsons, in-laws and friends. Seeing his kinsmen established in opposition, Arjuna was overcome by sorrow. Despairing, he spoke these words:
>
> ARJUNA: O Krishna, I see my own relations here anxious to fight, and my limbs grow weak; my mouth is dry, my body shakes, and my hair is standing on end. My skin burns, and the bow Gandiva has slipped from my hand. I am unable to stand; my mind seems to be whirling. These signs bode evil for us. I

do not see that any good can come from killing our relations in battle . . .

O Krishna, what satisfaction could we find in killing Dhritarashtra's sons? We would become sinners by slaying these men, even though they are evil. The sons of Dhritarashtra are related to us; therefore, we should not kill them. How can we gain happiness by killing members of our own family?

Though they are overpowered by greed and see no evil in destroying families or injuring friends, *we* see these evils. Why shouldn't we turn away from this sin? When a family declines, ancient traditions are destroyed. With them are lost the spiritual foundations for life, and the family loses its sense of unity. Where there is no sense of unity, the women of the family become corrupt; and with the corruption of its women, society is plunged into chaos. Social chaos is hell for the family and for those who have destroyed the family as well. It disrupts the process of spiritual evolution begun by our ancestors. The timeless spiritual foundations of family and society would be destroyed by these terrible deeds, which violate the unity of life.

It is said that those whose family dharma has been destroyed dwell in hell. This is a great sin! We are prepared to kill our own relations out of greed for the pleasures of a kingdom. Better for me if the sons of Dhritarashtra, weapons in hand, were to attack me in battle and kill me unarmed and unresisting.

SANJAYA: Overwhelmed by sorrow, Arjuna spoke these words. And casting away his bow and his arrows, he sat down in his chariot in the middle of the battlefield.[193]

With royal Arjuna incapacitated by indecision, it fell to his charioteer to counsel the wavering warrior and embolden him for battle. This Krishna proceeds to do. He chides that despair and weakness ill befit the warrior-prince. Though the body may be destroyed, the Self within survives, so there is no true "killing" anyway. It is Arjuna's dharma as *kṣatriya* (a warrior) to fight; refusal would tarnish his honor and offer his enemies opportunity to mock. If he fights he wins whatever the outcome: should he die in battle he enters heaven; should he survive he acquires a kingdom. Arjuna's course, therefore, is to do his duty and fight, unconcerned about whether he win or lose.

Krishna's counsel applies to all of life and not just this particular battle. Arjuna asks as much: "My will is paralyzed, and I am utterly confused. Tell me which is the better path for me. Let me be your disciple. I have fallen at your feet; give me instruction" (2.7). As charioteer counsels chieftain, Krishna reveals that he is no mere mortal, and thus his advice surpasses human opinion. Arjuna's questions then progress from whether to fight this battle and what his worldview should be, to how he should worship this god with whom he speaks: "Of those steadfast devotees who love you and those who seek you as the eternal formless Reality, who are the more established in yoga?" (12.1).

Yoga comes from *yuj*, Sanskrit for "yoke," "unite," or "bind together." Yoga is a state of union with God, or a discipline leading to such union. By asking who are more established in yoga, Arjuna wonders who is closer to God, or who is best pursuing being one with him. Put nontheistically, yoga seeks profound insight into the nature of existence, resulting in the yogin's or yoginī's transcendence of the limited ego to the experience of the true self; it is deep spiritual wholeness. There are four disciplines (*yogas*) or paths (*mārgas*) that the *Gītā* advises—*karma, jñāna*, *bhakti*, and *rāja*: action, knowledge, devotion, and concentration.[194] Following any one or any combination of these leads to union with God or profound insight.

Krishna expounds these yogas. Arjuna should pursue all four. First, he should practice karmayoga. That is, Arjuna should do his duty as best he can, unconcerned whether he gain or lose in the process. Krishna speaks:

> You have the right to work, but never to the fruit of work. You should never engage in action for the sake of reward, nor should you long for inaction. Perform work in this world, Arjuna, as a man established within himself—without selfish attachments, and alike in success and defeat. For yoga is perfect evenness of mind.
>
> Seek refuge in the attitude of detachment and you will amass the wealth of spiritual awareness. Those who are motivated only by desire for the fruits of action are miserable, for they are constantly anxious about the results of what they do. When consciousness is unified, however, all vain anxiety is left

> behind. There is no cause for worry, whether things go well or ill. Therefore, devote yourself to the disciplines of yoga, for yoga is skill in action.
>
> The wise unify their consciousness and abandon attachment to the fruits of action, which binds a person to continual rebirth. Thus they attain a state beyond all evil (2.47–51).
>
> There is nothing in the three worlds for me to gain, Arjuna, nor is there anything I do not have; I continue to act, but I am not driven by any need of my own. If I ever refrained from continuous work, everyone would immediately follow my example. If I stopped working I would be the cause of cosmic chaos, and finally of the destruction of this world and these people.
>
> The ignorant work for their own profit, Arjuna; the wise work for the welfare of the world, without thought for themselves. By abstaining from work you will confuse the ignorant, who are engrossed in their actions. Perform all work carefully, guided by compassion (3.22–26).
>
> Both renunciation of action and the selfless performance of action lead to the supreme goal. But the path of action is better than renunciation . . . It is not those who lack energy or refrain from action, but those who work without expectation of reward who attain the goal of meditation. Theirs is true renunciation (5.2; 6.1).
>
> As long as one has a body, one cannot renounce action altogether. True renunciation is giving up all desire for personal reward. Those who are attached to personal reward will reap the consequences of their actions: some pleasant, some unpleasant, some mixed. But those who renounce every desire for personal reward go beyond the reach of karma (18.11–12).

Thus, the *Bhagavad Gītā* does not commend withdrawal from society as the path to spiritual awakening. What the spiritual aspirant should relinquish is not action but selfish attachment to the results of action. Work for the welfare of others excels renunciation, or perhaps constitutes what true renunciation is. Just as in Daoism wu wei does not imply passivity, so in the *Gītā* neither does renunciation. Rather, freedom and perfection result from selfless service. Such service benefits doer, recipient, and observer. Krishna himself constantly works but remains unattached to the fruits of what he does. Selfless service is the path to freedom and peace.

Second, Arjuna should grow in the yoga of jñāna—knowledge or rational inquiry.

> There has never been a time when you and I and the kings gathered here have not existed, nor will there be a time when we will cease to exist. As the same person inhabits the body through childhood, youth, and old age, so too at the time of death he attains another body. The wise are not deluded by these changes.
>
> When the senses contact sense objects, a person experiences cold or heat, pleasure or pain. These experiences are fleeting; they come and go. Bear them patiently, Arjuna. Those who are not affected by these changes, who are the same in pleasure and pain, are truly wise and fit for immortality. Assert your strength and realize this!
>
> The impermanent has no reality; reality lies in the eternal. Those who have seen the boundary between these two have attained the end of all knowledge. Realize that which pervades the universe and is indestructible; no power can affect this unchanging, imperishable reality. The body is mortal, but he who dwells in the body is immortal and immeasurable. Therefore, Arjuna, fight in this battle.
>
> One man believes he is the slayer, another believes he is the slain. Both are ignorant; there is neither slayer nor slain. You were never born; you will never die. You have never changed; you can never change. Unborn, eternal, immutable, immemorial, you do not die when the body dies. Realizing that which is indestructible, eternal, unborn, and unchanging, how can you slay or cause another to slay?
>
> As a man abandons worn-out clothes and acquires new ones, so when the body is worn out a new one is acquired by the Self, who lives within.
>
> The Self cannot be pierced by weapons or burned by fire; water cannot wet it, nor can the wind dry it. The Self cannot be

pierced or burned, made wet or dry. It is everlasting and infinite, standing on the motionless foundations of eternity. The Self is unmanifested, beyond all thought, beyond all change. Knowing this, you should not grieve.

O mighty Arjuna, even if you believe the Self to be subject to birth and death, you should not grieve. Death is inevitable for the living; birth is inevitable for the dead. Since these are unavoidable, you should not sorrow. Every creature is unmanifested at first and then attains manifestation. When its end has come, it once again becomes unmanifested. What is there to lament in this? (2.12–28).

When your mind has overcome the confusion of duality, you will attain the state of holy indifference to things you hear and things you have heard. When you are unmoved by the confusion of ideas and your mind is completely united in deep samadhi, you will attain the state of perfect yoga (2.52–53).

The offering of wisdom is better than any material offering, Arjuna; for the goal of all work is spiritual wisdom.

Approach someone who has realized the purpose of life and question him with reverence and devotion; he will instruct you in this wisdom. Once you attain it, you will never again be deluded. You will see all creatures in the Self, and all in me.

Even if you were the most sinful of sinners, Arjuna, you could cross beyond all sin by the raft of spiritual wisdom. As the heat of a fire reduces wood to ashes, the fire of knowledge burns to ashes all karma. Nothing in this world purifies like spiritual wisdom. It is the perfection achieved in time through the path of yoga, the path which leads to the Self within.

Those who take wisdom as their highest goal, whose faith is deep and whose senses are trained, attain wisdom quickly and enter into perfect peace. But the ignorant, indecisive and lacking in faith, waste their lives. They can never be happy in this world or any other.

Those established in the Self have renounced selfish attachments to their actions and cut through doubts with spiritual wisdom. They act in freedom. Arjuna, cut through this doubt

> in your own heart with the sword of spiritual wisdom. Arise; take up the path of yoga! (4.33–42).
>
> Those who know truly are free from pride and deceit. They are gentle, forgiving, upright, and pure, devoted to their spiritual teacher, filled with inner strength, and self-controlled. Detached from sense objects and self-will, they have learned the painful lesson of separate birth and suffering, old age, disease, and death (13.7–8).

In short, if Arjuna realized that killing the body does not harm the Self that inhabits it, he would not be troubled by slaying. Even should he believe the Self to be subject to birth and death, every living being is sure to die sometime, so what's the big deal? Or, to view it differently, Krishna has already determined who will perish in the upcoming battle. Arjuna's job is simply to carry out what Krishna has decreed: "I have already slain all these warriors; you will only be my instrument. Bhishma, Drona, Jayadratha, Karna, and many others are already slain. Kill those whom I have killed. Do not hesitate" (11.33–34). Believing all this will free Arjuna from indecision and regret, filling him instead with certainty and joy. Knowledge emancipates from evil, crushes karma, and rescues from rebirth as an independent entity. The goal of the *Gītā* is to gird Arjuna for life. Growth in knowledge is crucial to that process.

Hinduism is a collective term for a spectrum of beliefs and practices. Some Hindus espouse nondualism (*advaita*). That is, only one true reality, Brahman, exists. Nirguṇa Brahman has no qualities, since ascribing any attribute would differentiate Brahman from an entity that lacked it. Since all is one, there can be no individual self or soul (*jīva*), only the ultimate self (ātman), which is the same as Brahman. Realizing this oneness is what liberates. Hence for an *advaita* thinker such as Śaṅkara (c. 788–820 CE), knowledge (*jñāna*) is primary in leading to liberation.

Although the *Bhagavad Gītā* does promote knowledge as a productive path, its philosophy more closely reflects *viśiṣṭādvaita* (qualified nondualism) or *dvaita* (dualism). Both Rāmānuja (c. 1017–1137 CE), who developed viśiṣṭādvaita, and Madhva (c. 1296–1386), who championed dvaita, wrote commentaries on the *Gītā*. For Madhva three realities exist—God, soul, and inanimate nature. Ignorance can be dispelled and liberation achieved through the third yoga of devotion (bhakti) to a personal deity. The *Gītā* urges such bhakti toward Krishna:

Whatever I am offered in devotion with a pure heart—a leaf, a flower, fruit, or water—I partake of that love offering. Whatever you do, make it an offering to me—the food you eat, the sacrifices you make, the help you give, even your suffering. In this way you will be freed from the bondage of karma, and from its results both pleasant and painful. Then, firm in renunciation and yoga, with your heart free, you will come to me (9.26–28).

To those steadfast in love and devotion I give spiritual wisdom, so that they may come to me. Out of compassion I destroy the darkness of their ignorance. From within them I light the lamp of wisdom and dispel all darkness from their lives (10.10–11).

ARJUNA: Of those steadfast devotees who love you and those who seek you as the eternal formless Reality, who are the more established in yoga?

SRI KRISHNA: Those who set their hearts on me and worship me with unfailing devotion and faith are more established in yoga.

As for those who seek the transcendental Reality, without name, without form, contemplating the Unmanifested, beyond the reach of thought and of feeling, with their senses subdued and mind serene and striving for the good of all beings, they too will verily come unto me.

Yet hazardous and slow is the path to the Unrevealed, difficult for physical man to tread. But they for whom I am the supreme goal, who do all work renouncing self for me and meditate on me with single-hearted devotion, these I will swiftly rescue from the fragment's cycle of birth and death, for their consciousness has entered into me.

Still your mind in me, still your intellect in me, and without doubt you will be united with me forever (12.1–8).

Make every act an offering to me; regard me as your only protector. Relying on interior discipline, meditate on me always. Remembering me, you shall overcome all difficulties

> through my grace. But if you will not heed me in your self-will, nothing will avail you . . .
>
> I give you these precious words of wisdom; reflect on them and then do as you choose. These are the last words I shall speak to you, dear one, for your spiritual fulfillment. You are very dear to me.
>
> Be aware of me always, adore me, make every act an offering to me, and you shall come to me; this I promise, for you are dear to me. Abandon all supports and look to me for protection. I shall purify you from the sins of the past; do not grieve (18.57–58, 63–66).

For the International Society for Krishna Consciousness (ISKCON, the Hare Krishna movement), devotion is *the* message of the *Bhagavad Gītā*. Others also underscore the primacy of bhakti:

> Although knowledge, meditation, yoga, and other forms of self-effort are lauded in texts, eventually it is devotional forms of worship that become the distinguishing characteristic of Hindu traditions—transmitted for centuries to the masses through singing and dancing lyrics of devotion . . .
>
> The *Gita* says one may reach Vishnu/Krishna/God through devotion, knowledge, or selfless action. Later interpreters think of these as three paths, while others consider them to be three aspects of the one path of loving surrender to the supreme being.[195]

But while Krishna does assure Arjuna that "Those who set their hearts on me and worship me with unfailing devotion and faith are more established in yoga" (12.2), he says this to answer whether personal devotion to him or focus on Nirguṇa Brahman is better. Either path works, but personal devotion is easier. *Jñānamārga*—though hazardous, slow, and difficult—also leads to *mokṣa*.

The *Bhagavad Gītā* also mentions a fourth yoga, less frequently discussed—that of rāja or meditation:

> Those who aspire to the state of yoga should seek the Self in inner solitude through meditation. With body and mind

controlled they should constantly practice one-pointedness, free from expectations and attachment to material possessions.

Select a clean spot, neither too high nor too low, and seat yourself firmly on a cloth, a deerskin, and kusha grass. Then, once seated, strive to still your thoughts. Make your mind one-pointed in meditation, and your heart will be purified. Hold your body, head, and neck firmly in a straight line, and keep your eyes from wandering. With all fears dissolved in the peace of the Self and all desires dedicated to Brahman, controlling the mind and fixing it on me, sit in meditation with me as your only goal. With senses and mind constantly controlled through meditation, united with the Self within, an aspirant attains nirvana, the state of abiding joy and peace in me.

Arjuna, those who eat too much or eat too little, who sleep too much or sleep too little, will not succeed in meditation. But those who are temperate in eating and sleeping, work and recreation, will come to the end of sorrow through meditation. Through constant effort they learn to withdraw the mind from selfish cravings and absorb it in the Self. Thus they attain the state of union.

When meditation is mastered, the mind is unwavering like the flame of a lamp in a windless place. In the still mind, in the depths of meditation, the Self reveals itself. Beholding the Self by means of the Self, an aspirant knows the joy and peace of complete fulfillment. Having attained that abiding joy beyond the senses, revealed in the stilled mind, he never swerves from the eternal truth. He desires nothing else, and cannot be shaken by the heaviest burden of sorrow.

The practice of meditation frees one from all affliction. This is the path of yoga. Follow it with determination and sustained enthusiasm. Renouncing wholeheartedly all selfish desires and expectations, use your will to control the senses. Little by little, through patience and repeated effort, the mind will become stilled in the Self.

Wherever the mind wanders, restless and diffuse in its search for satisfaction without, lead it within; train it to rest in

> the Self. Abiding joy comes to those who still the mind. Freeing themselves from the taint of self-will, with their consciousness unified, they become one with Brahman . . .
>
> Meditation is superior to severe asceticism and the path of knowledge. It is also superior to selfless service. May you attain the goal of meditation, Arjuna! Even among those who meditate, that man or woman who worships me with perfect faith, completely absorbed in me, is the most firmly established in yoga (6.10–27, 46–47).
>
> When you make your mind one-pointed through regular practice of meditation, you will find the supreme glory of the Lord . . .
>
> There is merit in studying the scriptures, in selfless service, austerity, and giving, but the practice of meditation carries you beyond all these to the supreme abode of the highest Lord (8.8, 28).

These paths—each of them a response to Krishna's gracious self-revelation and the desire to know better the god so revealed—are all acceptable, since "As men approach me, so I receive them. All paths, Arjuna, lead to me" (4.11). But variety can confuse. Early in the *Gītā* Arjuna asks, "O Krishna, you have said that knowledge is greater than action; why then do you ask me to wage this terrible war? Your advice seems inconsistent. Give me one path to follow to the supreme good" (3.1–2). He later inquires who are the more established in yoga. Are the paths distinct, or different aspects of one? Perhaps action, knowledge, devotion, and meditation together constitute one mārga, since "The immature think that knowledge and action are different, but the wise see them as the same. The person who is established in one path will attain the rewards of both. The goal of knowledge and the goal of service are the same; those who fail to see this are blind" (5.3–5). Individuals may follow a favorite, but in the end the four are one, just as the goal is one. Knowledge, for example, should generate devotion, desire to meditate, and selfless service. As Sri Swami Sivananda puts it,

> In the Vishnu Purana, Bhagavan Vishnu is highly eulogised and a secondary place is given to Lord Siva. In the Siva Purana,

> Lord Siva is immensely praised and a secondary place is given to Lord Hari. In Devi Bhagavatam, Devi is highly praised and a secondary place is given to Lord Siva and Lord Hari. This is done in order to create intense and unswerving faith in the aspirant for his Ishta Devata or favourite deity. Siva, Hari and Devi are one. They are different aspects of the Lord. It is simply absurd if you believe that Siva is inferior to Hari or Hari is inferior to Siva.
>
> Even so, in one place Lord Krishna praises Karma Yoga. "Yoga of action is verily better than renunciation of action." In another place He praises Yoga. "The Yogi is greater than the ascetic; he is thought to be even greater than the wise; the Yogi is greater than the man of action; therefore, become thou a Yogi, O Arjuna." In another place, the Lord praises Bhakti Yoga. "He, the Highest Spirit, O Partha, may be reached by unswerving devotion to Him alone." In another place, He praises Jnana Yoga. "Noble are all these, but I hold the wise as verily Myself; he, self-united, is fixed on Me, the highest path."
>
> A neophyte will be confused when he comes across these verses. But there is no room for any confusion if you think deeply. Lord Krishna has praised each Yoga in order to create interest in the aspirant in his particular Marga or path. You must remember that the Gita is a book for the people of the world at large. It was not meant for Arjuna alone. Each Yoga is as efficacious and potent as the other.[196]

Be that as it may, Arjuna has glimpsed the divine and now desires to delve deeper into this deity. Krishna's gracious self-revelation has prompted Arjuna's devoted response. Without Krishna's initiative no effort by Arjuna would have availed:

> Arjuna, through my grace you have been united with me and received this vision of my radiant, universal form, without beginning or end, which no one else has ever seen.
>
> Not by knowledge of the Vedas, nor sacrifice, nor charity, nor rituals, nor even by severe asceticism has any other mortal seen what you have seen, O heroic Arjuna . . .

> It is extremely difficult to obtain the vision you have had; even the gods long always to see me in this aspect. Neither knowledge of the Vedas, nor austerity, nor charity, nor sacrifice can bring the vision you have seen. But through unfailing devotion, Arjuna, you can know me, see me, and attain union with me. Whoever makes me the supreme goal of all his work and acts without selfish attachment, who devotes himself to me completely and is free from ill will for any creature, enters into me (11.47–48, 52–55).

One need not be a theist to respond with awe to the majesty of the universe. Many nontheists labor alongside Arjuna to understand reality, devote themselves to enjoying the cosmos and its creatures, and live lives meaningful to themselves and helpful to others. Highly respected Vietnamese monk Thich Nhat Hanh, promoter of Engaged Buddhism, recalls:

> During a conference on religion and peace, a Protestant minister came up to me toward the end of one of our meals together and said, "Are you a grateful person?" I was surprised. I was eating slowly, and I thought to myself, Yes, I am a grateful person. The minister continued, "If you are really grateful, how can you not believe in God? God has created everything we enjoy, including the food we eat. Since you do not believe in God, you are not grateful for anything." I thought to myself, I feel extremely grateful for everything. Every time I touch food, whenever I see a flower, when I breathe fresh air, I always feel grateful. Why would he say that I am not? I had this incident in mind many years later when I proposed to friends at Plum Village that we celebrate a Buddhist Thanksgiving Day every year. On that day, we practice real gratitude—thanking our mothers, fathers, ancestors, friends, and all beings for everything. If you meet that Protestant minister, I hope you will tell him that we are not ungrateful. We feel deeply grateful for everyone and everything.
>
> Every time we eat a meal, gratitude is our practice. We are grateful for being together as a community. We are grateful

> that we have food to eat, and we really enjoy the food and the presence of each other. We feel grateful throughout the meal and through the day, and we express this by being fully aware of the food and living every moment deeply. This is how I try to express my gratitude to all of life.[197]

Similarly, one can be a theist who holds neither to the storyline of the *Bhagavad Gītā* nor such concepts as Brahman, atman, karma, and reincarnation, and yet agree that the *Song of the Lord* outlines appropriate responses to God. If God has graciously met us, as Krishna did Arjuna, in our hour of need, we should reciprocate by pursuing paths that draw us closer to him. If, beyond the *Gītā*'s vision, God has met us with substitutionary sacrifice, our debt is greater still. Dr. Dilip Joseph was captured in Afghanistan by the Taliban on 05 December 2012 and anticipated death. But US SEAL Team Six stormed in. During the rescue, twenty-eight-year-old SEAL Nicolas Checque was killed. Joseph later reflected, "He died to save my life. It is hard to live with the idea that somebody died for my sake. The best that you can do is to honor them through your life, and that's exactly what I want to do."[198]

Our response to a graciously self-revealing God should naturally begin with accepting and acknowledging the way things are—who he is and what he has done. Then it should mature into a determined effort to know him better, love him more, and selflessly serve others. The Hindus are right—grace calls for thanks, and for effort to enjoy deeper union with the divine.

Zen master in Thiên Mụ Pagoda, Hué.

11

LIVING TRUMPS TALKING

(*Zen*)

> The World-Honored One long ago instructed the assembly on Vulture Peak by holding up a flower. At that time everyone in the assembly remained silent; only Mahākāśyapa broke into a smile. The World-Honored One stated: "I possess the treasury of the true Dharma eye, the wondrous mind of *nirvāṇa*, the subtle dharma-gate born of the formlessness of true form, not established on words and letters, a special transmission outside the teaching. I bequeath it to Mahākāśyapa."[199]

This is the Buddha's "Flower Sermon" or *nengemishō* (literally "pick up flower, subtle smile"). It first surfaces in the eleventh-century *Ching-te Record of the Transmission of the Lamp.* The "lamp" is Śākyamuni Buddha's enlightenment experience and its accompanying insight.[200] How will he pass these on to succeeding generations? Not with words, but by direct transmission from mind of master to mind of student.

> In the person of a genuine master, able to expound the Buddha's Dharma with a conviction born of a profound, personal experience of truth, is to be found the embodiment of Zen's wisdom and authority. Such a teacher is a guide whose spirit-heart-mind is identical with that of all Buddhas and Ancestral Teachers, separated though they be by centuries in time. Without such people Zen's past is lifeless, its future "powerless to be born." Zen, as a transmission from mind to mind,

> cherishes pulsating, living truth—truth in action. Like sound imprisoned in a record or tape, needing electrical energy and certain devices to reproduce it, so the Heart-mind of the Buddha, entombed in the sutras, needs a living force in the person of an enlightened teacher to re-create it.[201]

Enlightenment must be transmitted through living mentors who do not rely upon words to share their insight. An individual experiencing enlightenment resembles a deaf-mute dreaming—neither can verbalize his vision.[202]

The Mahākāśyapa story is foundational for all forms of Zen.[203] Whether the event actually occurred is questionable; the tale may have been composed to legitimize a movement within Ch'an away from reasoned explanations of reality (as expressed in the sūtras) to an epistemology bypassing logic and speech. This movement taught that since words cannot communicate enlightenment, mysticism surpasses logic. The nengemishō conceivably arose so that the idea of "special transmission outside the teaching" could be attributed to Śākyamuni himself and invested with his authority. If so, the resulting text is invoked to undermine the authority of texts.

Regardless of how the Flower Sermon originated, as an emic perspective it epitomizes Zen self-understanding. Mahākāśyapa became the first in a line of twenty-eight Indian Zen patriarchs. The last was Bodhidharma, who migrated east and became the first Chinese patriarch. Enlightenment and investiture pass wordlessly from master to disciple, apart from texts. Because of the putatively unbroken line from Mahākāśyapa onward, the Buddha's ineffable enlightenment remains accessible today.

Thus arises Zen, which poses as Buddhist but treats all its ancient writings "as mere waste paper whose utility consists in wiping off the dirt of the intellect and nothing more."[204] Creeds, doctrines, analysis, and intellectual effort matter less than direct personal experience. Not only texts, but all other authorities outside experience are rejected. When a novice monk respectfully mentions the Buddha the master may scold, "Wash out your mouth and never say that dirty word again!" In fact, "If you meet the Buddha, kill the Buddha!"[205]

These interjections, of course, exaggerate. Zen is fond of shock and overstatement, with *rōshis* verbally abusing novices and knocking them on the head to accelerate their approach to enlightenment. Nevertheless, masters do insist that their followers find truth within themselves, outside of texts or other sources of authority such as traditional logic:

> Empty-handed I go, and behold the spade is in my hands;
> I walk on foot, and yet on the back of an ox I am riding;
> When I pass over the bridge,
> Lo, the water floweth not, but the bridge doth flow.

Zen proposes this sixth-century verse to urge "that the so-called common-sense way of looking at things is not final, and that the reason why we cannot attain to a thoroughgoing comprehension of the truth is due to our unreasonable adherence to a 'logical' interpretation of things."[206] Compared with experience, words are weak:

> [T]he deepest truths of Zen . . . are to be experienced in the inmost soul . . .
>
> Personal experience, therefore, is everything in Zen. No ideas are intelligible to those who have no backing of experience . . . A baby has no ideas, for its mentality is not yet so developed as to experience anything in the way of ideas. If it has them at all, they must be something extremely obscure and blurred and not in correspondence with realities. To get the clearest and most efficient understanding of a thing, therefore, it must be experienced personally. Especially when the thing is concerned with life itself, personal experience is an absolute necessity. Without this experience nothing relative to its profound working will ever be accurately and therefore efficiently grasped. The foundation of all concepts is simple, unsophisticated experience . . .[207]

Or as Thich Nhat Hanh says,

> [N]othing can be talked about, perceived, or described by representation. If you talk about things you have not experienced, you are wasting your and other people's time. As you continue the practice of looking deeply, you will see this more

> and more clearly, and you will save a lot of paper and publishing enterprises and have more time to enjoy your tea and live your daily life in mindfulness.[208]

What, then, can words contribute?

> I don't say that [through words] the truth can be conveyed. But some hints, some indications, some gestures can be communicated, so that the other becomes ready to take the jump. The truth cannot be conveyed but the thirst can be given. No teaching worth the name can give the key through words.[209]

Two major Japanese branches of Zen follow different routes to *satori.* Sōtō stresses *zazen*, or quiet, seated meditation, the desired result of which is gradual awakening. Sōtō draws upon the thought and practice of Dōgen (1200–1253). Rinzai utilizes shouts and blows and *kōan*, word puzzles that defy logic. Such tactics often jar the seeker to sudden enlightenment. Eisai (1141–1215) and Hakuin (1686–1769) are important in Rinzai. Other sects use the methods of both Sōtō and Rinzai. Ōbaku combines Rinzai with nembutsu practice.

Whichever sect is followed, viscerally grasping one's true nature often does not come easily. Years may be invested sitting in zazen or wrestling over kōan before the truth dawns. "The great merit of koans, which range over the vast area of the Mahayana teachings, is that they compel us, in ingenious and often dramatic fashion, to learn these doctrines not simply with our head but with our whole being, refusing to permit us to sit back and endlessly theorize about them in the abstract."[210] Throughout his quest the seeker must endure sometimes intimidating interviews (dokusan) with one's rōshi, verbal harangues, and corrective blows from a kyōsaku.

Since its publication in 1965, Philip Kapleau's *Three Pillars of Zen* has helped introduce Zen to the West. Sixty pages are devoted to transcripts of interviews between devotees and their rōshi. Many illustrate the effort expended to achieve enlightenment. The following student was a woman of thirty-three:

> STUDENT: If I understood you correctly, at one time you told me to keep my mind in my palm, another time to focus it in the region below the navel, and again, when I become sleepy,

to place it between my eyes. I am confused. I don't even know what my mind is, so how can I put it in any of these places?

ROSHI: When I told you to put your mind in the palm of your hand, what I meant was to focus your *attention* at that point. You must not constantly change the focal point of your concentration. Both Dogen and Hakuin recommend focusing the mind in the palm of the hand. If you want to increase the intensity of your zazen, you can do so by directing your attention to your tanden. A good way to overcome sleepiness is to concentrate your attention between your eyes.

STUDENT: But what is mind, anyway? I mean, I know what it is theoretically, because I have read many of the sutras and other books on Buddhism. But can I really find out what mind is by asking "Who am I?"

ROSHI: A theoretical understanding of mind is not enough to resolve the question "Who am I?" and through it the problem of birth-and-death. Such understanding is merely a portrait of reality, not reality itself. If you persistently question yourself "Who am I?" with devotion and zeal—that is to say, moved by a genuine desire for self-knowledge—you are bound to realize the nature of Mind.

Now, mind is more than your body and more than what is ordinarily called mind. The inner realization of mind is the realization that you and the universe are not two. This awareness must come to you with such overwhelming certainty that you involuntarily slap your thigh and exclaim: "Oh, of course!"

STUDENT: But I don't know who it is that is asking "Who am I?" and not knowing this—or who it is that is being asked—how can I find out who I am?

ROSHI: The one asking the question is You and You must answer. The truth is, they are not two. The answer can only come out of persistent questioning with an intense yearning to know. Up to the present you have been wandering aimlessly, uncertain of your destination, but now that you have been given a map and have your bearings, don't stop to admire the sights—march on!

. . .

ROSHI: Is there anything you wish to say or ask?

STUDENT: From five this morning up to now [3 P.M.] I have been steadily asking myself "Who am I?" Sometimes the question has absorbed me, but most of the time I have been just plain bored. Why do I get bored?

ROSHI: Probably because you are not yet convinced that through such questioning you can perceive your True-nature and thus attain lasting peace of mind. When those who have experienced a great deal of pain in life hear the truth of Buddhism and begin to practice zazen, they usually want to get kensho quickly in order to relieve their own sufferings as well as those of others.

STUDENT: Part of the reason I find it so hard to concentrate is that the new monitor we have is roaring at us all and clouting everyone so hard.

ROSHI: You need only ask yourself "*Who* is listening to all this shouting?" Don't make a problem of it; it is no concern of yours.

STUDENT: It is impossible for me to be indifferent to it. On either side of me the sitters are being struck so hard that I shudder every time I hear the kyosaku. I tried to ask myself "*Who* is listening to all this horrible shouting?" but I was so upset I couldn't continue.

ROSHI: These people around you are close to kensho, that is why they are being struck so hard—to spur them on to a last desperate effort. If you don't want to be hit because it interferes with your zazen, I can have a "Do not strike" sign placed over you.

STUDENT: Yesterday when Mr. K______ struck me it was helpful, as he knows how and when to strike, but this man hits without rhyme or reason and his shouting is so frightening it makes me sick in my stomach.

ROSHI: Of course some of the wielders of the kyosaku are more capable than others. Mr. K______, having had long experience, is quite accomplished. Do you wish a sign placed over you?

STUDENT: The funny thing is that half of me wants to be

hit, because I think I'll get kensho quicker that way, and half of me dreads it. If Mr. K______ returns, I would like him to strike me occasionally.

ROSHI: We can have a sign put over your place, and when you wish to be struck you can signal with your hands raised over your head, palms together. But don't concern yourself with what happens around you, only concentrate on your own problems.

From now on you can reduce "Who am I?" to "Who?" since the whole question has sunk into your subconscious.

. . .

ROSHI: There is no real answer to "Who?" "What?" or "Why?" Why is sugar sweet? Sugar is sugar. Sugar!

STUDENT: You told me earlier, "You are You!" All right, I am I—I accept that. Isn't this enough? What more need I do? Why must I keep struggling with this question?

ROSHI: Because this understanding is external to you—you don't really know what you mean by "I am I." You must come up against this question with the force of a bomb, and all your intellectual notions and ideas must be annihilated. The only way to resolve this question is to come to the explosive inner realization that everything is [ultimately reducible to] Nothing. If your understanding is merely theoretical, you will forever ask "Who?" "What?" and "Why?"[211]

Or this testimony is from Mr. A.K., a twenty-five-year-old Japanese insurance adjuster who did ultimately achieve kenshō:

The fourth day had come. Again and again I was walloped by the kyosaku, once so hard that my mind and body became momentarily paralyzed. This day I "fought" the hardest. But in spite of everything, I still could not come to kensho. Now it was the fifth day; only a day and a half remained to me. On the sixth day I threw my last ounce of energy into the "battle," allowing nothing whatever to sidetrack me. After the morning chores, and just before the roshi's talk, a university student sitting near

> me (who got kensho at this sesshin), suddenly yelled out: "You foolish, foolish, stupid guy!" referring to himself. "Go on, on! One more step, only one! The summit! Die if need be, die!" The strength of his desperation flowed into me and I began to concentrate as though my very life depended on it.[212]

The point is not that Zen lacks ideas or a worldview. Rather, it urges that genuine grasp of these transcends the cerebral. Truth is not to be parroted, even in correct formulae, but holistically and internally embraced.

> Zen expresses itself concretely because Zen is above all interested in facts, not theories, in realities and not those pallid counters for reality which we know as concepts. "Fact" may suggest to the Western mind something merely quantitative, or statistical—therefore also a lifeless and abstract thing. Zen wants, rather, the facts as living and concrete. In this sense, Zen may be described as Radical Intuitionism—if the Westerner wishes a handle by which to lay hold of it.[213]

This is why although students in Kapleau's book are often able to articulate Zen ideas, their words do not necessarily satisfy the rōshi. They must agonize to seize—or perhaps be seized by—a more inner grasp of Zen reality.

In short, truth in Zen is not a troupe of dancers who pirouette in the mind and twirl lightly out of the mouth, but a troop of soldiers who have stormed and seized the heart. Such captivation occurs only through patient practice of Zen disciplines:

> At its profoundest level Zen, like every other great religion, transcends its own teachings and practices, yet at the same time there is no Zen apart from these practices. Attempts in the West to isolate Zen in a vacuum of the intellect, cut off from the very disciplines which are its *raison d'être*, have nourished in places a pseudo-Zen that is little more than a mind-tickling diversion.[214]

Since truth thus embraces the whole person, it must not only permeate heart and mind, but be practiced hand and foot. "Ch'an is not content with mere doctrine, or exposition. Ch'an must be lived, must be experienced concretely every single moment of the day."[215]

> For thought to be of value, Zen holds, it must be translated into action: understanding, while important, is nowhere near as important as acting . . . Zen Buddhism is not so much a theoretical philosophy to be discussed and debated at leisure as it is a way of action, a philosophy to be practiced and realized every moment of our daily life . . .
>
> Many people think that the Zen Buddhist turns his back upon the world to submerge himself in abstract meditation. This is a misconception . . . The Zen way is not to withdraw from life into an isolated utopia, but to get into life and change it from the inside by action.
>
> The following story illustrates the importance of action in Zen Buddhism. Once in ancient China, there lived a great Buddhist scholar. He had studied the scriptures with diligence, knew whole passages by heart and could expound the texts at length both by mouth and by pen. Yet, despite his learning, he had fallen into confusion because of the many contradictory things he encountered in his studies. He went from one teacher to another seeking to resolve his doubts, but this only left him more confused. Then one day he heard that a famous Zen master was residing in a nearby temple. He went to see the Master and, after greeting him respectfully, asked: "Could you please tell me, Venerable Sir, what is the essence of Buddhism? I have read many books and have only become confused. Please help to resolve my doubts." The Master smiled at him and replied: "I too have read many books and practiced for many years, but cannot tell you anything of my own. But let me recite for you a little *gāthā* ("poem") which may contain the answer you are seeking." The scholar was delighted, and the master recited:
>
> Not to commit evils,
> To practice all the good,
> And to keep the mind pure:
> That is the teaching of the Buddhas.

> The scholar immediately exclaimed: "What, is that all you have to answer? Why, any child of three knows that!" "True," the Master answered, "any child of three knows that, but even an old man of eighty finds it difficult to practice." This statement suddenly made sense to the scholar. He realized that studying treatises on philosophy is not the key to understanding Buddhism; the key lies rather in practice. Joyfully he expressed his gratitude to the Master and returned home, his mind at last set at rest.[216]
>
> If we do not live Zen, we know nothing about it. Even if we study Zen philosophy extensively, if we do not practice it, we know very little about Zen. Intellectual understanding is second-hand knowledge; it is not direct experience. In order to have direct experience one must practice. Just as the student of calligraphy must hold the brush, dip it into ink and draw it across the paper, stroke by stroke, so must the Zen student practice his sitting meditation and apply it to his daily life. One can study Zen academically from a teacher, professor, or if fortunate enough, from a Master, or Roshi. One can study Zen by research, reading books about Zen or listening to the lectures of the Zen Masters. Nonetheless, the student of Zen must remember that intellectual understanding is not the heart of Zen. It is mere knowledge, indirect understanding; it is not an actual experience or true realization of Zen.[217]

This idea emerges from the Ox-Herding Pictures, one of the most familiar depictions of Zen. Many variants exist. The following introductions and verses are attributed to Kuoan Shiyuan of the twelfth century, and the pictures themselves to Tenshō Shūbun of the fifteenth.[218]

I ***Searching for the Ox.*** The beast has never gone astray, and what is the use of searching for him? The reason why the oxherd is not on intimate terms with him is because the oxherd himself has violated his own inmost nature. The beast is lost, for the oxherd has himself been led out of the way through his deluding senses. His home is receding farther away from him, and byways and crossways are ever confused. Desire for gain and fear of loss burn like fire; ideas of right and wrong shoot up like a phalanx.

Alone in the wilderness, lost in the jungle, the boy is searching, searching!
The swelling waters, the far-away mountains, and the unending path;
Exhausted and in despair, he knows not where to go,
He only hears the evening cicadas singing in the maple-woods.

II ***Seeing the Traces.*** By the aid of the sutras and by inquiring into the doctrines, he has come to understand something, he has found the traces. He now knows that vessels, however varied, are all of gold, and that the objective world is a reflection of the Self. Yet, he is unable to distinguish what is good from what is not, his mind is still confused as to truth and falsehood. As he has not yet entered the gate, he is provisionally said to have noticed the traces.

By the stream and under the trees, scattered are the traces of the lost;
The sweet-scented grasses are growing thick—did he find the way?
However remote over the hills and far away the beast may wander,
His nose reaches the heavens and none can conceal it.

III ***Seeing the Ox.*** The boy finds the way by the sound he hears; he sees thereby into the origin of things, and all his senses are in harmonious order. In all his activities, it is manifestly present. It is like the salt in water and the glue in color. [It is there though not distinguishable as an individual entity.] When the eye is properly directed, he will find that it is no other than himself.

On a yonder branch perches a nightingale cheerfully singing;
The sun is warm, and a soothing breeze blows,
on the bank the willows are green;
The ox is there all by himself, nowhere is he to hide himself;
The splendid head decorated with stately horns
what painter can reproduce him?

IV ***Catching the Ox.*** Long lost in the wilderness, the boy has at last found the ox and his hands are on him. But, owing to the overwhelming pressure of the outside world, the ox is hard to keep under control. He constantly longs for the old sweet-scented field. The wild nature is still unruly, and altogether refuses to be broken. If the oxherd wishes to see the ox completely in harmony with himself, he has surely to use the whip freely.

With the energy of his whole being, the boy has at last taken hold of the ox:
But how wild his will, how ungovernable his power!
At times he struts up a plateau,
When lo! he is lost again in a misty impenetrable mountain-pass.

V *Herding the Ox.* When a thought moves, another follows, and then another—an endless train of thoughts is thus awakened. Through enlightenment all this turns into truth; but falsehood asserts itself when confusion prevails. Things oppress us not because of an objective world, but because of a self-deceiving mind. Do not let the nose-string loose, hold it tight, and allow no vacillation.

The boy is not to separate himself with his whip and tether,
Lest the animal should wander away into a world of defilements;
When the ox is properly tended to, he will grow pure and docile;
Without a chain, nothing binding, he will by himself follow the oxherd.

VI *Coming Home on the Ox's Back.* The struggle is over; the man is no more concerned with gain and loss. He hums a rustic tune of the woodman, he sings simple songs of the village-boy. Saddling himself on the ox's back, his eyes are fixed on things not of the earth, earthy. Even if he is called, he will not turn his head; however enticed he will no more be kept back.

Riding on the animal, he leisurely wends his way home:
Enveloped in the evening mist, how tunefully the flute vanishes away!
Singing a ditty, beating time, his heart is filled with a joy indescribable!
That he is now one of those who know, need it be told?

VII *The Ox Forgotten, Leaving the Man Alone.* The dharmas are one and the ox is symbolic. When you know that what you need is not the snare or set-net but the hare or fish, it is like gold separated from the dross, it is like the moon rising out of the clouds. The one ray of light serene and penetrating shines even before days of creation.

Riding on the animal, he is at last back in his home,
Where lo! the ox is no more; the man alone sits serenely.
Though the red sun is high up in the sky, he is still quietly dreaming,
Under a straw-thatched roof are his whip and rope idly lying.

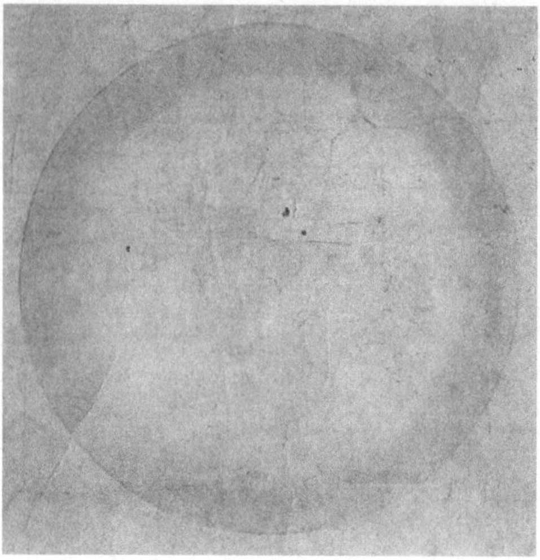

VIII ***The Ox and the Man Both Gone out of Sight.*** All confusion is set aside, and serenity alone prevails; even the idea of holiness does not obtain. He does not linger about where the Buddha is, and as to where there is no Buddha he speedily passes by. When there exists no form of dualism, even a thousand-eyed one fails to detect a loop-hole. A holiness before which birds offer flowers is but a farce.

All is empty—the whip, the rope, the man, and the ox:
Who can ever survey the vastness of heaven?
Over the furnace burning ablaze, not a flake of snow can fall:
When this state of things obtains, manifest is the spirit of the ancient master.

IX *Returning to the Origin, Back to the Source.* From the very beginning, pure and immaculate, the man has never been affected by defilement. He watches the growth of things, while himself abiding in the immovable serenity of non-assertion. He does not identify himself with the maya-like transformations [that are going on about him], nor has he any use of himself [which is artificiality]. The waters are blue, the mountains are green; sitting alone, he observes things undergoing changes.

To return to the Origin, to be back at the Source—already a false step this!
Far better it is to stay at home, blind and deaf, and without much ado;
Sitting in the hut, he takes no cognizance of things outside,
Behold the streams flowing—whither nobody knows;
and the flowers vividly red—for whom are they?

X *Entering the City with Bliss-bestowing Hands.* His thatched cottage gate is closed, and even the wisest know him not. No glimpses of his inner life are to be caught; for he goes on his own way without following the steps of the ancient sages. Carrying a gourd [symbol of emptiness] he goes out into the market, leaning against a staff [no extra property he has, for he knows that the desire to possess is the curse of human life] he comes home. He is found in company with wine-bibbers and butchers, he and they are all converted into Buddhas.

Bare-chested and bare-footed, he comes out into the market-place;
Daubed with mud and ashes, how broadly he smiles!
There is no need for the miraculous power of the gods,
For he touches, and lo! the dead trees are in full bloom.

Our true mind or self (the ox) has always been with us. Nevertheless, because ignorance and illusion permeate the heart, discovering and controlling that self is often achieved only after an arduous effort under an enlightened master. Some versions of the ox-herding pictures delete the tenth and reverse the eighth and ninth.[219] Such enneads end with an empty circle suggesting śūnyatā and the enlightenment of grasping it. Other versions drop the tenth but add one in the middle. In such decades the circle of individual enlightenment again constitutes the final goal, leaving nothing further to achieve. For many practitioners, however, the tenth step of Entering the City with Bliss-bestowing Hands is essential:

> [A] buddha is not a buddha if he cannot come back to ordinary humanity, if he cannot again become simple, innocent, carrying his nirvana, carrying his ecstasy in the bottle of wine, utterly drunk with the divine but still going toward the marketplace . . .
>
> Without [the tenth picture], ending in nothingness looks a little sad, looks a little serious, looks empty.
>
> All this effort of finding yourself, meditating, going beyond the mind, realizing your being and ending up in the desert of nothingness . . . no, there must be something more to it, something more beyond it, where flowers blossom, where songs arise, where dance is again possible—of course, on a totally different level.[220]

Thus, once an individual achieves satori, she must reenter the world and aid the unenlightened. Zen is not complete until the newly awakened does that. Truth must be understood cognitively, grasped viscerally, and lived practically. More than a set of tidy tenets, truth is a reality that fills the mind, flows in the veins, and fashions the actions of fingers and toes. It has not been grasped unless it does all three. Living the truth trumps talking about it. "[T]he disciplined mind obtained from zazen must be carried into everyday life. That purified mind must be transformed into action. Every day becomes a day of practice."[221] Because truth must be lived as well as known, and despite popular misconceptions, it is "emphatically not true . . . that today the principal occupation of Zen monks is sitting. Except for a total of six weeks or so in the year when they are in *sesshin*, Japanese Zen monks in training spend most of their time working, not sitting . . ."[222]

This mosaic of spiritual search and prosaic practice is portrayed in *The Zen Life*. The monks' meticulous tending of monastery gardens and graveyard, chopping firewood, constantly cleaning corridor floors so they shine as if waxed, tea ceremonies, and kitchen chores are as much a part of their lives as is meditation. All activities are undertaken mindfully. "The 'Zen life' is and must be expressed as fully in carrying firewood as in the practice of zazen. The deeper the monk's awareness of this fact becomes, the stronger his practice will be."[223] Flower arranging, calligraphy, painting, and martial arts are other traditional Zen practices.

So, increasingly, is social service. The author of *The Zen Life* lamented that Buddhism and Zen were deficient in this area:

> Zen is a religion which is inclined to be somewhat highbrowed and ascetic. However, if one truly takes seriously the Bodhisattva vow to save others even at the expense of throwing away one's own peace, then one ought to become even more earnestly engrossed in compassionate practices as expressed by "entering the marketplace with helping hands." In this regard I think Zen could learn a great deal from the social-oriented activities of the Quakers . . .
>
> When one reflects seriously upon the first vow of the Bodhisattva—to save all sentient beings though their number be limitless—it is impossible not to regret that there is not a single Dr. Schweitzer to be found in present-day Japanese Zen or in Japanese Buddhism in general. This lack was vividly illustrated by the fact that when a Japanese medical assistance team was recently sent to Nepal, the area in which the Buddha was born, it was not sent by Japanese Buddhists but by Japanese Christians.[224]

That complaint, however, is not as valid today as when raised in the 1970s. Since then a movement of socially engaged Buddhists has emerged, particularly in East and Southeast Asia. Some, such as Vietnam's Thich Nhat Hanh, are clearly Zen; others, such as Taiwan's Cheng Yen, the founder of Tzu Chi and known as the Chinese world's Mother Teresa, have been influenced by and show affinity to it.[225]

To summarize: in Zen truth must be both internally grasped and externally lived. Words alone will not do. "Because language and intellectual knowledge are indirect tools, they are not the heart of Zen."[226]

> To attain Nirvāṇa all we need is practice and action. From practice and action we will transcend our limited mind and teach the enlightened mind. From that state of mind we will experience Nirvāṇa here in this world of Saṃsāra in the present moment. Now there are no words—only action, only Nirvāṇa.[227]

Buddhism—its words, sūtras, doctrines—is a finger pointing to the moon. No finger is or can reach that heavenly body. If we wish to observe the moon, we may start by following the direction the finger indicates. But eventually our eyes must leap from the finger and focus on the orb itself.[228]

There is much to commend in this concept of truth. Applying it to our path means that we should deal with duḥkha not as a dry doctrine but a desperate disease. If, as Islam insists, God exists—transcendent, personal, righteous, all-seeing—then wisdom suggests paying him more than lip service. If humanity has so lost itself that we require divine intervention to bring us home, then with the Daoists we should accept that fact and not pretend otherwise. As Krishna counseled Arjuna, grace elicits thanks. And now Zen points out that such ideas, if true, should grip our souls and shape our lives. Truth must be lived. On this point Zen offers a welcome alternative to that curious Western proposal that one's beliefs should not affect his politics. Of course what a person believes shapes values and actions! Thus it is crucial to thoughtfully weigh what one chooses to believe.

It is unnecessary to denigrate thought in order to appreciate this insight. Is reason, that most distinguishing of human capacities, our enemy? Must indeed the mind be "emptied of all ideas" before a person can respond with her whole being?[229] Is thinking what prompts the worst in human attitudes and actions?[230] The mind is part of our being; why should its testimony alone be singled out and rejected? Logic, thought, discussion, and words instead play essential roles in the discovery and communication of truth, as the vast corpus of Zen literature itself suggests. The mind is not an alien to be repulsed, though Zen masters are correct in urging that religious truth must move beyond mental formulations and creedal statements. With these provisos Zen is right: truth must be grasped within and practiced without.

The all-seeing Divine Eye at the Cao Đài temple in Da Nang.

12

WIRED TO CONNECT

(*Bahá'í, Cao Đài*)

Tetsin Ani did not want to marry. But what could she do? Her suitor's social stature empowered him to practically compel her consent. She escaped by clambering down the hole of a cliffside latrine and fleeing to a Buddhist monastery. There she spent the next forty-five years in solitary retreat, endlessly reciting three mantras (particularly *oṃ maṇi padme hūṃ*) and dedicating the resulting merit to the benefit of all sentient beings. Local Sherpas considered her a legend, and on their way to Mount Everest they would first stop at her hut to pay homage.[231]

Something about solitary ascetics enshrouds them in an otherworldly aura in the eyes of outsiders. Their disciplined determination dumbfounds the uninitiated. But does saintliness automatically stem from abusing the body? Are isolation and austerity ideals in themselves? Do they produce anything positive? Is it indeed *holiness* that the sādhu achieves by smearing himself with ashes, sleeping in cemeteries, supping from skulls, and suspending his body from meat hooks?

The words *monk, monastic,* and cognates derive from the Greek *monos*, "alone, solitary." Many religions include adherents who engage in solitary practice. Some, such as Jainism, naturally lend themselves to it, whereas others, such as Sikhism and Zoroastrianism, do not. All faiths, by contrast, encourage community. They outline ideals for relationships among adherents, within families and clans, and then with the world at large. Ancient Israel urged loyalty to tribe and nation. The New Testament seeks oneness within the church. Islam values its *ummah* or community, and Sunnis in particular stress the importance of *ijmā'* or consensus in formulating interpretations and laws. Even Theravāda, which exalts the arhat, includes the *saṅgha* or monastic community among its three jewels.

Celebrating community is good. Humans are, after all, wired to connect. We innately enjoy interaction, which anthropologists argue was important for our species' survival. We learn from observing others. Mirror neurons in the human brain "reflect back an action we observe in someone else, making us mimic that action or have the impulse to do so." As such, they

> appear to be essential to the way children learn. Imitative learning has long been recognized as a major avenue of childhood development. But findings about mirror neurons explain how children can gain mastery simply from watching. As they watch, they are etching in their own brains a repertoire for emotion, for behavior, and for how the world works.

From earliest childhood and throughout our lives interaction makes us what we are. "[W]e humans are the social animal par excellence." We value how we fit in with others: "the brain's default activity—what happens automatically when nothing much else goes on—seems to be mulling over our relationships . . . Rehashing our social lives may rate as the brain's favorite downtime activity."[232]

Socialization is central to our souls. We thrive on meaningful relations. At least two faiths go beyond any limited vista and urge unity for all humanity. Bahá'í, a child of nineteenth-century Islam, and Cao Dai, born within twentieth-century Buddhism, make universal unity their chief objectives.

Insistence on oneness—of God, religion, and humanity—suffuses Bahá'í. John Esslemont (1875–1925) embraced Bahá'í around 1915 and was posthumously named one of its Hands of the Cause. In his *Bahá'u'lláh and the New Era*, "by far the most comprehensive and accurate introduction ever produced,"[233] Esslemont outlines Bahá'í's vision for itself and the world.

Decrying the upheavals of his own day, prompted as they were by selfish parochialism, Esslemont offers Bahá'í's universalism as an alternative. Bahá'í's founder Bahá'u'lláh (1817–1892) had declared himself to be "the long-expected educator and teacher of all peoples, the channel of a wondrous Grace that would transcend all previous outpourings, in which all previous forms of religion would become merged." Bahá'u'lláh's program promises a quest for "truth, the oneness of mankind, unity of religions, of races, of nations, of East and West, the reconciliation of religion and science, the eradication of prejudices and superstitions, the equality of men and women, the establishment of justice and righteousness, the setting up of a supreme international tribunal, the unification of languages, the compulsory diffusion of knowledge." His program is necessary because the other religions offer only "violently opposed views" to solving the world's deep problems. But the adoption of Bahá'í "would obviously make the world a paradise."

Other religions are exclusive, limited by the historical nature of their origins; Bahá'í is inclusive. "The scientific must associate with the simple and unlearned, the rich with the poor, the white with the colored, the mystic with the literalist, the Christian with the Jew, the Muslim with the Parsee . . ." A clannish, defensive mentality stifles the human spirit, keeping it from fully blossoming.

> But the love of God removes fear; the removal of fear establishes the latent power, and association with others in spiritual love brings these powers into vital, positive expression. A Bahá'í community is a gathering where this process can take place in this age, slowly at first, as the new impetus gathers force, more rapidly as the members become conscious of the powers unfolding the flower of unity among men . . . [Someday, however, Bahá'í] shall forge ahead, undivided and unimpaired, till it embraces the whole of mankind.

Previous paradigms for world order have not worked. But unity is no longer an option, for we have reached "an age which must either achieve the unity of the world, as adumbrated by Bahá'u'lláh, or perish . . . Some form of a world Super-State must needs be evolved" in which federated nations cede their rights to wage war and levy certain taxes. It would be headed by "an International Executive adequate to enforce supreme and unchallengeable authority." In this New World Order

> all economic barriers will have been permanently demolished and the interdependence of Capital and Labor definitely recognized; . . . the clamor of religious fanaticism and strife will have been forever stilled; . . . the flame of racial animosity

> will have been finally extinguished; . . . a single code of international law—the product of the considered judgment of the world's federated representatives—shall have as its sanction the instant and coercive intervention of the combined forces of the federated units; and . . . the fury of a capricious and militant nationalism will have been transmuted into an abiding consciousness of world citizenship.

Such a system is not intended to homogenize humanity by eradicating "legitimate allegiances" or "a sane and intelligent patriotism . . . It does not ignore, nor does it attempt to suppress, the diversity of ethnical origins, of climate, of history, of language and tradition, of thought and habit, that differentiate the peoples and nations of the world." It only superimposes upon these a "wider loyalty" and "larger aspiration." The practice of such unity would represent "the consummation of human evolution," the "coming of age of the entire human race." More than simply another spiritual revival, Bahá'í comprises "the last and highest stage in the stupendous evolution of man's collective life on this planet."

The "bewildered followers of bankrupt and broken creeds" must abandon their antiquated systems before it is too late, although a world catastrophe or fiery ordeal may be required before they do so. No past religious or political system has approached Bahá'í' vision. It would be wise not to mock or dismiss Bahá'í while it is still small, since it is founded upon "God's immutable Purpose for mankind in this day." The watchword of this New World Order is "the unification of the human race; its standard the 'Most Great Peace.'"

Esslemont mentions some practical steps that this world unity will entail:

> A world metropolis will act as the nerve center of a world civilization, the focus towards which the unifying forces of life will converge and from which its energizing influences will radiate. A world language will either be invented or chosen from among the existing languages and will be taught in the schools of all the federated nations as an auxiliary to their mother tongue. A world script, a world literature, a uniform and universal system of currency, of weights and measures,

> will simplify and facilitate intercourse and understanding among the nations and races of mankind. In such a world society, science and religion, the two most potent forces in human life, will be reconciled, will cooperate, and will harmoniously develop. The press will, under such a system, while giving full scope to the expression of the diversified views and convictions of mankind, cease to be mischievously manipulated by vested interests . . . The causes of religious strife will be permanently removed . . . Destitution on the one hand, and gross accumulation of ownership on the other, will disappear. The enormous energy dissipated and wasted on war . . . will be consecrated to such ends as will extend the range of human inventions and technical development.

Bahá'í is "a system in which Force is made the servant of Justice, whose life is sustained by its universal recognition of one God and by its allegiance to one common Revelation."[234]

Such a vision takes us beyond isolated unified communities to oneness with the world. Who would not like peace on earth; goodwill among men; the eradication of superstitions, prejudices, and racial and religious animosities; the end of gender and economic exploitation; and the establishment of justice and righteousness? Who can calculate the waste wrought by wars—to our souls, our *joie de vivre*, our progress in arts and sciences, our environment, and our wealth? These are immensely important questions. The goals of equity, education, justice, opportunity, and peace are noble. We may ask, however, whether the Bahá'í vision will actually achieve such global harmony.

What about religious oneness? Bahá'í purportedly desires Christians to be better Christians, Muslims better Muslims, etc. But what it in fact proposes is that all convert to Bahá'í Faith. Theravādists would be required to abandon their atheism for theism. Christians who believe Jesus to be the unique revelation of God, and Muslims who hold that Muḥammad is the seal of the prophets, would have to abandon these commitments and embrace Bahá'u'lláh as having surpassed them. This is not a unity comprised of distinct parts functioning harmoniously together, but uniformity; not a collage but conversion. Such homogeneity may mean that the "causes of religious strife will be permanently removed," but it removes them by eliminating other religions.

Further, talk of the "compulsory diffusion of knowledge," "control [of] the entire resources of all the component nations," "unchallengeable authority," "a system in which Force is made the servant of Justice," and of a humanity that "stubbornly refuses to embrace the light and acknowledge the sovereign authority of the one Power that can extricate it from its entanglements" hints at the compulsion of belief in Bahá'u'lláh and Bahá'u'lláh's god, since they form the foundation of the system. This proposed path to Oneness, then, consists of conversion to the theology and practice of Bahá'í, not the peaceful coexistence of different ideologies that it purports to be. It is doubtful that all non-Bahá'í will tread that path.

A second proposal for religious and social unity emerged eight decades later, in Southeast rather than West Asia, stemming from séance and spirit communication instead of visions and the writing of tablets; out of Buddhism rather than Islam. It is called Cao Dai.

> April 24, 1926
>
> JADE EMPEROR, or CAO DAI TIEN ONG DAI BO TAT MA HA TAT, TEACHING THE GREAT WAY FOR THE SOUTHERN QUARTER:
>
> Formerly, people lacked transportation and therefore did not know each other, I then founded at different epochs and in different areas, five branches of the Great Way: Confucianism, Shintoism, Christianity, Taoism and Buddhism, each based on the customs of the race. In present days, transportation has been improved, and people have come to know each other. But people do not always live in harmony because of the very multiplicity of those religions. That is why I have decided to unite all those religions into one to bring them to the primordial unity. Moreover, the Holy Doctrine has been, through centuries, more and more denatured by the people responsible for spreading it. I am so broken-hearted to see that human beings, for the last ten thousand years, have sinned and subsequently suffered life after life in Hell.
>
> I have now firmly resolved to come Myself to save you and not to leave anymore the Holy Doctrine in human hands.

You have to be well organized to guide and support each other on your way to Nirvana.

I create then the "Giao Tong" position (Pope) who is the eldest brother of all dignitaries from the "Giao Huu" (Priest) to the "Dau Su" (Cardinal). No one in this world is allowed to have My authority to manage the human spirits. Whoever has well self cultivated will be worth the position I give. Otherwise, all disciples are all equal, and should not establish any sect or party; whoever commits crimes will be excluded from the religion.

. . .

Truong Sanh Temple (Can Giuoc) Sunday, May 30, 1926

(The 19th Day of the 4th Month of the Year of the Yang Fire Tiger)

JADE EMPEROR, or CAO DAI TIEN ONG DAI BO TAT MA HA TAT, TEACHING THE GREAT WAY FOR THE SOUTHERN QUARTER:

I could not believe that you, My disciples, could be so confused!

What is the meaning of "Chieu Ky Trung do dan Hoai Sanh" (Raise high the flag of guidance for all living beings—the born and the unborn)? It means that you have to help all living beings, including even the unborn.

Why did you chase disciples away?

Promise to admit! Open the door!

Listen, all living beings:

Formerly, I incarnated and created Buddhism almost six thousand years ago, and the Buddhist teachings have now been almost denatured. People even used to say that the Buddha did not teach. Today, I have decided not to incarnate anymore, but instead to use miracles to perfect Buddhism and to teach people.

Thus, those living beings who do not wish to spiritually improve themselves and who will subsequently be punished in Hell will not deny their crimes and will not have any basis to blame Me by claiming that Buddha did not teach.

You must know that if you do not take the opportunity of this third universal salvation to improve yourself spiritually, you will have no more hope to be saved.

I will now reorganize the manner of worship:

You will set up an altar for Me in the middle of the temple between the altars of Quan Am Bo Tat and Quan Thanh De Quan. Thus, the statue of Quan Am Bo Tat will be on my right, and the statue of Quan Thanh De Quan will be on my left.

On the next row beneath will be different statues of other Buddhas, Immortals, and Saints.

The Temple will now be named, "Jade Emperor Temple."

. . .

July 5, 1926
CAODAI

K . . . Listen to Me, your Master.

People on earth, in order to be rich, you find ways to make money. This is solely from the material point of view. The Angels, Saints, Immortals, and Buddhas, in order to be enlightened, must gain service credits.

I come to save you by establishing a school of credits and of virtues for your spiritual development and enlightenment. Whether or not you become enlightened is totally up to you. Listen to Me! K . . . If you don't go through My school, you can never be enlightened anywhere else.

My child K . . .! Very few people go by the White Pearl Gate, but many go to Hell. Think about it and cultivate your spirit. As much as I love you now, so much more will you regret in the future not listening to me when you could.

I have already forgiven you because I know that you will have repented.

Your mission is great. Wait for My orders at the Ngoc Dan (name of a séance).

. . .

Saturday, July 17, 1926
(The 8th of the sixth month of the year of the Yang Fire Tiger)
JADE EMPEROR, or CAO DAI TIEN ONG DAI BO TAT

MA HA TAT, TEACHING THE GREAT WAY FOR THE SOUTHERN QUARTER:

Lady Duong, I, your Master, assign you to establish the female College. Your gender alone does not condemn you to the kitchen. At this 3rd salvation, there will be much hard work for everyone. Male and female are of equal number. Not only males work to become Immortals and Buddhas. As I have said, at the Bach Ngoc Kinh (White Pearl Palace), there are both male and female, and frequently, females are predominant.

So follow My order to establish the female college.

Listen and obey!

I will always be with you. Don't worry.

H., I assign you to teach and guide all the females.

I will share some responsibility with you.

Ngoc Dan (Can Giuoc) Saturday, July 17, 1926
(The 8th day of the sixth month of the year of the Yang Fire Tiger)
JADE EMPEROR, or CAO DAI TIEN ONG DAI BO TAT MA HA TAT, TEACHING THE GREAT WAY FOR THE SOUTHERN QUARTER:

My greetings to all disciples.

Great Joy! Great joy!

The Dau Su of the Confucian Branch may teach secret principles. Whoever practices vegetarianism for more than ten days per month may receive these secret, precious teachings.

All disciples should practice vegetarianism. Why? It is not simply that I wish to adhere to tradition and enforce an old law, but that this law is important, or you could never reach the stage of Immortal or Buddha without it.

Allow Me to explain:

Everyone on this earth has two bodies. The earthly one is called the physical; the sacred body, the spiritual. The spiritual body is formed from the earthly body and therefore may be visible or invisible. This miraculous spiritual body is formed from "Tinh," "Khi" and "Than" by spiritual self-cultivation. This spiritual body is lighter than air. When it leaves the physical body, it retains the impression of physicality as if it were molded in the body.

You cannot become fully enlightened and return to Nirvana if you have "Tinh" and "Khi," but not "Than." You cannot make a spiritual body for the return to Nirvana if you have "Than" but not "Tinh" or "Khi."

For the spiritual body to be created and enlightenment to occur, one must have all three elements: "Tinh," "Khi," and "Than" united. "Tinh" and "Khi" are all materials and will interact with cosmic ether where there is electricity. To reach the universe, the soul must be pure, advanced and therefore lighter than atmospheric air. It must also be as genuinely good as the Saints, Immortals and Buddhas in order to reach those levels.

A pure "Than" is produced by a pure body. Meat-eating creates difficulties for one practicing meditation, inasmuch as it prevents the practitioner from effectively resolving complications which arise from meditation. Even if you have no such complications, an impure physical body will create an impure spiritual body, which cannot conduct electricity well. As a result, it will then be struck by lightning and be destroyed in the atmosphere. Even if the impure spiritual body is wise and remains on the earth to avoid the lightning, it will remain an Immortal and never proceed to Buddhahood.

This is why I recommend the practice of complete vegetarianism before attempting meditation.[235]

What we discover when we compare Bahá'í and Cao Dai is two quite different proposals for world unity:

Issues	Bahá'í	Cao Dai
Meaning	Properly an adjective ("The Bahá'í Faith") from Arabic bahā' Glory, Splendor.	Cao Đài = High Tower. Đại Đạo Tam Kỳ Phổ Độ = The Great Religion of Third-Period Salvation.

Dates	1844 Declaration of the Báb. 1863 Declaration of Bahá'u'lláh.	1920 first séance appearance to Ngo Van Chieu of the spirit Cao Dai. 1926 formal establishment of Caodaism by Le Van Trung.
Source Region and Religion	Iran. Shi'a Islam.	Vietnam. Mahāyāna Buddhism, as well as Daoism, Catholicism, Confucianism, and spirit/ancestor religions.
Divinely-appointed Revealer	Husayn-'Alí of Núr (1817–92), *Bahá'u'lláh* (Glory of God), a Manifestation prophesied by 'Alí-Muhammad of Shīrāz (1819–50), the *Báb* (Gate).	Ngo Van Chieu, later known as Ngo Minh Chieu (1878–1932).
Scriptures	~2,000 surviving works by the Báb, and ~18,000 works by Bahá'u'lláh. Of lesser stature: ~30,000 works by 'Abdu'l-Bahá.	*Thanh Ngon Hiep Tuyen* ("Compilation of Divine Messages"), two volumes of messages to Cao Dai leaders given during séances.
Method of Revelation	Báb—religious visions, including one of drinking seven drops of blood of the martyred Imám Husayn. Lengthy compositions written quickly and spontaneously. Bahá'u'lláh—dramatic religious experiences when imprisoned in Tehran. Revelation of the sacred books, sometimes visually, sometimes quickly.	Séances, including use of devices.

Past Revealers	Manifestations (individuals who can reflect all the attributes of God perfectly, and whose primary purpose is education) whom Bahá'u'lláh acknowledged are Abraham, Zoroaster, Moses, Jesus, Muḥammad, the Báb, and himself. 'Abdu'l-Bahá later added the Buddha; Shoghi Effendi added Krishna and an unnamed Sabaean Manifestation. Others are possible.	Three periods of salvation in which God sent Ambassadors of his kingdom. The first two were socially and culturally specific, but the third is universal. First stage included Moses; second included Śākyamuni Buddha, Lao-tze, Confucius, Jesus, and Muḥammad. Sun Yat-sen, Joan of Arc, Victor Hugo, and Louis Pasteur are among others honored. In the third stage spirits are used to communicate truth.
Present Leaders	Universal House of Justice—nine members elected every five years.	A pope and hierarchy.
God	One God.	Dieu Tri Kim Mau or Duc Phat Mau (Mother Goddess) and Cao Dai (God).
Organizational Structure	No clergy; importance of consultation; elected 9-member local, regional, and national spiritual assemblies, and Universal House of Justice (which is infallible in protecting the Bahá'í Faith).	Similar to Roman Catholic Church: pope, cardinals, bishops, priests.
Headquarters	Haifa, Israel. (US headquarters = Wilmette, Illinois).	Long Hoa, Tay Ninh province, Vietnam.

Rituals	Daily individual ablutions, obligatory prayers, and 95-fold repetition of "Alláh-u-Abhá"; an annual fast from 2–20 March; the Nineteen Day Feast—a regular gathering for worship, consultation, and socializing; pilgrimage to Bahá'í holy places.	Celibate priesthood, vegetarianism, daily prayers, incense offerings, meditation, exorcism. Symbol = the divine eye.
Goal for Individuals	Each individual's ability to "manifest all the potential forces with which his inmost true self has been endowed." Since the true self consists of all the attributes of God in potential form, self-realization results in understanding God. Release from saṃsāra to nirvāṇa.	Escape saṃsāra; achieve enlightenment and self-liberation from sins and evil desires; nurture pure love, justice, compassion, and truth. These are achieved through focus meditation and supporting socio-ethical activities.
Social Agenda	The Most Great Peace in which the world is united and human potential can be fully expressed.	The universe is a network of evolution operating under cause and effect, yang and yin, the cycle of birth-growth-aging-death. Religion must help build a world of love, justice, compassion, fraternity, and human progress without discrimination. Universal harmony for all peoples.

Advancement Agenda	Various multiple-year plans proposed by the Universal House of Justice, including education, public discourse, and social action projects. Clear objectives of planting the Bahá'í Faith in many countries.	Little focused effort to reach beyond the Vietnamese community.
Status of Women	Equal with men, including political and spiritual leadership.	No woman can become pope or other top leader. Men and women enter the temple through different doors and sit on different sides.
Opposition	External: the Báb executed 1850. Bahá'u'lláh exiled and imprisoned. Numerous martyrdoms. Persecution and confiscation of property in Iran following 1979 Islamic revolution and continuing to today. Internal: opposition from rival factions.	External: French colonial and North Vietnamese opposition. Internal: various sects and excommunications.
Factions	Yahyá, half-brother and rival to Bahá'u'lláh. Muhammad-'Alí, half-brother and rival to 'Abdu'l-Bahá. Ibrahim George Kheiralla (1849–1929). Charles Mason Remey (1874–1974).	Various religious and political/military factions formed throughout the years. Largest sect is the Tay Ninh.

If we are to accept Bahá'í and Cao Dai as revelations from God, it seems God has proposed two incompatible paths to unity. Adding Sun Myung Moon's Unification Church means that God actually offers three.

Such dissonant harmony grates on the ear. The ideal of unity is good; certainly world peace and the quelling of suspicion, hostility, and war would benefit us all. People are wired to connect, and we are happiest, longest lived, most productive, most fulfilled, and most human when they do. "When a man pursues a way which separates him from men, it is not Nature's way."[236]

But it is doubtful that all will drop their commitment to Jesus or Muḥammad, for example, and welcome Bahá'u'lláh as the superseding Manifestation of God, or that all will believe it was actually God who spoke to Ngo Van Chieu in séances or to Sun Myung Moon on a Korean mountainside. Accepting Bahá'u'lláh would entail embracing his thesis of multiple Manifestations throughout history, that these agree with and build upon one another, and that he is the latest and final Manifestation. Bahá'u'lláh spoke of Abraham, Zoroaster, Moses, Jesus, Muḥammad, the Báb, and himself as Manifestations; 'Abdu'l-Bahá added the Buddha; Shoghi Effendi added Krishna. But these eight do not teach the same ideas or practices; numerous chasms divide them. Krishna values ātman while the Buddha teaches anātman. Zoroaster taught the existence of two eternal forces, good and evil, whereas Moses conceived of one—God as the source of all. For Christians the death of Jesus is essential, whereas the Qur'ān denies it happened. One writer who apparently embraces neither Christianity nor Buddhism, and whose description of the Christian God could benefit from editing, nevertheless captures a key discontinuity between these:

> [I]f you're a Christian, you believe that a man who breathed his last on a cross two thousand years ago was the son of a vast and immortal being hovering somewhere above the visible sky, and that someday this long-departed soul will return to earth and usher in an entirely new order of things. If you're a Buddhist, you know with absolute certainty that this is a figment of the Christian's imagination.[237]

One may find similar ethics among various religions. But similarity does not imply identity. "The same thing done by two different people is not the same thing."[238]

It is hard enough to conceive of this salad of earlier "Manifestations" as undifferentiated and complementary without having to top it with Bahá'u'lláh as the final garnish. Or, practically speaking, we may ask, for example, why his year of nineteen nineteen-day months is better than the traditional twelve-month year? Cao Dai, with its history of internal divisions and its focus on ethnic Vietnamese, fares worse than Bahá'í as a candidate for the foundation of universal human unity.

In short, Bahá'í, Cao Dai, and the Unification Church are right—peace and unity would be a wonderful gift to humanity. But the fact that three incompatible proposals for attaining these lie on the table suggests that at least two, and perhaps all three, are not the divine plan they purport to be, and that another way must be found.

Jesus and children at St. Joseph's Cathedral in Hanoi.

13

DISAGREEING AGREEABLY

(*Christianity*)

"Disciples can usually be depended upon to wreck the teachings of a master."[239] Sad but true. However, though wreckers have wreaked ruin in all religions, they have not entirely erased the originals.

Christianity serves as an example. The practice of some who profess to follow Christ is not only unrelated to what Jesus intended but antithetical to it. How can they claim to be his disciples yet do what they do? Nowhere is this clearer than in the way the church has sometimes treated those with whom it disagrees.

In its early centuries and still in places today, Christianity has been a minority religion viewed by the empowered majority with suspicion or hostility. But when tables are turned and Christians gain the upper hand, they sometimes morph from persecuted to persecutor. The phrase "Spanish Inquisition" still evokes images of mindless brutality. An example from 1683:

> There was among the sufferers a young Jewess of exquisite beauty, and but seventeen years of age. Being on the same side of the scaffold where the queen was seated, she addressed her, in hope of obtaining pardon, in the following pathetic speech:—"Great Queen! will not your royal presence be of some service to me in my miserable condition? Have regard to my youth; and, oh! consider that I am about to die for professing a religion imbibed from my earliest infancy!" Her majesty seemed greatly to pity her distress, but turned away her eyes,

> as she did not dare speak a word on behalf of a person who had been declared a heretic by the Inquisition.[240]

Protestants joined Catholics in destroying those they disliked, as Zwingli's drowning of Manz and Calvin's burning of Servetus illustrate. Such butchery, though practiced by broad swaths of the midmillennium church, hardly represents what Jesus intended.

Christians are instead supposed to practice peace and unity. A call for these suffuses Jesus's final counsel for his apostles—his Upper Room Discourse. Note particularly the prayer with which it ends:

> I pray they will be one, Father, just as you are in me and I am in you. I pray that they also will be in us, so that the world will believe that you sent me. I've given them the glory that you gave me so that they can be one just as we are one. I'm in them and you are in me so that they will be made perfectly one. Then the world will know that you sent me and that you have loved them just as you loved me.[241]

Not only do the gospels stress unity, the New Testament letters do as well. Ephesians consists of two halves. The first outlines the church's nature; the second, its practices. Unity heads the list:

> Therefore, as a prisoner for the Lord, I encourage you to live as people worthy of the call you received from God. Conduct yourselves with all humility, gentleness, and patience. Accept each other with love, and make an effort to preserve the unity of the Spirit with the peace that ties you together. You are one body and one spirit just as God also called you in one hope. There is one Lord, one faith, one baptism, and one God and Father of all who is over all, through all, and in all.[242]

Thus Christianity's founding documents urge both unity and the humility and deference that nurture it. The kind of oneness it envisions can only emerge among those who hold common ideas and agendas. Organic unity is impossible among those whose core values conflict:

> Don't be tied up as equal partners with people who don't believe. What does righteousness share with that which is outside the Law? What relationship does light have with darkness? What harmony does Christ have with Satan? What does a believer have in common with someone who doesn't believe? What agreement can there be between God's temple and idols? Because we are the temple of the living God. Just as God said, I live with them, and I will move among them. I will be their God, and they will be my people. Therefore, come out from among them and be separated, says the Lord. Don't touch what is unclean. Then I will welcome you. I will be a father to you, and you will be my sons and daughters, says the Lord Almighty. My dear friends, since we have these promises, let's cleanse ourselves from anything that contaminates our body or spirit so that we make our holiness complete in the fear of God.[243]

The New Testament therefore urges unity among Christians who share a common understanding and allegiance. But how should they relate to those outside their convictions? Here is where past inquisitors and present abortionist killers have it so wrong.

Following a quasi-formal rejection of his Messiahship by the religious leaders of his day, Jesus began to picture in parables a new form of his kingdom. In one of these he addresses how to handle imposters:

> The kingdom of heaven is like someone who planted good seed in his field. While people were sleeping, an enemy came and planted weeds among the wheat and went away. When the stalks sprouted and bore grain, then the weeds also appeared.
>
> The servants of the landowner came and said to him, "Master, didn't you plant good seed in your field? Then how is it that it has weeds?"
>
> "An enemy has done this," he answered.
>
> The servants said to him, "Do you want us to go and gather them?"
>
> But the landowner said, "No, because if you gather the weeds, you'll pull up the wheat along with them. Let both grow

> side by side until the harvest. And at harvest time I'll say to the harvesters, 'First gather the weeds and tie them together in bundles to be burned. But bring the wheat into my barn.'"

In case we don't get the point, he explains:

> The one who plants the good seed is the Human One [or "the Son of Man," the title Jesus most frequently used when referring to himself]. The field is the world. And the good seeds are the followers of the kingdom. But the weeds are the followers of the evil one. The enemy who planted them is the devil. The harvest is the end of the present age. The harvesters are the angels. Just as people gather weeds and burn them in the fire, so it will be at the end of the present age. The Human One will send his angels, and they will gather out of his kingdom all things that cause people to fall away and all people who sin. He will throw them into a burning furnace. People there will be weeping and grinding their teeth. Then the righteous will shine like the sun in their Father's kingdom. Those who have ears should hear.[244]

It is clear that Jesus did not authorize anything resembling an Inquisition, with its torture and executions. His errant church invented that. Jesus was not so naive that he failed to anticipate persecution. His church would receive it but was not to practice it. Though He acknowledged that pretenders and heretics would thrive after his departure, his orders were, "Don't harm them physically. God through his angels will sort things out in the end." The most the church could do was excommunicate them, as Paul made clear:

> Everyone has heard that there is sexual immorality among you. This is a type of immorality that isn't even heard of among the Gentiles—a man is having sex with his father's wife! And you're proud of yourselves instead of being so upset that the one who did this thing is expelled from your community. Though I'm absent physically, I'm present in the spirit and I've already judged the man who did this as if I were present. When

> you meet together in the name of our Lord Jesus, I'll be present in spirit with the power of our Lord Jesus. At that time we need to hand this man over to Satan to destroy his human weakness so that his spirit might be saved on the day of the Lord.
>
> Your bragging isn't good! Don't you know that a tiny grain of yeast makes a whole batch of dough rise? Clean out the old yeast so you can be a new batch of dough, given that you're supposed to be unleavened bread. Christ our Passover lamb has been sacrificed, so let's celebrate the feast with the unleavened bread of honesty and truth, not with old yeast or with the yeast of evil and wickedness.
>
> I wrote to you in my earlier letter not to associate with sexually immoral people. But I wasn't talking about the sexually immoral people in the outside world by any means—or the greedy, or the swindlers, or people who worship false gods—otherwise, you would have to leave the world entirely! But now I'm writing to you not to associate with anyone who calls themselves "brother" or "sister" who is sexually immoral, greedy, someone who worships false gods, an abusive person, a drunk, or a swindler. Don't even eat with anyone like this. What do I care about judging outsiders? Isn't it your job to judge insiders? God will judge outsiders. Expel the evil one from among you![245]

In this passage "handing someone over to Satan" means excommunicating that person from the church (where God is particularly active) and back into the world (where Satan, "the god of this world," holds sway under God's providence). The last sentence in the chapter confirms this understanding.

Inquisitors showed no evidence of having listened to Jesus's parable, nor to the Jewish leader Gamaliel's sage advice when the ruling council sought to exterminate the infant church:

> When the council members heard this, they became furious and wanted to kill the apostles. One council member, a Pharisee and teacher of the Law named Gamaliel, well-respected by all the people, stood up and ordered that the men be taken outside for a few moments. He said, "Fellow Israelites, consider

> carefully what you intend to do to these people. Some time ago, Theudas appeared, claiming to be somebody, and some four hundred men joined him. After he was killed, all of his followers scattered, and nothing came of that. Afterward, at the time of the census, Judas the Galilean appeared and got some people to follow him in a revolt. He was killed too, and all his followers scattered far and wide. Here's my recommendation in this case: Distance yourselves from these men. Let them go! If their plan or activity is of human origin, it will end in ruin. If it originates with God, you won't be able to stop them. Instead, you would actually find yourselves fighting God!" The council was convinced by his reasoning.[246]

This tolerant approach, though accompanied by a pointed verbal warning of God's future judgment, contrasts with commands often encountered in the Tanakh (or Old Testament). The Tanakh urges the extermination of whole communities and of individuals who teach or practice error:

> Thus says Yahweh of hosts, "I remember what Amalek did to Israel, how he laid wait for him in the way, when he came up from Egypt. Now go and smite Amalek, and utterly destroy all that they have, and spare them not; but slay both man and woman, infant and suckling, ox and sheep, camel and ass."[247]

> If there arise among you a prophet, or a dreamer of dreams, and give you a sign or a wonder, and the sign or the wonder of which he spoke to you come to pass saying, "Let us go after other gods, which you have not known, and let us serve them;" you shall not hearken unto the words of that prophet, or that dreamer of dreams: for Yahweh your God is testing you, to know whether you love Yahweh your God with all your heart and with all your soul. You shall walk after Yahweh your God, and fear him, and keep his commandments, and obey his voice, and you shall serve him, and cleave unto him. And that prophet, or that dreamer of dreams, shall be put to death; because he has spoken to turn you away from Yahweh your God, who brought

> you out of the land of Egypt, and redeemed you out of the house of bondage, to thrust you out of the way which Yahweh your God commanded you to walk in. So you shall put the evil away from your midst.
>
> If your brother, the son of your mother, or your son, or your daughter, or the wife of your bosom, or your friend, which is as your own soul, entice you secretly, saying, "Let us go and serve other gods," which you have not known, you, nor your fathers; namely, of the gods of the people which are round about you, nigh unto you, or far off from you, from the one end of the earth even unto the other end of the earth; you shall not consent unto him, nor hearken unto him; neither shall your eye pity him, neither shall you spare, neither shall you conceal him: but you shall surely kill him; your hand shall be first upon him to put him to death, and afterwards the hand of all the people. And you shall stone him with stones, that he die; because he has sought to thrust you away from Yahweh your God, who brought you out of the land of Egypt, from the house of bondage. And all Israel shall hear, and fear, and shall do no more any such wickedness as this is among you.[248]

Such commands were addressed to national, theocratic Israel. Christianity, by contrast, was never intended to be a nation, but a people called out from among the nations.[249] The constitution and rules for the nation of Israel do not apply to the transnational church. God's morality does not change, but the mechanisms through which his morality is mediated may. The church learns by observing Old Testament patterns and examples but does not find in them its own structural mandate. In some cases it is required to disregard Old Testament directives and do the opposite. This is the case in dealing with false teachers and immoral members.

The principle of the church's freedom from the Mosaic Law is the point of the first church council:

> Some believers from among the Pharisees stood up and claimed, "The Gentiles must be circumcised. They must be required to keep the Law from Moses."

The apostles and the elders gathered to consider this matter. After much debate, Peter stood and addressed them, "Fellow believers, you know that, early on, God chose me from among you as the one through whom the Gentiles would hear the word of the gospel and come to believe. God, who knows people's deepest thoughts and desires, confirmed this by giving them the Holy Spirit, just as he did to us. He made no distinction between us and them, but purified their deepest thoughts and desires through faith. Why then are you now challenging God by placing a burden on the shoulders of these disciples that neither we nor our ancestors could bear? On the contrary, we believe that we and they are saved in the same way, by the grace of the Lord Jesus."

The entire assembly fell quiet as they listened to Barnabas and Paul describe all the signs and wonders God did among the Gentiles through their activity. When Barnabas and Paul also fell silent, James responded, "Fellow believers, listen to me. Simon reported how, in his kindness, God came to the Gentiles in the first place, to raise up from them a people of God. The prophets' words agree with this; as it is written,

> After this I will return, and I will rebuild David's fallen tent; I will rebuild what has been torn down. I will restore it so that the rest of humanity will seek the Lord, even all the Gentiles who belong to me. The Lord says this, the one who does these things known from earliest times.

"Therefore, I conclude that we shouldn't create problems for Gentiles who turn to God. Instead, we should write a letter, telling them to avoid the pollution associated with idols, sexual immorality, eating meat from strangled animals, and consuming blood. After all, Moses has been proclaimed in every city for a long time, and is read aloud every Sabbath in every synagogue."

The apostles and the elders, along with the entire church, agreed to send some delegates chosen from among themselves to Antioch, together with Paul and Barnabas. They selected

Judas Barsabbas and Silas, who were leaders among the brothers and sisters. They were to carry this letter:

> The apostles and the elders, to the Gentile brothers and sisters in Antioch, Syria, and Cilicia. Greetings! We've heard that some of our number have disturbed you with unsettling words we didn't authorize. We reached a united decision to select some delegates and send them to you along with our dear friends Barnabas and Paul. These people have devoted their lives to the name of our Lord Jesus Christ. Therefore, we are sending Judas and Silas. They will confirm what we have written. The Holy Spirit has led us to the decision that no burden should be placed on you other than these essentials: refuse food offered to idols, blood, the meat from strangled animals, and sexual immorality. You will do well to avoid such things. Farewell.[250]

Thus, while it values and learns from the Torah, the New Testament Church is not obliged to obey it, as the nation of Israel once was. The first covenant is "obsolete . . . old and outdated . . . close to disappearing."[251] So instead of executing the one who prophesies falsely or who breaks Torah by gathering wood on the Sabbath, the church at most excludes from its number those who err. It then urges repentance, all the while allowing the weeds to grow and awaiting unerring divine judgment.[252]

In sixteenth-century Europe, both Catholic and Protestant Christians failed to grasp the difference between Israel and the church, ignored the New Testament Scriptures they professed, and executed heretics. One who protested such practice, and who himself ended up burning at the stake, was Anabaptist theologian Balthasar Hubmaier:

> [Heretics] should be overcome with holy instruction, not contentiously but gently, even though the Holy Scripture also includes wrath . . . Should they not yield to words of authority or gospel reasons, then avoid them and let them go on to rant and rage so that those who are filthy may become yet more filthy. The law which condemns heretics to [execution by] fire

> is based upon Zion in blood and Jerusalem in wickedness . . . It follows now that the inquisitors are the greatest heretics of all, because counter to the teaching and example of Jesus, they condemn heretics to fire; and before it is time they pull up the wheat together with the tares. For Christ did not come to slaughter, kill, burn, but so that those who live should live yet more abundantly . . . [I]t is well and good that the secular authority puts to death the criminals who do physical harm to the defenseless. But no one may injure the atheist [*Gotssfind*] who wishes nothing for himself other than to forsake the gospel . . . Therefore to burn heretics appears to be confessing Christ, but indeed it is to deny him . . . Now it appears to anyone, even to a blind person, that the law [which provides] for the burning of heretics is an invention of the devil.[253]

The church pursues an organic unity that grows out of inner conviction, not external coercion. It further anticipates a unity that will one day embrace all humanity. It draws upon prophetic images that the earth will someday be filled with the knowledge of Yahweh as the water covers the sea, and that

> in the last days it shall come to pass that
> the mountain of the house of Yahweh
>   shall be established in the top of the mountains;
> it shall be exalted above the hills,
>   and people shall flow unto it.
> Many nations shall come and say,
> "Come, and let us go up to the mountain of Yahweh,
>   and to the house of the God of Jacob;
> he will teach us of his ways,
>   and we will walk in his paths."
> For the law shall go forth out of Zion,
>   and the word of Yahweh from Jerusalem.
> He shall judge among many people,
>   and rebuke strong nations afar off;
> they shall beat their swords into plowshares,

and their spears into pruninghooks:
nation shall not lift up a sword against nation,
neither shall they learn war any more.
But they shall sit every man under his vine and under his fig tree;
and none shall make them afraid:
for the mouth of Yahweh of hosts has spoken it.[254]

The penultimate chapter of the New Testament describes a new heaven, new earth, and new Jerusalem:

> The city doesn't need the sun or the moon to shine on it, because God's glory is its light, and its lamp is the Lamb. The nations will walk by its light, and the kings of the earth will bring their glory into it. Its gates will never be shut by day, and there will be no night there. They will bring the glory and honor of the nations into it. Nothing unclean will ever enter it, nor anyone who does what is vile and deceitful, but only those who are registered in the Lamb's scroll of life.[255]

This image envisions a global unity that does not imply uniformity. The kings of the earth differ from one another. The envisioned unity is organic, deep, grounded upon a similar vision of reality and the divine, and parallel in its moral practice. But the kings remain different kings and the nations varied nations.

So although the New Testament vision for unity may at first seem circumscribed when compared with the Bahá'í vision, its ultimate outcome is just as universal. But the New Testament's more immediate focus is on producing unity of faith, conduct, and mutual acceptance among Christian believers here and now.

Other New Testament passages underscore that Christians should communicate their faith with words and commend it with works rather than compel "converts" with sword and flame. Examples abound in Jesus's ministry. When Matthew sought a prophetic passage to characterize Messiah's ministry, he chose Isaiah:

Look, my Servant whom I chose,
the one I love, in whom I find great pleasure,

I'll put my Spirit upon him,
    and he'll announce judgment to the Gentiles.
He won't argue or shout,
    and nobody will hear his voice in the streets.
He won't break a bent stalk,
    and he won't snuff out a smoldering wick,
until he makes justice win.
    And the Gentiles will put their hope in his name.[256]

Matthew uses *pais mou* to translate Isaiah's Hebrew *'abdi*; both mean "my servant", but pais can also mean "my child." When meaning "servant," pais implies a closer relationship and a more kindly regard than do *diakonos* or *doulos*, other Greek words for "servant." Jesus is a pais, not a crusader. As such, his ministry will be characterized by unambiguous proclamation—he will neither avoid nor dilute the truth. But he will make this proclamation gently, neither brashly, sarcastically, nor arrogantly. "What is pictured is a ministry so gentle and compassionate that the weak are not trampled on and crushed till justice, the full righteousness of God, triumphs. And for such a Messiah most Jews were little prepared."[257]

> Jesus did not . . . stay around "to show them" who is lord or to flaunt his divinely given powers . . . He is not the kind of person who seeks dramatic confrontations for the glory of God . . . He prefers to do his work quietly and inconspicuously. This is the way *God's* Messiah works, in contrast to all false Messiahs . . .
>
> Jesus' quiet tactics have turned people away from John's day to ours. But maybe Jesus' way, beautifully outlined for us in this Isaiah quote, has more to suggest for revolution and reform than we credit. To be sure, its failure "to shout and scream," as revolutionaries and the Spirit-filled of all times are wont to do, its failure to work in the middle of the streets (as contemporary revolutionary and revivalist strategies both advise), and its strange penchant for working with bruised rather than with polished reeds, with flickering rather than with glowing flames, will often turn some people away from Jesus . . .

> Jesus' method clear to the end will be the method of quiet revolution, the unlikely tactic of treating persons with great respect—the method of gentleness. There is nothing sensational or special about this method—but it has been determined ever since his baptism at least that this is the way Jesus will go, and Matthew now certifies this way as the *prophetic* way . . . And though Matthew's emphasis in the last two verses (following Isaiah) has been on what the Servant of the Lord will *not* do (stressed no less than four times), nevertheless, this Servant will never rest in his nonviolent zeal until he brings *justice* to earth . . . The Servant is quiet but not quietistic; nonviolent but not noninvolved; gentle but passionate for justice—a justice, we are promised, that he shall one day successfully bring to victory.[258]

The difference between Jesus's approach and that of his enthusiastic apostles emerged as they traveled through Samaria. The Samaritans refused Jesus hospitality because Jerusalem was his destination. "When the disciples James and John saw this, they said, 'Lord, do you want us to call fire down from heaven to consume them?' But Jesus turned and spoke sternly to them, and the went on to another village." Burn them? No, leave them in their opposition and move on. Later, while being nailed to the cross Jesus prayed, "Father, forgive them, for they don't know what they're doing." Peter, by contrast, had swung a sword.[259]

Fortunately, in time, the writers of the New Testament got the idea and elaborated on Jesus's approach:

> God's slave shouldn't be argumentative but should be kind toward all people, able to teach, patient, and should correct opponents with gentleness. Perhaps God will change their mind and give them a knowledge of the truth. They may come to their senses and escape from the devil's trap that holds them captive to do his will.
>
> They shouldn't speak disrespectfully about anyone, but they should be peaceful, kind, and show complete courtesy toward everyone. We were once foolish, disobedient, deceived, and slaves to our desires and various pleasures too.

> Whenever anyone asks you to speak of your hope, be ready to defend it. Yet do this with respectful humility, maintaining a good conscience. Act in this way so that those who malign your good lifestyle in Christ may be ashamed when they slander you.
>
> No one can tame the tongue, though. It is a restless evil, full of deadly poison. With it we both bless the Lord and Father and curse human beings made in God's likeness. Blessing and cursing come from the same mouth. My brothers and sisters, it just shouldn't be this way! . . . What of the wisdom from above? First, it is pure, and then peaceful, gentle, obedient, filled with mercy and good actions, fair, and genuine. Those who make peace sow the seeds of justice by their peaceful acts.[260]

Christianity neither proposes that all beliefs are true nor promotes an institutional unity that pretends they are. Christians are free to argue that other beliefs are wrong.[261] But Christianity, properly practiced, does not attempt to compel "conversion" to its own point of view. One of the most often cited verses of the Qur'ān agrees: "Let there be no compulsion in religion." This is because "religion depends upon faith and will, and these would be meaningless if induced by force."[262] An open letter from Islamic authorities to Pope Benedict XVI elucidates the meaning of this phrase:

> *There is no compulsion in religion* was not a command to Muslims to remain steadfast in the face of the desire of their oppressors to force them to renounce their faith, but was a reminder to Muslims themselves, once they had attained power, that they could not force another's heart to believe. *There is no compulsion in religion* addresses those in a position of strength, not weakness. The earliest commentaries on the Qur'an . . . make it clear that some Muslims of Medina wanted to force their children to convert from Judaism or Christianity to Islam, and this verse was precisely an answer to them **not** to try to force their children to convert to Islam. Moroever [sic], Muslims are also guided by such verses as *Say: The truth is from your Lord; so whosoever will, let him believe, and whosoever will,*

> *let him disbelieve.* (*al-Kahf* 18:29); and *Say: O disbelievers! I worship not that which ye worship; Nor worship ye that which I worship. And I shall not worship that which ye worship. Nor will ye worship that which I worship. Unto you your religion, and unto me my religion* (*al-Kafirun*: 109:1–6).[263]

Or from the Hindu perspective,

> There is nothing wrong with disagreement. In fact, where relationships are concerned, it is a necessary part of love to disagree when the other person is about to do something he or she will later regret. What upsets us in such situations is simply lack of detachment: we don't know how to disagree with complete respect.[264]

Or from Zen,

> We must learn to respect the differences between people, to see that points of view alien to our own may be valid to those who hold them. Too often we are inclined to believe that a peaceful society must be a homogeneous society, a society where everyone thinks, acts and speaks alike. However, it is better to have a variegated society, provided we can come to recognize that variety does not of necessity exclude harmony. In music, in order to achieve harmony there must be different notes; if all notes are the same, what results is not harmony but monotony. Variety is more than the spice of life: it is the very substance of meaningful existence.[265]

It is criminal that confessing Christians have not consistently conducted themselves according to Christ's commands. Christians, of course, are not alone in harboring adherents who perpetrate a violence contradictory to their core principles. Some Hindus and Buddhists also speak and act in ways hard to reconcile with their traditions' more tolerant and peaceful reputations.[266] But at least the founding documents have it right. Disagreements necessarily imply neither hatred ("miso-") nor fear ("-phobia"). Verbalizing them is not necessarily a sign of narrow-mindedness, nor does it constitute a hate crime. Articulating differences is fine; hubris and violence in doing so are not.

> Put crudely, the non-judgmental inclusivist seems to believe that you can only be nice to people if you agree with them. This seems clearly false. It is both logically and practically possible for us . . . to respect and revere worthy representatives of other traditions while still believing—on rational grounds—that some aspects of their world-view are simply mistaken. On a rather less exalted level, we can trust and respect, even have as a friend who can be relied on, a member of the Flat Earth Society, even though we know that his cosmological views are less than accurate.[267]

Stephen Prothero is right: various religions teach different things.[268] Christians are right, at least in their founding documents: we may discuss our differences. We may even discuss them pointedly and vigorously. But physical force, condescension, misrepresentation, and intimidation play no legitimate part in the process. Where we disagree, we must disagree agreeably.

Rock carvings in the American Southwest.

14

THE EARTH IS OUR MOTHER

(*Native American Practices*)

> It may seem absurd to believe that a "primitive" culture in the Himalaya has anything to teach our industrialized society. But our search for a future that works keeps spiraling back to an ancient connection between ourselves and the earth, an interconnectedness that ancient cultures have never abandoned.[269]

Cultures other than Himalayan also prize interconnectedness. The Nahua of Mexico and El Salvador value

> existential ties between humans, seeds, natural settings, and the gods through communications with the Cemanahuac, "that which surrounds us" . . .
>
> For us, the narratives of the supernatural . . . symbolize all that which escapes Western reason, but which in our world possesses a deep and substantial meaning. The narratives are about a mythical and almost miraculous existence. There is an intimate connection between the myths, the sacred stories of the indigenous people, their villages, rituals, moral behavior, social organization, and daily activities. Myth is neither a dark fantasy nor a senseless infusion of vain dreams; rather, it represents a laborious and important cultural force . . .
>
> The first agricultural rite consists in preparing Totlaltonantzin, "our mother earth," or *Totlaltzin*, "our earth," to be impregnated by the seed . . .

[T]he farmer approaches his garden in constant dialogue with nature. This dialogue takes many forms. He listens to the birds, especially Mezutechitl, Cenzontle, and Huerecoch, understanding that their song announces the arrival of the first rains. The Nahua know how to interpret nature's messages announcing the arrival of the new season: humid soils in the gardens, the smell of moisture in the air, and the splendor of the leaves on the holm oaks and buddle trees . . .

The indigenous Nahua farmer is in dialogue throughout the agricultural cycle with the living beings of Cemanahuac, "that which surrounds us." He seeks to hear the communications of the birds, the insects, and other animals and to learn of their knowledge regarding the approach of good and bad weather. He converses with the beings that inhabit the forest to request rain, wood, and other foods that they provide.

The garden is the place where various types of knowledge come together. The interpretation of weather, the words of the animals, the knowledge of soils, the coexistence with other animals all converge in the relationship with seeds, with whom the gardener pleads, "Give us our flesh and food" (*tonacayotl*). The Nahua speak with the gods in their gardens. This is where rites and songs acquire significance . . .

The Cemanahuac is where we live. It is our home. Because the tree is the brother of Cemanahuac, one must ask permission before using its wood. If this is not done, the substance that lives within the tree and in the forest can do harm to the peasant or his family by causing disease and even death. If the gifts of the forest are overexploited, there will come a time when the forest will cease to produce, because all living things become tired. Even the earth must be given time to rest so that it might produce better crops in the following year. Everything that exists in nature has its limits, can be exhausted, and is invaluable. We must take care not to misuse nature's resources so that we do not suffer one day.

By conceiving Cemanahuac, "that which surrounds us," to be our home, all of its members, including animals and plants, become mutually important for the existence of any one being.

> This is why the hunting of animals that prey on crops is limited to controlling their presence and not to eliminating them . . .
>
> Indigenous people also believe that there should be food for both animals and humans. For this reason, a diverse number of plants should be grown in the fields. Above, I noted that weeding within the agricultural cycle is selective. Left to grow between the furrows of maize are other legumes, such as the pumpkin, beans, *chilacayote*, chili, and chícharos. Edible wild plants, including quelite and quiltoniles (amaranth), chivitos, and jaltomatoes, as well as medicinal plants used to remove *tenamitiliztli* (bad air), are also permitted growing space. Farmers also allow plants to grow between the rows that are used as fodder for their beasts of burden. Finally . . . the Indians try to copy the natural habitat of plants in their fields.[270]

Native American traditions posit spirits that inhabit plants, animals, and specific locations. Relationships must be maintained

> not only among people, but also nature and deities . . . [T]he highest value is harmony with the earth . . . The plant, animal, or crystal some ethnopharmacologist may want to collect may, in fact, encompass, contain, or be the manifestation of the ancestral spirit—even the healer's grandmother . . .
>
> The same is true for the Mazatecs of Southern Mexico, whose shamans and *curandeiros* confer with the plant spirits in order to heal: successful curers must above all else learn to listen to the plants talk . . .
>
> These links between life, land, and society are identified by David Suzuki and Peter Knudtson as the "Sacred Balance." Science, with its quantum mechanics methods, they say, can never address the universe as a whole; and it certainly can never adequately describe the holism of indigenous knowledge and belief. In fact, science is far behind in the environmental movement. It still sees nature as objects ("components" of biodiversity is the term used in the Convention on Biological Diversity, or CBD) for human use and exploitation. Technology has used the

> banner of scientific "objectivity" to mask the moral and ethical issues that emerge from such a functionalist, anthropocentric philosophy. Marilyn Strather makes this clear when discussing the ethical dilemmas raised (or avoided) when embryos are "decontextualized" as human beings to become "objects" of scientific research.[271]

Parallel to this "Sacred Balance" is the idea of a "Sacred Trust," which is

> an ethic passed down through countless generations of forefathers and mothers. The Sacred Trust holds holy all things in the natural world; the wind that brings the rain that grows the grasses that feeds the buffalo that sustain the man. All natural things are interdependent and contribute to a universal state of balance and harmony. For the Coyote Warriors, it is impossible to love the Creator and desecrate the Creation. The natural world is the great mystery, the religion before religion . . .
>
> "[M]y father . . . taught me that playing games against nature is always counterproductive. Indians know how to play games *with* nature. Europeans—Whites—have been at odds with nature for many centuries. The Man vs. Nature argument is a contrived dichotomy with ancient roots in Christianity, Descartes and Francis Bacon. What you end up with is a race of people trapped by myth, striving to claw its way back to Eden against ever-growing odds. The project of nature is ongoing, we are a part of it, yet the European continues to set himself outside of it. Its [sic] brought a crippling exhaustion and anxiety to the White culture, exhaustion with the notion that we can achieve utopia by our own efforts.
>
> "Four hundred years of Cartesian-utopist thinking gets you a civilization of people lost in shopping malls, spiritually adrift in the meaninglessness of their lives, with no connection to the Earth."[272]

Talk of nature spirits may strike outsiders as pagan, puerile, or prescientific. A nonnative observer may thus dismiss any hope that Nahua or Native

American practice might contribute anything useful to our map of reality today. However, study of Traditional Ecological Knowledge (TEK) has unearthed not only intriguing case studies of human thought but also helpful values and paradigms. These may complement or reverse modern Western views of our natural environment and of how humanity can best function within and as part of it. Sacred groves, for example, may at first glance seem to represent nothing more than relics of a superstitious past. But in fact

> [h]abitats protected by sacred locales may be recruitment areas, for example for populations of seed-dispersing birds and bats, that are of importance for renewal of surrounding ecosystems. They are also important for birds controlling insect outbreaks on adjacent crop fields, and may serve as seed banks for locally adapted crop varieties and medicinal plants. Even small sacred groves may be surprisingly effective in conserving biodiversity. A botanical survey in a Nigerian sacred grove yielded 330 plant species as compared to only 23 in surrounding nonprotected areas.[273]

So, perhaps unintentionally, the maintenance of sacred groves has proven ecologically valuable.

Further, traditional methods may better encourage an ecosystem's resilience, the gradual loss of which "is often masked by the development of fossil-fuel-dependent technologies to maintain yields" or by "financial insurance to fishermen and farmers in periods of resource crisis, thereby removing incentives for building an ecological knowledge base."[274]

Native practice is not perfect. It has advanced over centuries by trial and error. Massive mistakes have been made, such as hunting to extinction the giant ground sloth,[275] or the depletion of caribou by the Cree in the early twentieth century. In other words, the image of the Noble Savage is a myth, and "exaggerated claims on behalf of traditional ecological wisdom require a reality check." Despite these caveats there is much in a Native American worldview that might help us understand our own humanity, our world, and how best to dwell together.

> The pervasive cosmology of traditional societies may be characterized as a "community of beings" world view in which

> humans are part of an interacting set of living things, a view that was also common in Europe up until Medieval times. Such a cosmology does have similarities to a holistic ecological view of the world, as opposed to the Newtonian mechanical model, except that traditional world views often also have a spiritual component . . .
>
> Cultural values such as respect (for humans as well as for nature), sharing, reciprocity, and humility characterize a diversity of systems of traditional knowledge and practice, including those of American aboriginal groups . . .[276]

> Indigenous and traditional peoples frequently view themselves as guardians and stewards of nature. Harmony and equilibrium among components of the cosmos are central concepts in most cosmologies . . . [T]he highest value is harmony with the earth.
>
> [There is a] "sacred balance" between all life . . . [I]ndigenous and traditional peoples maintain [kinship relationships] with their "extended family" of all living things.[277]

Rachel Carson's 1962 *Silent Spring* helped awaken ecological concern in the United States, though this book was not the first to confront environmental degradation. *Silent Spring* facilitated banning DDT a decade later, but other problems continue to arise. Warnings of how humanity is soiling its nest have been voiced by both religious and scientific groups. The Dalai Lama, for example, issued the following message for World Environment Day, June 5, 1986:

> Peace and the survival of life on earth as we know it are threaten [sic] by human activities which lack a commitment to humanitarian values. Destruction of nature and nature resources results from ignorance, greed and lack of respect for the earth's living things.
>
> This lack of respect extends even to earth's human descendants, the future generations who will inherit a vastly degraded planet if world peace does not become a reality, and destruction of the natural environment continues at the present rate.

> Our ancestors viewed the earth as rich and bountiful, which it is. Many people in the past also saw nature as inexhaustibly sustainable, which we now know is the case only if we care for it.
>
> It is not difficult to forgive destruction in the past, which resulted from ignorance. Today, however, we have access to more information, and it is essential that we re-examine ethically what we have inherited, what we are responsible for, and what we will pass on to coming generations. Clearly this is a pivotal generation. Global communication is possible, yet confrontations take place more often than meaningful dialogues for peace.
>
> Our marvels of science and technology are matched if not out-weighed by many current tragedies, including human starvation in some parts of the world, and extinction of other life forms.
>
> Exploration of outer space takes place at the same time as the earth's own oceans, seas, and freshwater areas grow increasingly polluted, and their life forms are largely unknown or misunderstood.
>
> Many of the earth's habitats, animals, plants, insects, and even microorganisms that we know of as rare or endangered, may not be known at all by future generations. We have the capacity, and the responsibility. We must act before it is too late.[278]

Half a dozen years later, 1,575 scientists, including more than half of all living scientists awarded the Nobel Prize, signed the World Scientists' Warning to Humanity. It warned that

> many of our current practices put at serious risk the future that we wish for human society and the plant and animal kingdoms, and may so alter the living world that it will be unable to sustain life in the manner that we know . . .
>
> Our massive tampering with the world's interdependent web of life—coupled with the environmental damage inflicted by deforestation, species loss, and climate change—could

> trigger widespread adverse effects, including unpredictable collapses of critical biological systems whose interactions and dynamics we only imperfectly understand . . .
>
> A new ethic is required—a new attitude towards discharging our responsibility for caring for ourselves and for the earth. We must recognize the earth's limited capacity to provide for us. We must recognize its fragility. We must no longer allow it to be ravaged.[279]

Along with profit-driven industrialists, Western theistic religions stand accused of culpably disregarding our planet and its future. "[T]he Christian location of salvation and divinity in a transcendent realm has led to an under-appreciation of the natural world whose ecological, moral-scientific, and even race and gender consequences are among the most challenging problems we now face."[280] "Our Native American culture has been strip-mined by the European's Judeo-Christian ethic . . . It is clear to indigenous peoples that we are dealing with a desperate society trapped inside a crumbling mythology."[281]

While it is lamentably true that many theists present and past have disdained and abused the natural world, such a sorry stance is not a natural corollary of theism. It is another sad case of disciples wrecking the teachings of their masters. The Genesis account portrays Yahweh's thoughtfully and logically creating the natural world and stepping back at the end of each "day" and saying, "That is good . . . that is good . . . that is very good," as would an artist at the easel admiring her brushstrokes.

Judaism's wisdom literature describes the wonder of nature and of God's joy in it:

> The heavens declare the glory of God,
> and the sky above proclaims his handiwork.
> Day to day pours out speech,
> and night to night reveals knowledge.
> There is no speech, nor are there words,
> whose voice is not heard.
> Their voice goes out through all the earth,
> and their words to the end of the world.

In them he has set a tent for the sun,
    which comes out like a bridegroom leaving his chamber,
    and, like a strong man, runs its course with joy.
Its rising is from the end of the heavens,
    and its circuit to the end of them,
    and there is nothing hidden from its heat.[282]

You make springs gush forth in the valleys;
    they flow between the hills;
they give drink to every beast of the field;
    the wild donkeys quench their thirst.
Beside them the birds of the heavens dwell;
    they sing among the branches.
From your lofty abode you water the mountains;
    the earth is satisfied with the fruit of your work.
You cause the grass to grow for the livestock
    and plants for man to cultivate,
that he may bring forth food from the earth
    and wine to gladden the heart of man,
oil to make his face shine
    and bread to strengthen man's heart.
The trees of Yahweh are watered abundantly,
    the cedars of Lebanon that he planted.
In them the birds build their nests;
    the stork has her home in the fir trees.
The high mountains are for the wild goats;
    the rocks are a refuge for the rock badgers.
He made the moon to mark the seasons;
    the sun knows its time for setting.
You make darkness, and it is night,
    when all the beasts of the forest creep about.
The young lions roar for their prey,
    seeking their food from God.
When the sun rises, they steal away
    and lie down in their dens.
Man goes out to his work

and to his labor until the evening.
O Yahweh, how manifold are your works!
In wisdom have you made them all;
the earth is full of your creatures . . .
May the glory of Yahweh endure forever;
may Yahweh rejoice in his works . . .[283]

"Where were you when I laid the foundation of the earth?
Tell me, if you have understanding.
Who determined its measurements—surely you know!
Or who stretched the line upon it?
On what were its bases sunk,
or who laid its cornerstone,
when the morning stars sang together
and all the sons of God shouted for joy? . . .
"Who has let the wild donkey go free?
Who has loosed the bonds of the swift donkey,
to whom I have given the arid plain for his home
and the salt land for his dwelling place?
He scorns the tumult of the city;
he hears not the shouts of the driver.
He ranges the mountains as his pasture,
and he searches after every green thing . . .
"Do you give the horse his might?
Do you clothe his neck with a mane?
Do you make him leap like the locust?
His majestic snorting is terrifying.
He paws in the valley and exults in his strength;
he goes out to meet the weapons.
He laughs at fear and is not dismayed;
he does not turn back from the sword.
Upon him rattle the quiver,
the flashing spear and the javelin.
With fierceness and rage he swallows the ground;
he cannot stand still at the sound of the trumpet.
When the trumpet sounds, he says 'Aha!'

He smells the battle from afar,
the thunder of the captains, and the shouting.
"Is it by your understanding that the hawk soars
and spreads his wings toward the south?
Is it at your command that the eagle mounts up
and makes his nest on high?
On the rock he dwells and makes his home,
on the rocky crag and stronghold.
From there he spies out the prey;
his eyes behold it from far away.
His young ones suck up blood,
and where the slain are, there is he."[284]

Such passages picture God's pleasure in what he produced—all of it, including the wild ass and hawk, who interact minimally if at all with humanity. They suggest the complexity of nature and humanity's place within it. Jesus's parables often invoked the natural world—birds of the air, lilies of the field, fertile soil. The Tanakh and New Testament commend wilderness as an arena for renewing the spirit and communing with God. To take God's commission in Genesis to "fill the earth, master it, and rule" as an invitation or license to trash the world is to skew the commission: a wider picture of Judeo-Christian teaching makes this clear. Anyone who knows this God who delights in his creation will treasure it as he does. Israel was not to imagine herself owner of the land, but steward who enjoyed and used it for a time. Her sabbatical year permitted both people and land to rest; the weekly sabbath benefitted man and beast. Theists who devalue this world because they anticipate a next might profit from pondering one basis of God's judgment: "The time came for the dead to be judged. The time came to reward your servants, the prophets and saints, and those who fear your name, both small and great, and to destroy those who destroy the earth."[285]

Fortunately, since devaluing the earth does not naturally devolve from devotion to deity, not all theists have promoted such perversion. In 1970, the year of the first Earth Day, evangelical writer Francis Schaeffer published *Pollution and the Death of Man—The Christian View of Ecology*. Decades before that, C.S. Lewis wrote his fictional Space Trilogy. All three stories celebrate the beauty of nature and lament the demonic forces that deface it.

This love of nature is particularly poignant in *Perelandra*. The protagonist, Ransom, finds himself wandering in the bowels of that planet:

> [H]e came through a vast cathedral space which was more like the work of art than that of Nature, with two great thrones at one end and chairs on either hand too large for human occupants. If the things were real, he never found any explanation of them. There was a dark tunnel in which a wind from heaven knows where was blowing and drove sand in his face. There was also a place where he himself walked in darkness and looked down through fathom below fathom of shafts and natural arches and winding gulfs on to a smooth floor lit with a cold green light. And as he stood and looked it seemed to him that four of the great earth-beetles, dwarfed by distance to the size of gnats, and crawling two by two, came slowly into sight. And they were drawing behind them a flat car, and on the car, upright, unshaken, stood a mantled form, huge and still and slender. And driving its strange team it passed on with insufferable majesty and went out of sight. Assuredly the inside of this world was not for man. But it was for something. And it appeared to Ransom that there might, if a man could find it, be some way to renew the old Pagan practice of propitiating the local gods of unknown places in such fashion that it was no offence to God Himself but only a prudent and courteous apology for trespass. That thing, that swathed form in its chariot, was no doubt his fellow creature. It did not follow that they were equals or had an equal right in the under-land.[286]

Later, as Ransom discusses the Great Dance of the universe with Perelandra's Adam, Eve, and tutelary spirit, the latter observes:

> Though men or angels rule them, the worlds are for themselves. The waters you have not floated on, the fruit you have not plucked, the caves into which you have not descended and the fire through which your bodies cannot pass, do not await your coming to put on perfection, though they will obey you when you come. Times without number I have circled Arbol

> while you were not alive, and those times were not desert. Their own voice was in them, not merely a dreaming of the day when you should awake. They also were at the centre. Be comforted, small immortals. You are not the voice that all things utter, nor is there eternal silence in the places where you cannot come. No feet have walked, nor shall, on the ice of Glund; no eye looked up from beneath on the Ring of Lurga, and Iron-plain in Neruval is chaste and empty. Yet it is not for nothing that the gods walk ceaselessly around the fields of Arbol.[287]

Lewis's 1943 *Perelandra* denies Lynn White's 1967 speculations that Christianity believes "God planned [creation] explicitly for man's benefit and rule: no item in the physical creation had any purpose save to serve man's purposes" and that Christianity therefore entails an unappreciative "arrogance toward nature."[288] Arrogance toward nature instead misrepresents Christian faith, even though some Christians may practice it.

Perhaps Christians need not develop a new position on ecology as much as to recover what their founding documents teach and what faith in a Creator who enjoys his handiwork implies. "When earth is scorned, half heaven is lost."[289] Nature not only provides nourishment for our bodies but nectar for our souls. Wilderness is where the weary Elijah retired to hear the voice of God and renew his heart for life and labors. It is where Jesus sat with God before and during his ministry. It is not unspiritual to love the physical world and sense a vital connection between it and the divine. Though unfortunately some theists do look down on this world and life, such disdain misrepresents love for God. Berating the body does not sanctify the soul. In charting a path home among the world religions, both belief in God and love for the world he made constitute critical cairns.

We have much to learn from Native American love for nature. Ota K'te (Plenty Kill) was the son of a Lakota (Sioux) chief. Born in the Dakotas around 1868, he was raised in his tribe's traditions and practices before being sent at age eleven to the Carlisle Indian Industrial School. Later, writing autobiographically for children, he describes the Lakota ethos:

> Nature has given more of her secret knowledge to us than to the white man. Maybe this is so because we lived so close to her

> and appreciated her so much. Then another reason is because the Indian's senses of sight, hearing, and smell are keener than the senses of the white man. Life for the Indian is one of harmony with nature and the things which surround him. The Indian tried to fit in with Nature and to understand, not to conquer and to rule. We were rewarded by learning much that the white man will never know. Life was a glorious thing, for great contentment comes with the feeling of friendship and kinship with the living things about you. The white man seems to look upon all animal life as enemies, while we looked upon them as friends and benefactors. They were one with the Great Mystery and so were we. We could feel the peace and power of the Great Mystery in the soft grass under our feet and in the blue sky above us. All this made deep feeling with us, and the old wise men thought much about it, and this is how we got our religion . . .
>
> [T]he Indian has a friendly feeling toward all creatures. It is a feeling that he and all other things of earth are unified in nature. This is one of the reasons that the Indian has never been a wanton destroyer of wild life and wild growth. He has a respect for life that the white man does not seem to be able to conceive.[290]

In another book he writes that the

> beautiful story of the genesis of the Lakota people furnished the foundation for the love they bore for earth and all things of the earth. Wherever the Lakota went, he was with Mother Earth. No matter where he roamed by day or slept by night, he was safe with her. This thought comforted and sustained the Lakota and he was eternally filled with gratitude.
>
> From Wakan Tanka there came a great unifying life force that flowed in and through all things—the flowers of the plains, blowing winds, rocks, trees, birds, animals—and was the same force that had been breathed into the first man. Thus all things were kindred and brought together by the same Great Mystery.

Kinship with all creatures of the earth, sky, and water was a real and active principle. For the animal and bird world there existed a brotherly feeling that kept the Lakota safe among them. And so close did some of the Lakota come to their feathered and furred friends that in true brotherhood they spoke a common tongue.

The animal had rights—the right of man's protection, the right to live, the right to multiply, the right to freedom, and the right to man's indebtedness—and in recognition of these rights the Lakota never enslaved the animal, and spared all life that was not needed for food and clothing.

This concept of life and its relations was humanizing and gave to the Lakota an abiding love. It filled his being with the joy and mystery of living; it gave him reverence for all life; it made a place for all things in the scheme of existence with equal importance to all. The Lakota could despise no creature, for all were of one blood, made by the same hand, and filled with the essence of the Great Mystery. In spirit the Lakota was humble and meek. "Blessed are the meek: for they shall inherit the earth," was true for the Lakota, and from the earth he inherited secrets long since forgotten. His religion was sane, normal, and human . . .

I have come to know that the white mind does not feel toward nature as does the Indian mind, and it is because, I believe, of the difference in childhood instruction. I have often noticed white boys gathered in a city by-street or alley jostling and pushing one another in a foolish manner. They spend much time in this aimless fashion, their natural faculties neither seeing, hearing, nor feeling the varied life that surrounds them. There is about them no awareness, no acuteness, and it is this dullness that gives ugly mannerisms full play; it takes from them natural poise and stimulation. In contrast, Indian boys, who are naturally reared, are alert to their surroundings; their senses are not narrowed to observing only one another, and they cannot spend hours seeing nothing, hearing nothing, and thinking nothing in particular. Observation was certain in its rewards; interest, wonder, admiration grew, and the fact was appreciated that life was more than mere human manifestation; that it was expressed in a multitude of forms. This appreciation enriched Lakota existence. Life was vivid and pulsing; nothing was casual and commonplace. The Indian lived—lived in every sense of the word—from his first to his last breath . . .[291]

The Indian was a natural conservationist. He destroyed nothing, great or small. Destruction was not a part of Indian thought and action; if it had been, and had the man been the ruthless savage he has been accredited with being, he would have long ago preceded the European in the labor of destroying the natural life of this continent. The Indian was frugal in the midst of plenty. When the buffalo roamed the plains in multitudes he slaughtered only what he could eat and these he used to the hair and bones . . .

I know of no species of plant, bird, or animal that were exterminated until the coming of the white man. For some years after the buffalo disappeared there still remained huge herds of antelope, but the hunter's work was no sooner done in the destruction of the buffalo than his attention was attracted toward the deer. They are plentiful now only where protected. The white man considered natural animal life just as he did the natural man life upon the continent, as "pests." There is no word in the Lakota vocabulary with the English meaning of this word.

There was a great difference in the attitude taken by the Indian and the Caucasian toward nature, and this difference made of one a conservationist and of the other a non-conservationist of life. The Indian, as well as all other creatures that were given birth and grew, were sustained by the common mother—earth. He was therefore kin to all living things and he gave to all creatures equal rights with himself. Everything of earth was loved and reverenced. The philosophy of the Caucasian was, "Things of the earth, earthy"—to be belittled and despised. Bestowing upon himself the position and title of

> a superior creature, others in the scheme were, in the natural order of things, of inferior position and title; and this attitude dominated his actions toward all things. The worth and right to live were his, thus he heartlessly destroyed. Forests were mowed down, the buffalo exterminated, the beaver driven to extinction and his wonderfully constructed dams dynamited, allowing flood waters to wreak further havoc, and the very birds of the air silenced. Great grassy plains that sweetened the air have been upturned; springs, streams, and lakes that lived no longer ago than my boyhood have dried, and a whole people harassed to degradation and death. The white man has come to be the symbol of extinction for all things natural to this continent. Between him and the animal there is no rapport and they have learned to flee from his approach, for they cannot live on the same ground.[292]

He summarizes, "Out of the Indian approach to existence there came a great freedom, an intense and absorbing love for nature . . . enriching faith in a Supreme Power; and principles of truth, honesty, generosity, equity, and brotherhood as a guide to mundane relations."[293]

Another Lakota, Lame Deer, describes differences between Anglo and Indian views of nature:

> You have made it hard for us to experience nature in the good way by being part of it. Even here we are conscious that somewhere out in those hills there are missile silos and radar stations. White men always pick the few unspoiled, beautiful, awesome spots for the sites of these abominations. You have raped and violated these lands, always saying, "Gimme, gimme, gimme," and never giving anything back. You have taken 200,000 acres of our Pine Ridge reservation and made them into a bombing range . . . The only use you have made of this land since you took it from us was to blow it up . . .
>
> There is power in an antelope, but not in a goat or in a sheep, which holds still while you butcher it, which will eat your newspaper if you let it. There was great power in a wolf, even

in a coyote. You have made him into a freak—a toy poodle, a Pekingese, a lap dog . . .

You have not only altered, declawed and malformed your winged and four-legged cousins; you have done it to yourselves. You have changed men into chairmen of boards, into office workers, into time-clock punchers. You have changed women into housewives, truly fearful creatures . . .

I think white people are so afraid of the world they created that they don't want to see, feel, smell or hear it. The feeling of rain and snow on your face, being numbed by an icy wind and thawing out before a smoking fire, coming out of a hot sweat bath and plunging into a cold stream, these things make you feel alive, but you don't want them anymore. Living in boxes which shut out the heat of the summer and the chill of winter, living inside a body that no longer has a scent, hearing the noise from the hi-fi instead of listening to the sounds of nature, watching some actor on TV having a make-believe experience when you no longer experience anything for yourself, eating food without taste—that's your way. It's no good . . .

To us life, all life, is sacred. The state of South Dakota has pest-control officers. They go up in a plane and shoot coyotes from the air. They keep track of their kills, put them all down in the little books. The stockmen and sheepowners pay them. Coyotes eat mostly rodents, field mice and such. Only once in a while will they go after a stray lamb. They are our natural garbage men cleaning up the rotten and stinking things. They make good pets if you give them a chance. But their living could lose some man a few cents, and so the coyotes are killed from the air. They were here before the sheep, but they are in the way; you can't make a profit out of them. More and more animals are dying out. The animals which the Great Spirit put here, they must go. The man-made animals are allowed to stay—at least until they are shipped out to be butchered. That terrible arrogance of the white man, making himself something more than God, more than nature, saying, "This animal must go, it brings no income, the space it occupies can be used in a better way. The

> only good coyote is a dead coyote." They are treating coyotes almost as badly as they used to treat Indians.

By contrast, Pete Catches says,

> I want to live as humbly, as close to the earth as I can. Close to the plants, the weeds, the flowers that I use for medicine. The Great Spirit has seen to it that man can survive in this way, and live as he is meant to live. So I and my wife are dwelling in a little cabin—no electricity, no tap water, no plumbing, no road. This is what we want. This simple log cabin knows peace . . .
>
> We live off nature, my wife and I; we hardly need anything. We will somehow live. The Great Spirit made the flowers, the streams, the pines, the cedars—takes care of them . . . He takes care of me, waters me, feeds me, makes me live with the plants and animals as one of them. This is how I wish to remain, an Indian, all the days of my life. This does not mean that I want to shut myself off. Somehow many people find their way to my cabin. I like this. I want to be in communication, reach out to people everywhere, impart a little of our Indian way, the spirit's way, to them.[294]

Benefits of Lakota ways are as potentially operative today as in the past. One author quotes Alex White Plume, a sixty-year-old Lakota activist:

> "Do you know what saved me from becoming a cold-blooded murderer? My language saved me. There is no way for me to be hateful in my language. It's such a beautiful, gentle language. It's so peaceful." Then White Plume started to speak in Lakota, and there was no denying the words came softly.[295]

Olowan Thunder Hawk Martinez continued:

> We're in dire distress, but we don't need anyone to come and save the Indian. When we honor our customs, and when we perform ceremonies, and when we listen to our ancestors, then

> we have everything we need to heal ourselves within ourselves . . . When the lights go out for good, my people will still be here. We have our ancient ways. We will remain.[296]

Even ardent ecologists acknowledge that, do what we will, the earth will someday die as the sun depletes its hydrogen and expands. But that does not keep them from joy in and care for what we have now. We need neither believe the earth itself to be alive, nor worship it, nor reject all civilization and insist that nature be left untouched to recognize that this world is our mother. We spring from her, our bodies are made from her, her environment and productivity sustain us, her beauty astounds us. She is not human property alone.

If we want to find home, we should remember that earth *is* home—the only planet we know that can sustain us. If someday we were to locate a viable alternative, would it do any good to migrate light-years to get there, only to stuff in our backpacks present destructive attitudes and practices and therefore similarly destroy a new home? The Native Americans are right: the earth is our mother, and we should treat her as such.

Mother and child at the Singapore Botanical Gardens.

15

REGARDLESS OF SIZE

(*Judaism*)

In a children's story a large creature cradles a community of smaller ones "Because, in my eyes, each being has value regardless of size." In a space saga a short sensei scolds his student for assessing significance on the basis of height, since stature matters not. As in fiction, so in reality. People matter regardless of "size"—physical, financial, educational, athletic. Little people have many reasons to live.

The Jewish Scriptures portray each human as reflecting the image of God. Genesis crowns the climatic day of creation with the emergence of humanity:

> Then God said, "Let us make mankind in our image, in our likeness, and let them rule over the fish in the sea and the birds in the sky, over the livestock and all the wild animals, and over all the creatures that move along the ground." So God created mankind in his own image, in the image of God he created them; male and female he created them.
>
> God blessed them and said to them, "Be fruitful and increase in number; fill the earth and subdue it. Rule over the fish in the sea and the birds in the sky and over every living creature that moves on the ground." Then God said, "I give you every seed-bearing plant on the face of the whole earth and every tree that has fruit with seed in it. They will be yours for food. And to all the beasts of the earth and all the birds in the sky and all the creatures that move along the ground—everything that has the breath of life in it—I give every green plant

> for food." And it was so. God saw all that he had made, and it was very good. And there was evening, and there was morning—the sixth day.[297]

This charge to master the earth and rule its creatures is not an invitation to disdain and destroy. All is God's good handiwork, though those who bear his image enjoy surpassing value. Noah's flood was sent because of violence against such image-bearers. Afterward God renewed and altered his mandate:

> Then God blessed Noah and his sons, saying to them, "Be fruitful and increase in number and fill the earth. The fear and dread of you will fall on all the beasts of the earth, and on all the birds in the sky, on every creature that moves along the ground, and on all the fish in the sea; they are given into your hands. Everything that lives and moves about will be food for you. Just as I gave you the green plants, I now give you everything.
>
> "But you must not eat meat that has its lifeblood still in it. And for your lifeblood I will surely demand an accounting. I will demand an accounting from every animal. And from each human being, too, I will demand an accounting for the life of another human being.
>
> "Whoever sheds human blood,
> by humans shall their blood be shed;
> for in the image of God
> has God made mankind."[298]

This new arrangement differs from the first one with Adam and Eve. God now grants animals as food but requires that human life be spared. Since humanity bears the divine image, murder is intolerable. Life is anyone's most valuable asset. Should one person maliciously snuff out another's, his own is forfeited. Capital punishment does not devalue human life (that of the assailant), but treasures it (that of the victim). A person's a person—bearing the image of God—regardless of size.

Throughout the Tanakh, caring for persons naturally springs out of cherishing the God whose image they bear. These twin attitudes intertwine: one cannot love God and loathe people. "The whole of Jewish teaching, it could be said, is grounded in a passionate concern for justice and compassion in human relations." Finding in God's nature and deeds the foundation for how people should treat each other may be what primarily distinguishes Jewish from more autonomous Greek ethics.[299]

The Talmud consequently cites imitation of God as foundational for ethics:

> God is the Pattern after which human life must be delineated. Conspicuous in Him are the qualities which should be prominent in human conduct.
>
> This doctrine is taught in several places: "What means the text, 'Ye shall walk after the Lord your God' (Deut. xii. 4)? Is it, then, possible for a man to walk after the *Shechinah* of which it is written, 'The Lord thy God is a devouring fire' (ibid. iv. 24)? But the meaning is to follow the attributes of the Holy One, blessed be He: as He clothed the naked (Gen. iii. 21), so do you clothe the naked; as He visited the sick (ibid. xviii. 1), so do you visit the sick; as He comforted mourners (ibid. xxv. 11), so do you comfort those who mourn; as He buried the dead (Deut. xxxiv. 6), so do you bury the dead (Sot. 14*a*) . . .
>
> "As the All-present is called compassionate and gracious, so be you also compassionate and gracious, and offering free gifts to all. As the Holy One, blessed be He, is called righteous (Ps. cxiv. 17), be you also righteous; as He is called loving (ibid.), be you also loving (Sifré Deut. § 49; 85*a*) . . .
>
> "Behold the Holy One, blessed be He, ignored (lofty) mountains and hills and caused his *Shechinah* to alight on Mount Sinai (which is lowly), and ignored all the fine trees and caused his *Shechinah* to alight upon a bush" (Sot. 5*a*). Similarly, man should not be haughty and should associate with the humble.
>
> The Rabbis, on the other hand, did not overlook that in the Bible qualities are attributed to God which should not be copied.[300]

Judaism's *n*^{e}*ḇî'îm* berate the blindness of devotion to deity wed to hubris toward humanity. One might think the prophets redundant, since the *tôrāh* taught the same. The tôrāh's Ten Words center around two themes: honoring God (1–4) and respecting people (5–10). The regulations that follow elaborate on both. Nevertheless, at times Israel abandoned this dual responsibility and paraded ritual devotion while oppressing people. Worshipping God is good and necessary, but worship does not cancel our responsibility to do justice and love mercy.

Isaiah indicts Judah for her unnatural union of worship and oppression:

> Hear the word of Yahweh, you rulers of Sodom
> [speaking metaphorically];
> give ear unto the law of our God, you people of Gomorrah.
> To what purpose is the multitude of your sacrifices unto me?
> says Yahweh:
> I am full of the burnt offerings of rams,
> and the fat of fed beasts;
> and I delight not in the blood of bullocks,
> or of lambs, or of he goats.
> When you come to appear before me,
> who has required this at your hand,
> to tread my courts?
> Bring no more vain oblations;
> incense is an abomination unto me;
> the new moons and sabbaths,
> the calling of assemblies, I cannot endure;
> it is iniquity, even the solemn meeting.
> Your new moons and your appointed feasts my soul hates:
> they are a trouble unto me;
> I am weary of bearing them.
> And when you spread forth your hands,
> I will hide my eyes from you:
> when you make many prayers,
> I will not hear: your hands are full of blood.
> Wash, make yourselves clean;
> put away the evil of your doings from before my eyes;
> cease to do evil; learn to do well;
> seek justice, relieve the oppressed,
> judge the fatherless,
> plead for the widow.[301]

In case Isaiah's introductory indictment fails to adequately affirm that religiosity does not replace responsibility, the prophet preaches even more poignantly:

> Shout it aloud, do not hold back.
> Raise your voice like a trumpet.
> Declare to my people their rebellion
> and to the descendants of Jacob their sins.
> For day after day they seek me out;
> they seem eager to know my ways,
> as if they were a nation that does what is right
> and has not forsaken the commands of its God.
> They ask me for just decisions
> and seem eager for God to come near them.
> "Why have we fasted," they say,
> "and you have not seen it?
> Why have we humbled ourselves,
> and you have not noticed?"
> Yet on the day of your fasting, you do as you please
> and exploit all your workers.
> Your fasting ends in quarreling and strife,
> and in striking each other with wicked fists.
> You cannot fast as you do today
> and expect your voice to be heard on high.
> Is this the kind of fast I have chosen,
> only a day for people to humble themselves?
> Is it only for bowing one's head like a reed
> and for lying in sackcloth and ashes?
> Is that what you call a fast,
> a day acceptable to Yahweh?
> Is not this the kind of fasting I have chosen:
> to loose the chains of injustice
> and untie the cords of the yoke,
> to set the oppressed free
> and break every yoke?
> Is it not to share your food with the hungry
> and to provide the poor wanderer with shelter—

when you see the naked, to clothe them,
  and not to turn away from your own flesh and blood?
Then your light will break forth like the dawn,
  and your healing will quickly appear;
then your righteousness will go before you,
  and the glory of Yahweh will be your rear guard.
Then you will call, and Yahweh will answer;
  you will cry for help, and he will say: Here am I.
If you do away with the yoke of oppression,
  with the pointing finger and malicious talk,
and if you spend yourselves in behalf of the hungry
  and satisfy the needs of the oppressed,
then your light will rise in the darkness,
  and your night will become like the noonday.[303]

Isaiah, of course, is not alone. Amos had already threatened:

There are those who turn justice into bitterness
  and cast righteousness to the ground.
He who made the Pleiades and Orion,
  who turns midnight into dawn and darkens day into night,
who calls for the waters of the sea
  and pours them out over the face of the land—
    Yahweh is his name.
With a blinding flash he destroys the stronghold
  and brings the fortified city to ruin.
There are those who hate the one who upholds justice in court
  and detest the one who tells the truth.
You levy a straw tax on the poor
  and impose a tax on their grain.
Therefore, though you have built stone mansions,
  you will not live in them;
though you have planted lush vineyards,
  you will not drink their wine.
For I know how many are your offenses
  and how great your sins.

There are those who oppress the innocent
    and take bribes and deprive the poor of justice in the courts.
Therefore the prudent keep quiet in such times,
    for the times are evil.
Seek good, not evil,
    that you may live.
Then Yahweh God Almighty will be with you,
    just as you say he is.
Hate evil, love good;
    maintain justice in the courts.
Perhaps Yahweh God Almighty will have mercy
    on the remnant of Joseph.
Therefore this is what the Lord, Yahweh God Almighty, says:
"There will be wailing in all the streets
    and cries of anguish in every public square.
The farmers will be summoned to weep
    and the mourners to wail.
There will be wailing in all the vineyards,
    for I will pass through your midst," says Yahweh.
Woe to you who long
    for the day of Yahweh!
Why do you long for the day of Yahweh?
    That day will be darkness, not light.
It will be as though a man fled from a lion
    only to meet a bear,
as though he entered his house
    and rested his hand on the wall
    only to have a snake bite him.
Will not the day of Yahweh be darkness, not light—
    pitch-dark, without a ray of brightness?
"I hate, I despise your religious festivals;
    your assemblies are a stench to me.
Even though you bring me burnt offerings and grain offerings,
    I will not accept them.
Though you bring choice fellowship offerings,
    I will have no regard for them.

Away with the noise of your songs!
    I will not listen to the music of your harps.
But let justice roll on like a river,
    righteousness like a never-failing stream!"[304]

Certainly the prophet neither devalues divine devotion nor condones idolatry. The following verses make that clear. But his primary objection here is injustice—particularly economic oppression—against one's fellow humans. Worship of God is a mockery when offered alongside exploitation of people. Better to stop the singing and sacrifices altogether. Better still to correct the injustice and resume the worship.

Financial exploitation is not the only injustice that invalidates devotion to God. Faithlessness in marriage does the same:

> Another thing you do: You flood Yahweh's altar with tears. You weep and wail because he no longer looks with favor on your offerings or accepts them with pleasure from your hands. You ask, "Why?" It is because Yahweh is the witness between you and the wife of your youth. You have been unfaithful to her, though she is your partner, the wife of your marriage covenant.
>
> Has not the one God made you? You belong to him in body and spirit. And what does the one God seek? Godly offspring. So be on your guard, and do not be unfaithful to the wife of your youth.
>
> "The man who hates and divorces his wife," says Yahweh, the God of Israel, "does violence to the one he should protect," says Yahweh Almighty.
>
> So be on your guard, and do not be unfaithful.[304]

Not only do tôrāh and n^{e}ḇî'îm agree that right religion requires justice, the *k^{e}tûḇîm* ("writings") concur. The Almighty Creator does not need what humans can offer him, but he does require that righteousness be practiced by those who speak in his name:

"Listen, my people, and I will speak;
    I will testify against you, Israel:

I am God, your God.
I bring no charges against you concerning your sacrifices
or concerning your burnt offerings, which are ever before me.
I have no need of a bull from your stall
or of goats from your pens,
for every animal of the forest is mine,
and the cattle on a thousand hills.
I know every bird in the mountains,
and the insects in the fields are mine.
If I were hungry I would not tell you,
for the world is mine, and all that is in it.
Do I eat the flesh of bulls
or drink the blood of goats?
"Sacrifice thank offerings to God,
fulfill your vows to the Most High,
and call on me in the day of trouble;
I will deliver you, and you will honor me."
But to the wicked person, God says:
"What right have you to recite my laws
or take my covenant on your lips?
You hate my instruction
and cast my words behind you.
When you see a thief, you join with him;
you throw in your lot with adulterers.
You use your mouth for evil
and harness your tongue to deceit.
You sit and testify against your brother
and slander your own mother's son.
When you did these things and I kept silent,
you thought I was exactly like you.
But I now arraign you
and set my accusations before you.
"Consider this, you who forget God,
or I will tear you to pieces, with no one to rescue you:
Those who sacrifice thank offerings honor me,
and to the blameless I will show my salvation."[305]

The Tanakh, then, demands justice.[306] Beyond that, it commends compassion. The weak lack voice and influence; the strong must proactively advocate for them. "Learn to do right; seek justice. Defend the oppressed. Take up the cause of the fatherless; plead the case of the widow." The able-bodied poor must be able to work to provide for themselves:

> And when you reap the harvest of your land, you shall not wholly reap the corners of your field, neither shall you gather the gleanings of your harvest. And you shall not glean your vineyard, neither shall you gather every grape of your vineyard; you shall leave them for the poor and stranger: I am Yahweh your God." Landowner Boaz ordered his harvesters, "Let [Ruth from Moab] gather among the sheaves and don't reprimand her. Even pull out some stalks for her from the bundles and leave them for her to pick up, and don't rebuke her.[307]

Kings in particular were commanded to pursue justice over ostentation. Jehoiakim, among others, failed:

> "Woe to him who builds his palace by unrighteousness,
> his upper rooms by injustice,
> making his own people work for nothing,
> not paying them for their labor.
> He says, 'I will build myself a great palace
> with spacious upper rooms.'
> So he makes large windows in it,
> panels it with cedar
> and decorates it in red.
> "Does it make you a king
> to have more and more cedar?
> Did not your father have food and drink?
> He did what was right and just,
> so all went well with him.
> He defended the cause of the poor and needy,
> and so all went well.

Is that not what it means to know me?"
    declares Yahweh.
"But your eyes and your heart
    are set only on dishonest gain,
on shedding innocent blood
    and on oppression and extortion."
Therefore this is what Yahweh says about
        Jehoiakim son of Josiah king of Judah:
"They will not mourn for him:
    'Alas, my brother! Alas, my sister!'
They will not mourn for him:
    'Alas, my master! Alas, his splendor!'
He will have the burial of a donkey—
    dragged away and thrown
    outside the gates of Jerusalem."[308]

In Israel's economy, poverty needed not permanently impair one's prospects. Periodically, indentured persons were to be freed, and forfeited family farms restored:

> Consecrate the fiftieth year and proclaim liberty throughout the land to all its inhabitants. It shall be a jubilee for you; each of you is to return to your family property and to your own clan. The fiftieth year shall be a jubilee for you; do not sow and do not reap what grows of itself or harvest the untended vines. For it is a jubilee and is to be holy for you; eat only what is taken directly from the fields.
>
> In this Year of Jubilee everyone is to return to his own property.
>
> If you sell land to any of your own people or buy land from them, do not take advantage of each other. You are to buy from your own people on the basis of the number of years since the Jubilee. And they are to sell to you on the basis of the number of years left for harvesting crops. When the years are many, you are to increase the price, and when the years are few, you are to decrease the price, because what is really being sold to you is

> the number of crops. Do not take advantage of each other, but fear your God. I am Yahweh your God.
>
> Follow my decrees and be careful to obey my laws, and you will live safely in the land. Then the land will yield its fruit, and you will eat your fill and live there in safety. You may ask, "What will we eat in the seventh year if we do not plant or harvest our crops?" I will send you such a blessing in the sixth year that the land will yield enough for three years. While you plant during the eighth year, you will eat from the old crop and will continue to eat from it until the harvest of the ninth year comes in.
>
> The land must not be sold permanently, because the land is mine and you reside in my land as foreigners and strangers.[309]

The Jubilee reminds us that relationships outrank riches. Disasters need not condemn those who suffer them to permanent poverty. Israel was structured to avert the emergence of a class of permanently endowed über-rich lolling atop strata of impoverished serfs. Unbridled accumulation does not ultimately enrich the rapacious:

> Woe to you who add house to house
> and join field to field
> till no space is left
> and you live alone in the land.
> Yahweh Almighty has declared in my hearing:
> "Surely the great houses will become desolate,
> the fine mansions left without occupants.
> A ten-acre vineyard will produce only a bath of wine;
> a homer of seed will yield only an ephah of grain."[310]

Individual initiative and industry were without doubt important. But ultimately the land and its inhabitants were God's. They were to be treated that way. A person is, after all, a person, regardless of size.

Because people are important, children are cherished. This theme runs throughout the Tanakh beginning with Eve, who exults upon the birth of Cain, "With the help of Yahweh I have brought forth a man."[311] The patriarch Abram was wealthy and powerful and lacked nothing—except children:

> Abram said, "Sovereign Yahweh, what can you give me since I remain childless and the one who will inherit my estate is Eliezer of Damascus?" And Abram said, "You have given me no children; so a servant in my household will be my heir."
>
> Then the word of Yahweh came to him: "This man will not be your heir, but a son who is your own flesh and blood will be your heir." He took him outside and said, "Look up at the sky and count the stars—if indeed you can count them." Then he said to him, "So shall your offspring be."
>
> Abram believed Yahweh, and he credited it to him as righteousness.[312]

Throughout the narrative about Abram's family that follows, a desire for children, and joy in them, recurs repeatedly.

> Unless Yahweh builds the house,
> the builders labor in vain.
> Unless Yahweh watches over the city,
> the guards stand watch in vain.
> In vain you rise early
> and stay up late,
> toiling for food to eat—
> for he grants sleep to those he loves.
> Children are a heritage from Yahweh,
> offspring a reward from him.
> Like arrows in the hands of a warrior
> are children born in one's youth.
> Blessed is the man
> whose quiver is full of them.
> They will not be put to shame
> when they contend with their opponents in court.
>
> Blessed are all who fear Yahweh,
> who walk in obedience to him.
> You will eat the fruit of your labor;
> blessings and prosperity will be yours.

Your wife will be like a fruitful vine
within your house;
your children will be like olive shoots
around your table.
Yes, this will be the blessing for the man
who fears Yahweh.
May Yahweh bless you from Zion;
may you see the prosperity of Jerusalem
all the days of your life.
May you live to see your children's children—
peace be on Israel.[313]

Parents were to instruct their children with care and diligence so that they would think and live wisely. This responsibility was central to Abraham's call into a unique covenant relationship with God:

> Shall I hide from Abraham what I am about to do? Abraham will surely become a great and powerful nation, and all nations on earth will be blessed through him. For I have chosen him, so that he will direct his children and his household after him to keep the way of Yahweh by doing what is right and just, so that Yahweh will bring about for Abraham what he has promised him.[314]

Centuries later, when Abraham's descendants had grown into a nation, their credo was immediately followed by the command that parents diligently impress it upon their children:

> Hear, O Israel: Yahweh our God, Yahweh is one. Love Yahweh your God with all your heart and with all your soul and with all your strength. These commandments that I give you today are to be on your hearts. Impress them on your children. Talk about them when you sit at home and when you walk along the road, when you lie down and when you get up.[315]

The wisdom literature abounds with examples of parents pleading with their little ones to listen and learn:

> Listen, my son, to your father's instruction
> and do not forsake your mother's teaching.
> They are a garland to grace your head
> and a chain to adorn your neck . . .
> Listen to your father, who gave you life,
> and do not despise your mother when she is old.
> Buy the truth and do not sell it—
> wisdom, instruction and insight as well.
> The father of a righteous child has great joy;
> a man who fathers a wise son rejoices in him.
> May your father and mother rejoice;
> may she who gave you birth be joyful![316]

Women were also valued in Israel. Male and female both bear the image of God. Daughters inherited property alongside sons. Women often outshone men and offered examples to them: Rahab in recognizing Jericho's impending doom and escaping death; Deborah and Jael over Barak in the defeat of Sisera; Abigail, whose discretion, courtesy, and character contrasted with the churlish Nabal; Ruth the Moabitess, who proved "more to [Naomi] than seven sons."[317]

This vision that a person's a person regardless of size is not, of course, a viewpoint unique to Judaism or the other Abrahamic faiths. Native American traditions reflect a similar perspective:

> The bands were governed, as were individuals, families, and the nation, by ancient and traditional customs. And these customs which had, through many years of time, become established in the minds of the people, were based upon human and individual needs. The central aim of the Lakota code was to bring ease and comfort in equal measure to all. There were no weak and no strong individuals from the standpoint of possessing human rights. It was every person's duty to see that the right of every other person to eat and be clothed was respected and there was no more question about it than there was about the free and ungoverned use of sunshine, pure air, and the rains with which they bathed their bodies. There were no groups of strength allied against groups of those weak in power.

The Lakotas were self-governors, and the rules and regulations that governed the conduct of people and established their duties as individuals, families, and bands came from a great tribal consciousness. Deep within the people, mingling with their emotions, was an inherent sense of solidarity—a tie between one and all others that the nation might be expressed . . .

Each and every individual regarded himself as the receiver and not the dispenser of ease and comforts. The source from which came all things beneficent was unlimited, and this made hoarding inconsistent. Strength was gained but from one source—nature—and until influenced, the Lakota mind was never blighted with the idea that strength was to be gained through the domination of other individuals. There was domination, but it was self-domination, the mother, father, sister, brother, and all, voluntarily placing their person in secondary importance to the needs of the band and nation. And by thus placing their interest the law worked that they themselves were never neglected. The result was that in the society of the Lakota there were no hungry and no overfed; no groveling and no arrogant; no jails, no judges, no poor houses, no brothels, and no orphan asylums . . .

Let me tell you a story of early days: Meat was once low in the village and a number of hunters went out to bring in some buffalo which were, at that particular time, scarce. Only three animals were found to be divided among every person in camp. Even the hunters who could have availed themselves of a feast did not do so, and though the portions were small, everyone was served.

Now, hunger is a hard thing to bear, but not so hard when all are sharing the same want in the same degree; but it is doubly hard to bear when all about is plenty which the hungry dare not touch. Sentences imposed upon those who, through hunger, take for their starving bodies, are to me inconceivably cruel, even to my now altered and accustomed viewpoint. For one man with full stomach to heap more misery upon one with an empty stomach is savage beyond compare. Perhaps I sense

> the degradation all the more, having tasted the sweetness of the life of my forefathers.[318]

Society's giants sometimes resent the small because they tend to bleed rather than build the public bankroll. But when the tall elevate the small they elevate themselves; when the strong humanize the weak they humanize themselves. Judaism is right: as God's image-bearers, all deserve dignity, justice, and care. Stature matters not. Each person has value regardless of size.

Time and change overwhelm a Buddha in Ayutthaya.

16

LIFE IS NOW

(Zen, Christianity)

"What day is it?" asked Pooh.
"It's today," squeaked Piglet.
"My favorite day," said Pooh.

Not only favorite, but in a sense the only day. Yesterday is gone; tomorrow may never come. Still, some people miss this world out of longing for a next, and lose their todays either pining for yesterday or panting for tomorrow.

Zen in particular does a good job of reminding us of the now:

> [I]t is not Buddhism in general that is intriguing the West so much as the specific school of Buddhism that is Zen. We understand the specific attraction of *Zen* Buddhism when we realize the extent to which the contemporary West is animated by "prophetic faith," the sense of the holiness of the *ought*, the pull of the way things could be and should be but as yet are not. Such faith has obvious virtues, but unless it is balanced by a companion sense of the holiness of the *is*, it becomes top-heavy. If one's eyes are always on tomorrows, todays slip by unperceived. To a West which in its concern to refashion heaven and earth is in danger of letting the presentness of life—the only life we really have—slip through its fingers, Zen comes as a reminder that if we do not learn to perceive the mystery and beauty of our *present* life, our *present* hour, we shall not perceive the worth of *any* life, of *any* hour.[319]

"Chinese Zen marked a distinct departure from the Mahayana texts that embody splendorous cosmic mythology and highly systematic theories. Instead, Chinese Zen leaders focused on a practitioner's experience of the very moment in each individual situation."[320] "To teach students the power of the present moment as the only moment is a skillful teaching of buddha ancestors."[321]

Though particularly noticeable in Zen, the priority of the present is promoted throughout other forms of Buddhism as well. In the Pāli sutra *Bhaddekaratta* (*A Single Excellent Night*) the Buddha advises:

> Let not a person revive the past
> Or on the future build his hopes;
> For the past has been left behind
> And the future has not been reached.
> Instead with insight let him see
> Each presently arisen state;
> Let him know that and be sure of it,
> Invincibly, unshakeably.
> Today the effort must be made;
> Tomorrow Death may come, who knows?
> No bargain with Mortality
> Can keep him and his hordes away,
> But one who dwells thus ardently,
> Relentlessly, by day, by night—
> It is he, the Peaceful Sage has said,
> Who has had a single excellent night.[323]

Buddhist "mindfulness" is closely tied to this preoccupation with the present:

> Mindfulness is present-moment awareness. It takes place in the here and now. It is the observance of what is happening right now, in the present. It stays forever in the present, perpetually on the crest of the ongoing wave of passing time. If you are remembering your second-grade teacher, that is memory. When you then become aware that you are remembering your second-grade teacher, that is mindfulness. If you

> then conceptualize the process and say to yourself, "Oh, I am remembering," that is thinking.[323]

Two early Pāli sūtras lay the foundation for mindfulness.[324] A monk gives full attention to whatever he is doing at the moment:

> Again, bhikkhus, a bhikkhu is one who acts in full awareness when going forward and returning; who acts in full awareness when looking ahead and looking away; who acts in full awareness when flexing and extending his limbs; who acts in full awareness when wearing his robes and carrying his outer robe and bowl; who acts in full awareness when eating, drinking, consuming food, and tasting; who acts in full awareness when defecating and urinating; who acts in full awareness when walking, standing, sitting, falling asleep, waking up, talking, and keeping silent.[325]

According to Vietnamese monk Thich Nhat Hanh, right mindfulness lies at the heart of both the Buddha's teachings and his own. It is

> the energy that brings us back to the present moment . . .
>
> According to Buddhist psychology (*abhidharma*, "super Dharma"), the trait "attention" (*manaskara*) is "universal," which means we are always giving our attention to something. Our attention may be "appropriate" (*yoniso manaskara*), as when we dwell fully in the present moment, or inappropriate (*ayoniso manaskara*), as when we are attentive to something that takes us away from being here and now.

A disciplined focus on now results in seven "miracles": the ability to be present and touch deeply, to make the other present also, to nourish, to relieve suffering, to look deeply, to understand, and to be transformed. Here is how Nhat Hanh describes the first two:

> The Sanskrit word for mindfulness, *smriti*, means "remember." Mindfulness is remembering to come back to the present

> moment. The character the Chinese use for "mindfulness" has two parts: the upper part means "now," and the lower part means "mind" or "heart." The First Miracle of Mindfulness is to be present and able to touch deeply the blue sky, the flower, and the smile of our child.
>
> The Second Miracle of Mindfulness is to make the other—the sky, the flower, our child—present, also. In the Vietnamese epic poem *Tale of Kieu*, Kieu returns to the apartment of her beloved, Kim Trong, and finds him fast asleep at his desk, his head resting on a pile of books. Kim Trong hears Kieu's footsteps, but, not quite awake, he asks, "Are you really there, or am I dreaming?" Kieu replies, "Now we have the opportunity to see each other clearly. But if we do not live deeply this moment, it will be only a dream." You and your loved one are here together. You have the chance to see each other deeply. But if you are not fully present, everything will be like a dream.[326]

By urging a mindfulness that focuses on the present the Buddha seeks to deliver us from the bane of busyness, from so multitasking for tomorrow that we miss today. We neither touch our "now" deeply nor experience the other "miracles." Our vision remains shallow. We fail to fully embrace the ones we say we love, who only pass us by as in a dream. "[T]here is never anything but the present, and if one cannot live there, one cannot live anywhere."[327]

A key early articulator of Zen, if an articulator is possible in a tradition suspicious of speech, is Dōgen (1200–1253). His masterwork *Shōbō Genzō—Treasury of the True Dharma Eye*—is a collection of fascicles on various topics composed in the last half of his life. One often-quoted fascicle is "Uji"—"The Time Being." Zen is not designed to be spoken but lived; *Shōbō Genzō* is deep in its thought and compact in its expression; and "Uji" is a particularly challenging fascicle. For those readers who would like a go at Dōgen's fascinating insight into the Zen way of being (not thinking), and its reasons for focusing on the present, the first half of Uji may be found in the appendix. But for the purposes of this chapter, it is enough to observe that in Uji and elsewhere, Dōgen urges that time and existence are one—time is established by existence, and nothing arises outside of time. All existences are linked and become time. No matter how many moments exist, only the present one is real. Time moves from present to present, generating an eternal present. There is no real present apart from human action. For those who make wise use of their time, every day is a good day. We must use each moment and hour without constantly thinking about tomorrow, and follow the Buddhist way today. The essence of religion consists of living truly in the present moment. Concern with life-and-death is the essence of religion, and we can transcend it by filling the present moment without constantly recalling the past or anticipating the future.[328]

Contemporary Zen thinkers echo and cite Dōgen. Nishitani wrote of time's "circuminsessional interpenetration" in which "all time enters into each moment," rendering both time and things "phantom-like." He continues:

> Dōgen crossed over into China and returned to Japan on a field where we can say that he never crossed into China nor returned to Japan. There, birth-*sive*-unbirth comes to be continually in time, in that "moment" that Kierkegaard referred to as the "atom of eternity" in temporality . . . Here each "time" is time because it is not time, because it is but an atom of eternity in temporality.
>
> The words of Dōgen's lecture, "I now while away my time, accepting whatever may come," refer to just such a time . . . [O]ne marks time, without so much as a single strand of the Buddha's Dharma, just taking things as they come—as they are fated to come—consigning oneself to the destiny of circumstances. This is simply daily life with the sun rising every morning and the moon rising every night: the daily life of King Samādhi, which is altogether different from any sort of fatalism or resignation.[329]

"Dogen pointed out that firewood does not become ashes and life does not become death, just as the winter does not become the spring. Every moment of time is 'self-contained and quiescent.'"[330]

Dōgen's thought is sometimes compared with Heidegger's, particularly in his 1927 *Sein und Zeit*. But because the latter excluded the soteriological dimension of time, Dōgen's conclusions may be "more universal . . . naturalistic . . . holistic . . . and existential."[331]

Christianity posits an ongoing self with a future existence. Critics suggest that such hope in a better tomorrow results in devaluing today. Certainly some Christians have neglected themselves in the present because they hoped by doing so to earn a better future. Others have skewed future hope into an excuse for present inaction, lending credence to Marx's critique of religion as an opiate.

Christianity does in fact teach a future, higher plane of existence, for which pursuit of present wealth or position may at times be wisely set aside. Nevertheless, Christianity also values the present, recognizing that in a sense it is the only time we have. Jesus, along with the Buddha, rejected a preoccupation with the future that overlooked the beauties of the now:

> Stop collecting treasures for your own benefit on earth, where moth and rust eat them and where thieves break in and steal them. Instead, collect treasures for yourselves in heaven, where moth and rust don't eat them and where thieves don't break in and steal them. Where your treasure is, there your heart will be also.
>
> The eye is the lamp of the body. Therefore, if your eye is healthy, your whole body will be full of light. But if your eye is bad, your whole body will be full of darkness. If then the light in you is darkness, how terrible that darkness will be! No one can serve two masters. Either you will hate the one and love the other, or you will be loyal to the one and have contempt for the other. You cannot serve God and wealth.
>
> Therefore, I say to you, don't worry about your life, what you'll eat or what you'll drink, or about your body, what you'll wear. Isn't life more than food and the body more than clothes? Look at the birds in the sky. They don't sow seed or harvest grain or gather crops into barns. Yet your heavenly Father feeds them. Aren't you worth much more than they are? Who among you by worrying can add a single moment to your life? And why do you worry about clothes? Notice how the lilies in the field grow. They don't wear themselves out with work, and they don't spin cloth. But I say to you that even Solomon in all of his splendor wasn't dressed like one of these. If God

> dresses grass in the field so beautifully, even though it's alive today and tomorrow it's thrown into the furnace, won't God do much more for you, you people of weak faith? Therefore, don't worry and say, "What are we going to eat?" or "What are we going to drink?" or "What are we going to wear?" Gentiles long for all these things. Your heavenly Father knows that you need them. Instead, desire first and foremost God's kingdom and God's righteousness, and all these things will be given to you as well. Therefore, stop worrying about tomorrow, because tomorrow will worry about itself. Each day has enough trouble of its own.[332]

Jesus is teaching that we may embrace today while anticipating an even greater tomorrow. The present, in fact, gains significance because of what is yet to be. "While it's daytime, we must do the works of him who sent me. Night is coming when no one can work."[333] Employing the present well is wise both in itself and because it can lead to hearing, "Excellent! You are a good and faithful servant! You've been faithful over a little. I'll put you in charge of much. Come, celebrate with me."[334]

In addition to the present, Christianity values the past, often as a source of instruction: "These things happened to them as an example and were written as a warning for us to whom the end of time has come."[335] Its central ceremony, the Eucharist, unites these three times: "Every time you eat this bread and drink this cup, you broadcast [acting in the present] the death of the Lord [recalling the past] until he comes [anticipating the future]."[336] So do summaries of the Christian life:

> The grace of God has appeared, bringing salvation to all people. It educates us so that we can live sensible, ethical, and godly lives right now [acting in the present] by rejecting ungodly lives and the desires of this world. At the same time we wait for the blessed hope and the glorious appearance of our great God and savior Jesus Christ [anticipating the future]. He gave himself for us [recalling the past] in order to rescue us from every kind of lawless behavior, and cleanse a special people for himself who are eager to do good actions.[337]

Christianity reflects its Jewish antecedents in this enjoyment of the present with an eye to the future:

> Go, eat your food with gladness, and drink your wine with a joyful heart, for God has already approved what you do. Always be clothed in white, and always anoint your head with oil. Enjoy life with your wife, whom you love, all the days of this meaningless life that God has given you under the sun—all your meaningless days. For this is your lot in life and in your toilsome labor under the sun. Whatever your hand finds to do, do it with all your might, for in the realm of the dead, where you are going, there is neither working nor planning nor knowledge nor wisdom . . .
>
> Remember your Creator
> in the days of your youth,
> before the days of trouble come
> and the years approach when you will say,
> "I find no pleasure in them"—
> before the sun and the light
> and the moon and the stars grow dark,
> and the clouds return after the rain;
> when the keepers of the house tremble,
> and the strong men stoop,
> when the grinders cease because they are few,
> and those looking through the windows grow dim;
> when the doors to the street are closed
> and the sound of grinding fades;
> when people rise up at the sound of birds,
> but all their songs grow faint;
> when people are afraid of heights
> and of dangers in the streets;
> when the almond tree blossoms
> and the grasshopper drags itself along
> and desire no longer is stirred.
> Then people go to their eternal home
> and mourners go about the streets.

> Remember him—before the silver cord is severed,
> and the golden bowl is broken;
> before the pitcher is shattered at the spring,
> and the wheel broken at the well,
> and the dust returns to the ground it came from,
> and the spirit returns to God who gave it.[338]

It is important to note that Zen Buddhism's focus on the present and denial of an ongoing self does not argue for irresponsible hedonism:

> That a strong sense of social and personal responsibility is inherent in the spiritual freedom of the deeply realized person was made clear by Yasutani-roshi in response to a question addressed to him in America by a group of university students: "If, as we have been led to believe, satori makes clear that past and future are unreal, is one not free to live as one likes in the present, unconcerned about the past and indifferent to the future?"
>
> In reply, Yasutani-roshi made a dot on the blackboard and explained that this isolated dot represented their conception of "here and now." To show the incompleteness of this view, he placed another dot on the board, through which he drew a horizontal line and a vertical one. He then explained that the horizontal line stood for time from the beginningless past to the endless future and the vertical for limitless space. The "present moment" of the enlightened individual, who stands at this intersection, embraces all these dimensions of time and space, he emphasized.
>
> Accordingly, the satori-realization that one is the focus of past and future time and space unavoidably carries with it a sense of fellowship and responsibility to one's family and society as a whole, alike to those who came before and those who will follow one. The freedom of the liberated Zen person is a far cry from the "freedom" of the Zen libertine, driven as the latter is by uncontrolled selfish desires. The inseparable bond with all human beings that the truly enlightened feels precludes any such self-centered behavior.[339]

In the final scenes of the 2001 film *K-PAX,* Dr. Mark Powell peers through the sunglasses Prot left behind upon returning to his home planet. Astrophysicists might question Prot's cyclical cosmology, but at least his parting counsel rings true: "Get it right this time around, because this time is all you have." Our current life is neither charade nor dress rehearsal; it and our actions in it matter in and of themselves. Prot, Jesus, and the Zen masters are right: the present is important; life is now.

One passageway opens to another and another at Hué.

THE JOURNEY

There is no conclusion. Life is a journey.

Three final thoughts, the first from Confucius:

> If there is righteousness in the heart,
> there will be beauty in the character.
> If there is beauty in the character,
> there will be harmony in the home.
> If there is harmony in the home,
> there will be order in the nation.
> If there is order in the nation,
> there will be peace in the world.

The second is from Einstein. The famous physicist fought to formulate a unified field theory that would fuse quantum mechanics with relativity. Hermann Weyl offered a proposal that originally impressed Einstein, but when experimental observation failed to confirm it, the latter wrote, "Your chain of reasoning is so wonderfully self-contained. Except for agreeing with reality, it is certainly a grand intellectual achievement."[340]

What holds in physics holds in religion. It is not enough to concoct a theory that coheres internally, or even one that produces a sense of well-being in the one who believes it. The theory must correspond to external reality. "[T]he best thing that can happen to a scientist" is "realizing that something that's happening in his or her mind exactly corresponds to something that happens in nature."[341] This is as true for a seeker after religion or worldview as it is for a physicist. A credo must correspond to what truly is, *yathā-bhūta-ñāna-dassana*, if it is to successfully help the one who believes it find home. Grand religious or intellectual achievements are ultimately useless unless they do.

Third, a personal reflection. Late one January afternoon I booked into an obscure guest house in Panaji, India. Not even the taxi drivers knew where it was. No other guests were there. After registering I picked up my ancient handheld GPS to mark the site and stroll the winding maze that comprised the neighborhood. After two hours of wandering, a naan, a lassi, and some chicken masala, it was time to return home. Easy—simply follow the outbound path backwards. As I neared the guesthouse neighborhood my screen suggested that my inbound path roughly paralleled the outbound one but was separated by a few blocks. No worries. Some daylight remained; I would stroll some different streets and approach from the opposite direction. A small lake appeared on the right that hadn't been there before, then an unkempt and unwelcoming neighborhood. Children gawked, and one cur would have bitten off my leg had a companion or two rallied to his yelps. Now it was getting dark, and the screen suggested that my guesthouse lay down an uninviting alley. This was utterly unfamiliar, and the alley soon petered out into a cluster of doorways. As I retreated, the realization arose: *My GPS is wrong! It doesn't know where home is!* It had not adequately tracked the satellites before it marked the guesthouse's location. Something similar had happened years before in Phnom Penh.

So now here I stood in the general vicinity of home, but on my own in an Englishless village with the need to locate my night's lodging. Fortunately, a building and then a turn in the road sparked a memory, and in a moment I was back. As I stood on the porch my GPS insisted that the guesthouse was still more than one hundred meters away. The moral: Know exactly what and where Home is, or even the best suggestions on finding it will get you lost.

Salaam, shalōm, shanti, may the grace of our Lord Jesus Christ be with you.

APPENDIX

EXTRACT FROM "UJI" BY DŌGEN

Translator's Introduction: *"Uji"* is Dōgen's discourse on the significance of *anatta* and *anicca*—the Buddhist terms for "no permanent, abiding self" and "continual change"—and their application to treading the paths of Right Understanding and Right Thought . . .

Because it is linguistically possible to translate the title as "Being and Time," some modern scholars have been led to assume that Dōgen was engaging in a form of philosophical speculation akin to that of some Western existentialists. Such an approach, however, would seem counter to the purpose behind a discourse given by a Buddhist Master, since speculative thinking—philosophical or otherwise—is a type of mentation that trainees are working to disengage themselves from so that they may progress toward realizing spiritual Truth, which lies beyond the reaches of speculation . . .

Underlying the whole of Dōgen's presentation is his own experience of no longer being attached to any sense of a personal self that exists independent of time and of other beings, an experience which is part and parcel of his "dropping off of body and mind." From this perspective of his, anything having existence—which includes every thought and thing—is inextricably bound to time, indeed, can be said to "be time," for there is no thought or thing that exists independent of time. Time and being are but two aspects of the same thing, which is the interrelationship of *anicca,* "the ever-changing flow of time" and *anatta,* "the absence of any permanent self existing within or independent of this flow of time" . . .

In the present discourse, Dōgen uses as his central text a poem by Great Master Yakusan Igen, the Ninth Chinese Ancestor in the Sōtō Zen lineage. In the Chinese version, each line of this poem begins with the word *uji*, which functions to introduce a set of couplets describing temporary conditions that appear to be contrastive, but which, in reality, do not stand against each other. These conditions comprise what might be referred to as "an I at some moment of time"; this is a use of the word "I" that does not refer to some "permanent self," abiding unchanged over time (as the Shrenikans maintained) but to a particular set of transient conditions at a particular time. In other words, there is no permanent, unchanging "Yakusan," only a series of ever-changing conditions, one segment of which is perceived as "a sentient being," which is, for convenience, conventionally referred to as "Yakusan." Both Yakusan and Dōgen understand *uji* (in its sense of "that which exists at some time") as a useful way of expressing the condition of *anatta*, and in this sense it is used to refer to a state of "being" that is neither a "permanent self" nor something separate from "other"; it is the "I" referred to in one description of a kenshō experience (that is, the experiencing of one's Buddha Nature) as "the whole universe becoming I." Hence, when the false notion of "having a permanent self" is abandoned, then what remains is just *uji*, "the time when some form of being persists" . . .

> **Dōgen, "Uji":** A former Buddha once said in verse:
> *Standing atop a soaring mountain peak is for the time being*
> *And plunging down to the floor of the Ocean's abyss is for the time being;*
> *Being triple-headed and eight-armed is for the time being*
> *And being a figure of a Buddha standing sixteen feet tall or sitting eight feet high is for the time being;*
> *Being a monk's traveling staff or his ceremonial hossu is for the time being*
> *And being a pillar supporting the temple or a stone lantern before the Meditation Hall is for the time being;*
> *Being a next-door neighbor or a man in the street is for the time being*
> *And being the whole of the great earth and boundless space is for the time being.*[1]

1 Dōgen appears to understand Yakusan's image of "a figure of a Buddha standing sixteen feet tall or sitting eight feet high" as referring to one who has realized

The phrase "for the time being" implies that time in its totality is what existence is, and that existence in all its occurrences is what time is. Thus, "being a golden body sixteen feet tall" refers to a time. And because it is a time, its time will have a wondrous luminosity—a point that we will be studying and learning about during the present twenty-four hours. "Being one with three heads and eight arms" also refers to a time. And because it is a time, it will be one and the same as the present twenty-four hours. Granted that we may not yet have measured the length of these twenty-four hours as to whether they are ever so long or as short as a sigh, still we speak of them as "the twenty-four hours of our day." The traces of this time having come and gone are clear, so people do not doubt that these hours have occurred. But, though people have no doubt about time having occurred, the past may be something that they have not known through their direct experience. And, just because sentient beings are always having their doubts about anything and everything that they have not directly experienced, this does not mean that what they may have previously doubted is the same as what they may now have doubts about, for doubts themselves are merely "just for the moment" kinds of time, and nothing more . . .

Since we human beings are continually arranging the bits and pieces of what we experience in order to fashion "a whole universe," we must take care to look upon this welter of living beings and physical objects as "sometime" things. Things do not go about hindering each other's existence any more than moments of time get in each other's way. As a consequence, the intention to train arises at the same time in different beings, and this same

---

his or her Buddha Nature and lives accordingly at all times. It is likely that "standing" and "sitting" are references to the Four Bodily Postures: standing, walking, sitting, and reclining. The first two represent active modes, the latter two passive ones: that is, "whether one is inwardly or outwardly active, whether one is awake or sleeping."

"Being triple-headed and eight-armed" is an allusion descriptive of several guardian beings who protect Buddhist temples and their trainees. The most likely candidates in the Zen tradition would be Achalanātha, the Steadfast Bodhisattva, and Rāgarāja, the Passionate Bodhisattva. The former is sometimes associated with the firm commitment of trainees to train until they have overcome all hindrances to realizing enlightenment as they persist in helping others to realize Truth. The latter has associations with a passionate desire to help all sentient beings realize Buddhahood.

intention may also arise at different times. And the same applies to training and practice, as well as to realizing the Way. In a similar manner, we are continually arranging bits and pieces of what we experience in order to fashion them into what we call "a self," which we treat as "myself": this is the same as the principle of "we ourselves are just for a time."

Because of this very principle of the way things are, the earth in its entirety has myriad forms and hundreds of things sprouting up, each sprout and each form being a whole earth—a point which you should incorporate into your study of the Way, for the recognition of the coming and going of things in this manner is a first step in training and practice. When you reach such a fertile field of seeing the way things really are, then the earth in its entirety will be "one whole sprouting, one whole form"; it will be comprised of forms that you recognize and forms that you do not, sproutings that you recognize and sproutings that you do not. It is the same as the times we refer to in "from time to time," which contain all forms of existence and all worlds. So take a moment to look around and consider whether there is any form of being, that is, any "world," that does or does not find expression at this very moment of time . . .

When ordinary, everyday people who do not take the Buddha's Teachings as their model hear the phrase "just for the time being" in Yakusan's poem, they customarily hold a view like the following:

> There was once a time when Yakusan had become what he describes as "someone with three heads and eight arms" and some other time when he had become "someone eight or sixteen feet tall." It is as though he were saying, "I have crossed the rivers and climbed over the mountains.[2] Even though those mountains and rivers may have existed in the past, I have completely gone beyond them and have now made a place for myself atop a vermilion pedestal in the Jeweled Palace.[3] I fancy

2 An allusion to surpassing hindrances by training oneself to live by the Precepts and to surmounting obstacles by practicing meditation.

3 A metaphor for being in the state of experiencing what "being enlightened" is. The reference is to a lotus pedestal upon which an awakened being sits when residing in the Western Pure Land.

> that the mountains and rivers on the one hand and I on the other are now as far apart as heaven and earth."

But such a view is not all there is to the principle of the case.

At the time when, proverbially, a mountain was being climbed and a river was being crossed, and I existed, and it was the time for that particular I.[4] Since such an I existed, time could not abandon it. If time did not have the characteristic of "coming and going, being continually in flux," then the time when this I was "climbing atop the mountain" would have remained forever, eternally comprised of that particular "time when." But, since time retains the characteristic of "coming and going, being continually in flux," there is a flow of ever-present "nows," each comprised of a time when an I exists. And this is what is meant by the phrase "just for the time being." Surely you don't think that the earlier time when the word "I" referred to "climbing the mountain" or "crossing the river" gulped up the later time when the word "I" referred to "being on a vermilion pedestal within the Jeweled Palace," or think that the former has vomited out the latter, do you?!?[5]

Yakusan's "being a triple-headed and eight-armed one" refers to a time that he would have called "yesterday": his "being someone eight or sixteen feet tall" refers to a time that he would have called "today." Be that as it may, this principle of a past and a present simply corresponds to the two periods of time when an I had headed straight into the mountains and when an I was now looking out from a vermilion pedestal over the thousands of

4 Dōgen's point in using the word "I" as a noun in this and the following paragraph is to indicate that there is no permanent, unchanging self that is being referred to, but rather a cluster of physical and mental characteristics that is flexible and fluid, undergoing change as the conditions and circumstances of what is existing change. Hence, this "I" refers to a series of manifestations over time, which are perceived as related to "a sentient being called Yakusan," but which have no unchanging, atemporal "permanent self" passing through them.

5 Most likely this sentence refers to common but erroneous views as to where the flowing moments of the ever-present now go to when they are no longer present, and where such moments come from. Dōgen is asserting that the past does not exist as an entity that "swallows up" the instances of present time once they are over, nor is the present something thrown out from such a past, as fatalism might suppose.

peaks and the thousands beyond them. Nor have such periods passed away. The time of an I being "triple-headed and eight-armed for the time being" had passed, but even though it seemed to be of another time and place, it was indeed a part of the ever-present now. The time of an I being "eight or sixteen feet tall for the time being" has also passed, but even though it now seems to be something distant from us, it is indeed part of the ever-present now. Thus, we speak of the pine as an analogy for time, as we also do of the bamboo[6] . . .

Do not look upon time as "something that just flies away": do not teach yourself that "flying away" is simply how time functions. Were we to endow time with the property of "flying away," there would undoubtedly be a gap left by the time that has flown. Should anyone have not yet heard teaching upon the principle expressed by the phrase "just for the time being," he may still think of time only as "something which has gone away" . . .

In short, everything whatsoever that exists in the whole universe is a series of instances of time. Since everything is for the time being, we too are for the time being . . .

Time has the virtue of continuity: it continuously flows from the today that we are talking about to a tomorrow, from a today to a yesterday, from a yesterday to a today. It flows from a today to a today and from a tomorrow to a tomorrow. Because continual, continuous flow is a function of time, past and present times do not pile atop each other nor do they form an accumulative line. Yet, even so, Seigen, too, represents a time, as does Ōbaku, and likewise Baso and Sekitō represent times.[7] Because we ourselves and

---

6 An allusion to the Zen saying, "The bamboo, all up and down its length, has joints (which mark the passage of the seasons); the pine (being ever-green) has no colors to differentiate past from present."

7 Seigen, Sekitō's Master, was already dead before Yakusan was born, and therefore represents a time that Yakusan did not know through direct experience. Ōbaku, whose Master was Baso Dōitsu, was a contemporary of Yakusan, and therefore "a time" simultaneous with Yakusan's time. Baso was contemporary with Sekitō, both together representing a time that included a past that Yakusan did not know directly, a past that he did, a present that was also 'his time', and a future time that was not theirs. Although Yakusan was Sekitō's disciple and ultimately his Transmission heir, at one point Sekitō sent Yakusan to train under Baso, who triggered Yakusan's realization of the Truth. These relation-

others, as previously stated, are already "beings for a time," our training and practice are times, as is also our awakening to Truth. Our "entering the mud or going into deep water"[8] is likewise a time . . .

The opinions of ordinary, everyday people today—as well as the source of those opinions—are based on what these people perceive. But this is not what ordinary people consider as being how things operate. For them, the way things operate is that they have "simply come about for a while." Because these people have convinced themselves that this time and this existence of theirs is not related to the way things really operate, they conclude that a golden body sixteen feet tall could not possibly be theirs.[9] Trying to free oneself from this opinion that "the golden body of a Buddha cannot be mine" is also a bit of what the phrase "just for the time being" implies, and is something about which a trainee who has not yet reached spiritual certainty may say, "Oh, I see, I get it!"

In the world today, we structure time by segments which we name, for instance, the Hours of the Horse or the Hours of the Sheep.[10] Be that as it may, these segments are merely persistent fluctuations in the here and now of thoughts and things which arise and fall. It is the same with the Hours of the Rat and the Hours of the Tiger, which are also "for a time."[11] And being an

---

ships represent various ways in which the time of a particular sentient being (Yakusan) relates to the times of other sentient beings.

8 A traditional Zen saying alluding to the actions of a bodhisattva who is willing to go anywhere to help ferry sentient beings to the Other Shore.

9 That is, they think, "I am no more than what I am right now, so I could not possibly be a Buddha, and being what I am now, I cannot see how I could possibly become a Buddha."

10 In medieval Japan, a full day was divided into twelve two-hour segments, named after the twelve signs of the Chinese zodiac. The Time of the Horse was 12:00 noon, and the Hours of the Horse were the hours preceding and following noon. Similarly, the Time of the Sheep was equivalent to 2:00 P.M. Except in the imperial court, where a water-clock was used for assuring that a ceremony was performed at the most auspicious time, determining time throughout medieval Japan was approximated based on the position of the sun in relation to the zenith.

11 The Time of the Rat was midnight, and that of the Tiger was 4:00 A.M., times which were still commonly referred to as "segments of time," even though they could not be determined, since the sun was not visible. Dōgen's point is that all such divisions are cultural conventions and do not constitute what time really is.

ordinary creature is also "for a time," as is being a Buddha. At such times as these, one will swear that being three-headed and eight-armed is the whole universe or that being a golden body sixteen feet tall is the whole universe. To universally penetrate the whole universe by means of the whole universe is called "complete realization." For us to give proof of a golden body sixteen feet tall by our attaining a golden body sixteen feet tall is to manifest our initial spiritual intention, our training and practice, our realizing of enlightenment, and our experiencing the freedom of nirvana—all of which comprises what existence is and what time is. It is a complete realization that the whole of time is what the whole of existence is, and that there is nothing more than this. Anything else would be a time when there was a partial "complete realization," which would be a full realization of a part of what "just for the time being" refers to . . .

Even at a stage where it would seem that you have taken a false step, this condition will be a state of "being." Further, should you leave the matter at this, your condition will still constitute a persistence of "a time being," which will include both a before and an after to this "having taken a false step." Dealing with thoughts and things while they persist, like a fish darting about through the water,[12] is indeed what "being just for the time being" is about. So, do not be upset over what is not, and do not be pressured by what is.[343]

12 A traditional Zen simile applied to a person who engages in the practice of all-acceptance and non-attachment.

NOTES

Religions vary in their orthographies as well as their orthodoxies. That variety is reflected throughout this book. Daoism is sometimes Taoism; Kṛṣṇa is Krishna; the Qur'ān the Quran or Koran; Chuang tzu is Chuang-Tzu or Chuang Tse or Chuang Chou or Zhuangzi or Zhuang Zhou; etc. Some transliterations include internal font changes such as italicizing a letter or two, as in sa*m*sâra. Such "inconsistencies" provide another opportunity to experience the diversity within religious and linguistic communities.

P. = Pāli, the language of the Theravāda canon
S. = Sanskrit, the classical language of India, comparable to Latin in the West

The Map

1 Abridged and adapted from Homer, *The Odyssey* 12:81–121, translated by Robert Fagles (New York: Penguin, 1996), 273–4.

2 John Steinbeck, *Travels with Charley in Search of America* (New York: Bantam, 1962), 272–3.

3 *Sirach* 34:11.

4 Neither Osama bin Laden nor Khalid Khawaja is an official spokesperson for his religion. Nevertheless each cites his faith as formative for his ideology and actions. The point here is not to paint all Islam with the agenda of these men. The point is rather to illustrate how vastly different people's thinking can be.

5 Paul Johnson, Prologue to *A History of Christianity* (New York: Simon & Schuster, 1976), viii.

6 Archie J. Bahm, *The Heart of Confucius: Interpretations of* Genuine Living *and* Great Wisdom, with a foreword by Thomé H. Fang, and sixteen Ming-dynasty Confucian prints (Berkeley: Asian Humanities Press, 1969, 1992), 63–4.

7 Of course the LEM "flew" above the surface of the moon, which has no atmosphere and hence no need for aerodynamics. But "flight" here means using an atmosphere for travel aloft.

8 Henry David Thoreau, *Walden, or Life in the Woods* (Boston: Ticknor and Fields, 1854; reprint edition, Edison, NJ: Castle Books, n.d.), 159, 163–4.

9 Lord Acton, *A Lecture on the Study of History*, delivered at Cambridge June 11, 1895 (London: MacMillan and Co., 1905), 45.

1: Things Could Be Better

10 The Buddha conceived of human beings, and all else, as having no "self" or independent existence. Instead, what we normally take as a human being only consists of the temporary concatenation of five "aggregates" or "bundles" of phenomena—(1) matter (*rūpa*, a physical body, translated a few paragraphs below as "form"); (2) sensations (*vedanā*, below "feelings," pleasant, unpleasant, or neutral); (3) perceptions of sense objects; concepts (S. *saṃjñā*; P. *saññā*); (4) mental formations; desires (*saṃskāras* or *sankhāras*); and (5) consciousness (*vijñāna* or *viññāṇa*). There is no "self" or ongoing being that underlies or suffuses these. Unfortunately, for the most part "sentient beings in their confusion become deeply attached to the view of an existent self, and therefore needlessly undergo transmigration." *Sutra for Resolving Doubts during the Age of the Semblance Dharma*, in Musō Soseki, *Dialogues in a Dream: The Life and Zen Teachings of Musō Soseki*, translated and annotated by Thomas Yūhō Kirchner (Somerville, MA: Wisdom Publications, 2015), 308. "[T]o grasp the Five Aggregates as though they constitute a self is suffering." Thich Nhat Hanh, *The Heart of the Buddha's Teaching: Transforming Suffering into Peace, Joy, and Liberation: The Four Noble Truths, The Noble Eightfold Path, and other Basic Buddhist*

Teachings (New York: Broadway Books, 1998), 258. See the final paragraph of this present quotation from the *Mahāsatipaṭṭhāna Sutta.*

11 22 *Mahāsatipaṭṭhāna Sutta: The Greater Discourse on the Foundations of Mindfulness*, in *The Long Discourses of the Buddha: A Translation of the Dīgha Nikāya*, translated by Maurice Walshe (Boston: Wisdom Publications, 1995) [*DN*], 344–6.

12 56 "*Saccasaṃyutta* Connected Discourses on the Truths," in *The Connected Discourses of the Buddha: A Translation of the Saṃyutta Nikāya*, translated by Bhikku Bodhi (Boston: Wisdom Publications, 2000), 1843–7.

13 63 *Cūḷamālunkya Sutta* The Shorter Discourse to Mālunkyāputta," in *The Middle Length Discourses of the Buddha: A Translation of the Majjhima Nikāya*, translated by Bhikkhu Ñāṇamoli and Bhikkhu Bodhi, 3rd ed. (Boston: Wisdom Publications, 2005), 534–6.

14 24 "*Pāṭika Sutta: About Pāṭikaputta* The Charlatan," in *DN*, 372.

15 Walpola Rahula, *What the Buddha Taught*, revised ed., with a foreword by Paul Demiéville (New York: Grove Press, 1974), 16–9.

16 Bhikku Bodhi, "The Buddha's Teaching," in *The Buddha and His Teachings*, edited by Samuel Bercholz and Sherab Chödzin Kohn (Boston: Shambhala, 2003), 62.

17 Eknath Easwaran, *The Upanishads*, translated with a general introduction by Eknath Easwaran, chapter introductions and concluding essay by Michael N. Nagler (Berkeley, CA: Nilgiri, 1987), 7.

18 Thich Nhat Hanh, *Going Home: Jesus and Buddha as Brothers* (New York: Riverhead, 1999), 161–3. Although Thây is not a Theravāda Buddhist, his comments on suffering parallel Theravāda thought.

19 Buddhadāsa Bhikkhu, *Handbook for Mankind* (Bangkok: Mahachula Buddhist University Press, n.d.), 42, 126.

2: Worth Knowing

20 K. N. Jayatilleke, *The Message of the Buddha*, edited by Ninian Smart (New York: The Free Press, 1974), 105.

21 Brian Greene, *The Hidden Reality: Parallel Universes and the Deep Laws of the Cosmos* (New York: Alfred A. Knopf, 2011), 33–4. Greene's statement does mention God, but his position that no reality exists beyond particles and their arrangement disallows his existence.

22 Many Muslims believe that the Qur'ān cannot be translated, because it is a copy of the original kept in heaven; Arabic was the language used by Gabriel; God said, "We have sent it down as an Arabic Qur'ān" (12.2 and ten other similar statements); and the literary beauty and cadences of the Arabic text cannot be replicated. However, various translations have in fact been made—often called "interpretations," or attempts to convey the Qur'ān's "meaning." I have consulted various editions of the work of 'Abdullah Yūsuf 'Alī, particularly the fourth US edition (Elmhurst, NY: Tahrike Tarsile Qur'an, Inc., 2002), the eleventh edition (Beltsville, MA: Amana Publications, 2004), and a paperback edition (Istanbul: Asir Media, 2002). I will use, among other things, the translation "God" instead of "Allah" employed in the first of these, modern rather than archaic English verb forms (e.g., "comes" rather than "cometh"), and American instead of British spelling (e.g., "honor" instead of "honour").

23 *Kalām*, or more fully *'ilm al-kalām*, is "speech" or "science of discourse" on God. Among the schools of kalām are the Mu'tazila, the Ash'arīya, and the al-Māturīdīya.

24 The first verse of every sūra in the Qur'ān except the ninth.

25 Caesar E. Farah, *Islam: Beliefs and Observances*, 7th ed. (Hauppauge, NY: Barron's, 2003), 6–7.

26 Farah, *Islam*, 109.

27 To study sunnah over theology is not necessarily wrong. Every faith includes some who specialize in theology or metaphysics and others who focus on ethics and practice.

28 Ali A. Allawi, *The Crisis of Islamic Civilization* (New Haven: Yale, 2009), 9, 61.

29 D.B. Macdonald, "Muslim Theology, Jurisprudence and Constitutional Theory," cited in Samuel M. Zwemer, *A Moslem Seeker After God: Showing Islam at Its Best in the Life and Teaching of Al-Ghazali, Mystic and Theologian of the Eleventh Century* (New York: Revell, 1920), 20.

30 http://www.ghazali.org/site/ihya.htm, accessed 10 June 2011.

31 Karen Armstrong, cited in Philip Jenkins, *The Lost History of Christianity: The Thousand-Year Golden Age of the Church in the Middle East, Africa, and Asia—and How It Died* (New York: HarperCollins, 2008), 200.

32 *Imam Ghazzali's Iḥyā' 'Ulūm-ud-din (The Revival of Religious Learnings)*, translated by Al-Haj Maulana Fazal-ul-karim, improved edition (Lahore, Pakistan: Sh. Muhammad Ashraf, 1993), book I, 14–106. A new English edition of *'Ulūm* is to be released soon by Fons Vitae. His work is also transliterated as *Iḥyā' 'Ulūm al-Dīn*.

33 *Iḥyā' 'Ulūm-ud-din*, book IV, 287, 300–1.

34 These three paragraphs summarize *Iḥyā' 'Ulūm-ud-din*, book IV, 290–336.

35 These three—love, *gnōsis*, and obedience—comprise the Ṣūfī ideal.

36 Radhakrishan. *The Hindu View of Life* (New Delhi: HarperCollins Publishers India, [1927] 1993), 16, 19.

3: Nobody's Perfect

37 Jacob Needleman, *Why Can't We Be Good?* (New York: Jeremy P. Tarcher, 2007). Charles Matthewes, "Why Evil Exists" (The Great Courses, 2011).

38 Tu Weiming, "Chinese Philosophy: A Synoptic View," chapter 1 (3–23) in *A Companion to World Philosophies*, ed. Eliot Deutsch and Ron Bontekoe. Blackwell Companions to Philosophy, vol. 10 (Malden, MA: Blackwell, 1997), 3.

39 Marietta Stepaniants, *Introduction to Eastern Thought*, ed. James Behuniak, trans. Rommela Kohanovskaya (Walnut Creek, CA: AltaMira, 2002), 41.

40 Tak-ling Terry Woo, "Women in Contemporary Chinese Religions," chapter 9 in *Chinese Religions in Contemporary Societies*, ed. James Miller (Santa Barbara, CA: ABC-CLIO, 2006), 233.

41 Julia Ching, *Chinese Religions* (Maryknoll, NY: Orbis, 1993), 58–9.

42 *The Analects of Confucius*, translated and annotated by Arthur Waley (New York: Macmillan 1938; Vintage, 1989), 33, 50.

43 Unless otherwise marked, sayings will be taken or adapted from James Legge, *The Chinese Classics: Translated into English, with Preliminary Essays and Explanatory Notes*. Vol. 1: *The Life and Teachings of Confucius*. Second ed. London: N. Trübner, 1869. Other translations cited are *The Analects of Confucius*, translated by A. Charles Muller (http://www.acmuller.net/con-dao/analects.html accessed 06 January 2016) [M]. *Analects*, Waley [AW]. *The Analects of Confucius*, translated by Burton Watson. Translations from the Asian Classics. (New York: Columbia University, 2007) [BW]. *The Analects of Confucius: An Online Teaching Translation*. version 2.2, translated by R. Eno: http://www.indiana.edu/~p374/Analects_of_Confucius_(Eno-2015).pdf accessed 06 January 2016 [E]. *The Sayings of Confucius*, translated by Leonard A. Lyall (New York: Longmans, Green and Co, n.d. [1909]) [LY]. William

Edward Soothall, *The Analects of Confucius* (n.p.: by the author, 1910) [S]. Sayings will generally omit such phrases as "The Master says," as well as questions regarding the dating of the various material. Comments or alternate translations, sometimes from footnotes, will be enclosed in square brackets. Verse numbers vary slightly among the translations. Citations are from 1.1 LY, 2, 8, 14 M; 2.2, 14 S; 3.7 S; 4.5, 16; 6.13 LY, 16 M; 7.36 M; 8.6 LY, 7; 9.13; 10.1; 12.2 E, 16 BW; 13.3, 19 S, 20 S, 25 LY, 26 S; 14.25 BW; 15.1, 20 LY, 36 BW; 16.7; 19.10; 20.2, 3.

44 Waley, *Analects*, 28.

45 13.12.

46 4.6 S; 7.29; 9.32 BW; 15.12 AW cp. 9.17; 15.3; 5.26; 19.5 S; 5.7 cp. 5.4, 10, 18; 5.23 AW; 7.33 S; 9.1 S; 14.30; 14.31 AW; 14.32 S.

47 Confucius, *Chung Yung* (Genuine Living) 7, in Archie J. Bahm, *The Heart of Confucius: Interpretations of* Genuine Living *and* Great Wisdom, with a foreword by Thomé H. Fang, and sixteen Ming-dynasty Confucian Prints (Berkeley: Asian Humanities Press, 1969, 1992), 79–82. Cp. Stephen Prothero, *God Is Not One: The Eight Rival Religions that Run the World—and Why Their Differences Matter* (New York: HarperOne, 2010), 129.

48 6.28 AW; 13.27 BW; 6.10; 9.10 S; 7.25 BW.

49 2.4; 7.16 S.

50 Waley, *Analects*, 74.

51 Confucius, *Genuine Living (Chung Yung)* 6, in Bahm, *Heart of Confucius*, 77.

52 *Hsün-tzu*, ch. 23, cited in Fung Y-Lan, *A Short History of Chinese Philosophy*, edited by Derk Bodde (New York: Free Press, 1948), 145.

53 5.12 LY.

54 Fung Yu-lan, *Short History*, 301–2.

55 Aleksandr I. Solzhenitsyn, *The Gulag Archipelago 1918–1956: An Experiment in Literary Investigation*, translated by Thomas P. Whitney (New York: Harper & Row, 1974), 168.

56 Howard Bloom, *The Lucifer Principle: A Scientific Expedition into the Forces of History* (New York: Atlantic Monthly Press, 1995).

57 Robert Oppenheimer, "The Added Cubit: A Talk in New York," *Encounter* 21/2 (August 1963): 46–7.

58 Robert Oppenheimer, "L'Intime et le Commun," Rencontres Internationales de Genève 19 (1964), *Comment Vivre Demain?* 22. http://www.rencontres-int-geneve.ch/volumes_pdf/rig19.pdf, accessed 10 December 2013.

59 Dōgen, *Treasury of the True Dharma Eye: Zen Master Dogen's* Shobo Genzo, edited by Kazuaki Tanahashi (Boston: Shambhala, 2012), 101.

60 Ecclesiastes 9:3.

61 Gimli the dwarf to Legolas the elf in J.R.R. Tolkien, *The Return of the King*, being the third part of *The Lord of the Rings*, 2nd ed. (Boston: Houghton Mifflin, 1955, 1983), 149.

4: Distance

62 Howard Bloom argues that "Evil is a by-product, a component, of creation. In a world evolving into ever-higher forms, hatred, violence, aggression, and war are a part of the evolutionary plan." Nature uses evil to build. "With it, she moves the human world to greater heights of organization, intricacy, and power." Hence "evil is woven into our most basic biological fabric." *The Lucifer Principle: A Scientific Expedition into the Forces of History* (New York: Atlantic Monthly Press, 1995), 2–3.

63 Walshe agrees that *sin* has "theistic connotations" and thus "is best avoided when translating Buddhist texts." *The Long Discourses of the Buddha: A Translation of the Dīgha Nikāya*, translated by Maurice Walshe (Boston: Wisdom Publications, 1995), 547, n. 137.

64 Philip Freund, *Myths of Creation* (New York: Washington Square, 1965), 41–2.

65 E.O. James, *The Worship of the Sky-God: A Comparative Study in Semitic and Indo-European Religion* (London: Atholone Press, 1963), v, 3, 6. See also *African Myths and Tales*, edited with an introduction by Susan Feldmann (New York: Dell, 1963), 31: "Before the arrival of the missionaries, if we asked, 'By what were these stones made?' it was said, 'They were made by Umvelinqangi [the omnipresent Zulu creator god].'" For an opposing view see Irving Hexam, "Lord of the Sky-King of the Earth: Zulu Traditional Religion and Belief in the Sky God," *Studies in Religion* 10/3 (Summer 1981): 273–85.

66 Ramesh Menon, *The Ramayana* (New York: North Point Press, 2001), 35.

67 Siraporn Nathaland, ed., *Thai Folklore: Insights into Thai Culture* (Bangkok: Chulalongkorn University Press, 2000), 103.

68 Siraporn Nathaland, ed., *Thai Folklore*, 103.

69 Maria Leach, *The Beginning: Creation Myths around the World*, illustrations by Jan Bell Fairservis (New York: Funk & Wagnalls, 1956), 143–4.

70 *African Myths*, ed. Feldmann, 37.

71 Maen Pongudom, "Creation of Man: Theological reflections based on Northern Thai Folktales," *East Asia Journal of Theology* 3/2 (1985), 223.

72 E.E. Evans-Pritchard, *Nuer Religion* (Oxford: Clarendon, 1956), 1–7.

73 Evans-Pritchard, *Nuer Religion*, 10.

74 Evans-Pritchard, *Nuer Religion*, 20.

75 *African Myths*, ed. Feldmann, 25.

76 Plato, *Critias*, in *The Dialogues of Plato*, vol. 3, 3rd ed., translated with Analyses and Introductions by B. Jowett (London: Humphrey Milford, 1892) 530, 542–3.

77 Jean C. Cooper, *An Illustrated Introduction to Taoism: The Wisdom of the Sages*, edited by Joseph A. Fitzgerald, foreword by William Stoddart (Bloomington, IN: World Wisdom, 2010), 16.

78 Taitetsu Unno, *River of Fire, River of Water: An Introduction to the Pure Land Tradition of Shin Buddhism* (New York: Doubleday, 1998), 162.

5: Preference

79 Psalm 103:8–18. In all citations from the Tanakh in this book, regardless of the translation used, [the] LORD or GOD has been replaced with Yahweh. The KJV citations have been further modified to reduce archaic diction.

80 Proverbs 3:11–2.

81 Lamentations 3:16–33.

82 Hosea 11:3–9 ESV.

83 Jonah 4:9–11.

84 Abraham Cohen, *Everyman's Talmud: The Major Teachings of the Rabbinic Sages* (New York: Schocken,1949), 16–20.

85 Ezekiel 18:25–32 ESV. Emphasis added.

6: Good

86 Although the Pāli word *bhikkhu* (fem. *bhikkhunī*; singular *bhikṣu*, fem. *bhikṣuṇī*) means "an ordained Buddhist monk," an ancient commentary says that in this passage it should be understood to include even laypersons who seriously try to follow the teaching. See *The Middle Length Discourses of the Buddha: A Translation of the Majjhima Nikāya*, translated by Bhikkhu Ñāṇamoli and Bhikkhu Bodhi, 3rd ed. (Boston: Wisdom Publications, 2005) [*MN*], 1189, n. 137.

87 *MN* 10 *Satipaṭṭhāna Sutta* The Foundations of Mindfulness 2–4, 145–6.

88 *MN* 10.10, 11, 14, 147–8.

89 *The Numerical Discourses of the Buddha: A Translation of the Aṅguttara Nikāya*, translated by Bhikkhu Bodhi (Boston: Wisdom Publications, 2012) [*AN*], The Book of Eights, IV, 245–7, 1174.

90 *AN* The Book of Eights, IV, 249–251, 1176–8.

91 Müller, 9.

92 *A Dictionary of Buddhism*, edited by Damien Keown (New York: Oxford, 2003), s.v. apramāda.

93 Adapted from *The Dhammapada: A Collection of Verses*, translated by F. Max Müller. *The Sacred Books of the East*, edited by F. Max Müller, vol. X (Oxford: Clarendon, 1881). The first part of verse 240 was reworked to allow "rust" to be substituted for "the impurity which springs from the iron."

94 16 *Mahāparinibbāna Sutta: The Great Passing* The Buddha's Last Days, in *The Long Discourses of the Buddha: A Translation of the Dīgha Nikāya*, translated by Maurice Walshe (Boston: Wisdom Publications, 1987, 1995) [*DN*], 245.

95 "Â*k*ârâṅga Sûtra," in G*aina Sûtras*, translated by Hermann Jacobi. Part I: The Â*k*ârâṅga Sûtra, The Kalpa Sûtra. The Sacred Books of the East, edited by F. Max Müller, vol. XXII (Oxford: Clarendon, 1884), 189.

96 "Kalpa Sûtra," in G*aina Sûtras*, translated by Jacobi, Part I, 262–4.

97 The text here and elsewhere repeats the entire list: "sinful, blamable, intent on works, acting on impulses, produces division and dissension, quarrels, faults, and pains, injures living beings, or kills creatures." For the sake of reducing redundancy I have included only the first word here and have edited out similar repetitions elsewhere.

98 Adapted from "Â*k*ârâṅga Sûtra," in G*aina Sûtras*, translated by Jacobi, Part I, 202–10.

99 Adapted from "Uttarâdhyayana Sûtra," in G*aina Sûtras*, translated by Hermann Jacobi. Part II: The Uttarâdhyayana Sûtra, The Sûtrak*ri*tâṅga Sûtra. The Sacred Books of the East, edited by F. Max Müller, vol. XLV (Oxford: Clarendon, 1895), 73–5.

100 See the criticism, for example, in 2 *Sāmaññaphala Sutta: The Fruits of the Homeless Life*, in *DN*, 91–109.

101 2 *Devaputtasaṃyutta*: Connected Discourses with Young Devas, in *The Connected Discourses of the Buddha: A Translation of the Saṃyutta Nikāya*, translated by Bhikkhu Bodhi (Boston: Wisdom Publications, 2000), 162.

102 Adapted from Max Arthur Macauliffe, *The Sikh Religion: Its Gurus, Sacred Writings and Authors*, vol. 1 (Oxford: Clarendon, 1909), verses 1, 6, 12–15, 20–21, 28, 32, 34, 38, Slok; 195–217.

103 Jonah 1:2; 3:10; Acts 24:25; Revelation 20:11–13; Qur'ān 79:36–41.

7: But Good Enough?

104 E.g., 16 Mahāparinibbāna Sutta: The Great Passing The Buddha's Last Days, in *The Long Discourses of the Buddha: A Translation of the Dīgha Nikāya,* translated by Maurice Walshe (Boston: Wisdom Publications, 1987, 1995), 245, cited above in chapter 6.

105 Not only is individual enlightenment selfish, but also anything else done in a proscribed way: "Foolish people, even when they worship a buddha, direct their devotion only to the particular buddha in whom they believe. When they make an offering, they do so in the same spirit. Whether they hold memorial services for their deceased parents or perform prayer rituals for their benefactors, their intentions are selfishly directed solely toward those to whom they are personally obliged, never toward the entire universe and all its sentient beings. As a result the merit produced is never great." Musō Soseki, *Dialogues in a Dream: The Life and Zen Teachings of Musō Soseki*, translated and annotated by Thomas Yūhō Kirchner (Somerville, MA: Wisdom Publications, 2015), 106.

106 Adapted from *The Saddharma-Pu*ndar*îka* or *The Lotus of the True Law*, translated by H. Kern. *The Sacred Books of the East*, edited by F. Max Müller, vol. XXI (Oxford: Clarendon, 1884), XXIV, 406–9.

107 Some vocabulary may help with this section. A *kalpa* in Hindu thought is a Day of Brahmā or 4,320,000,000 years. *Tathāgata* means "(one who has) thus come" or "thus gone" in conformity with the most profound way of things, a perfected one, a buddha. It is the term Siddhārtha Gautama most often used of himself. A *bhikṣu* is an ordained Buddhist monk. A *shravaka* is a hearer or disciple.

108 Adapted and abridged from "The Larger Sutra on Amitāyus," in *The Three Pure Land Sutras*, translated by Hisao Inagaki in collaboration with Harold Stewart, revised second ed., BDK English Tripiṭaka Series (Berkeley: Numata Center for Buddhist Translation and Research, 2003), Part 1.4–7, 8–18. http://www.bdk.or.jp/bdk/digitaldl.html, accessed 14 September 2015.

109 The time periods assigned to these three stages in the dharma vary.

110 *Hōnen's* Senchakushū: *Passages on the Selection of the Nembutsu in the Original Vow (Senchaku hongan nembutsu shū)*, translated and edited by the *Senchakushū* English Translation Project (Honolulu: University of Hawai'i, 1998), 77–8.

111 Hōnen, *Ichimai kishōmon* (The One-Page Document), *Shōwa shinshū Hōnen shōnin zenshū*, p. 416, cited in Hirikawa Takatoshi, Introduction to *Hōnen's* Senchakushū, 13.

112 Takatoshi, Introduction, 9.

113 Alfred Bloom. *Shinran's Gospel of Pure Grace*. The Association for Asian Studies: Monographs and Papers, No. XX. (Tucson: University of Arizona Press, 1965), 11. Taitetsu Unno, *River of Fire, River of Water: An Introduction to the Pure Land Tradition of Shin Buddhism* (New York: Doubleday, 1998), 29.

114 Takatoshi, Introduction, 13.

115 Yoshiko Ohtani, *The Life of Eshinni: Wife of Shinran Shonin*, translated by Taitetsu and Alice Unno (n.p., n.d.), 91.

116 *Shōwa shinshū Hōnen shōnin zenshū*, 462–3, cited in *Hōnen's* Senchakushū, 13–4.

117 *Wago-toroku*, cited in Ohtani, *Life of Eshinni*, 15–6.

118 Takatoshi, Introduction, 15.

119 "The more we become aware of the depths of our unawareness, the more we realize how impotent we are to realize Awakening through our own efforts. Accordingly, although the ideal of aspiring to attain Buddhahood is very important, in reality, it is practically impossible.

"It was in response to such hapless circumstances that Amida

Buddha showed compassion to us, and rather than wait for us to seek our Buddhahood, vowed to bring it about even before the idea occurred to us . . .

"We must clearly understand . . . that reliance, entrusting, and so on, does not come from ourselves, since we are deluded and easily led astray. Unless this is understood, you will not appreciate the spirit of 'Namo Amida Butsu.'

"Actually, the necessary 'reliance and entrusting' has already been accomplished on the part of Amida Buddha. That is why the Name of the Buddha already has contained within it the driving force of bringing about our complete liberation.

"Shinran states that *namo* means that Amida Buddha is calling out to us even before we have entrusted ourselves to Amida Buddha." *Jodo Shinshu: A Guide* (Kyoto: Hongwanji International Center, 2002), 67, 75.

120 *The Collected Works of Shinran*, vol. 1, *The Writings*, translated, with introductions, glossaries, and reading aids, by Dennis Hirota (Head Translator), Hisao Inagaki, Michio Tokunaga, and Ryushin Uryuzu (Kyoto: Jōdo Shinshū Hongwanji-Ha, 1997), 98.

121 *Jodo Shinshu: A Guide*, 79.

122 Unno, *River of Fire*, 19.

123 Bloom, *Shinran's Gospel*, 51.

124 Unno, *River of Fire*, 29–30, says, "While Shin Buddhism upholds the centrality of recitative nembutsu, it has nothing to do with the number of invocations. What is crucial is the quality of the heart inherent in each saying, the purity of response to the call of the Buddha of Immeasurable Light and Life. Thus, even a single utterance, or even the 'thought of wanting to say the nembutsu,' is sufficient."

125 *Collected Works of Shinran*, 1:494. This is Shinran's comment on the exclusion phrase of the eighteenth vow. Cp. *Jodo Shinshu: A Guide*, 73.

126 See Unno, *River of Fire*, 24–5.

127 "A Record in Lament of Divergences: *Tannishō*," in *Collected Works of Shinran*, 1:661–82. Numbers in parentheses indicate the sections from which the preceding paragraph(s) may be found.

128 K.N. Jayatilleke, *The Message of the Buddha*, a posthumous work edited by Ninian Smart (New York: Free Press, 1974), 105, 111.

129 Tai-Hsü, *Lectures on Buddhism* (Paris: n.p., 1928), 48.

130 Thomas J.J. Altizer, "Kenosis and *Śūnyatā* in the Contemporary Buddhist-Christian Dialogue," in *Masao Abe: A Zen Life of Dialogue*, ed. Donald W. Mitchell (Boston: Tuttle, 1998), 153, 157.

131 This fact alone raises questions in a system that teaches *anatman* or no-self.

132 Unno, *River of Fire*, 20.

133 *Collected Works of Shinran*, 95–6.

134 Unno, *River of Fire*, 20.

135 Unno, *River of Fire*, 27.

136 Unno, *River of Fire*, 20.

137 *Collected Works of Shinran*, 95; *Jodo Shinshu*, 81; Unno, *River of Fire*, 19.

138 *Unno, River of Fire*, 173–4, 208–9.

139 *The Three Pillars of Zen—Teaching, Practice, and Enlightenment,* compiled and edited by Philip Kapleau, updated and revised (New York: Anchor, 1989, 2000), 394.

140 *The Lotus Sutra*, translated by Burton Watson. Translations from the Asian Classics. (New York: Columbia University Press, 1993), 135–7.

8: What Works

141 John 1:29; Genesis 4:4; 8:20–22; 22:6–14; Exodus 12.

142 C.S. Lewis, *Till We Have Faces—A Myth Retold* (Grand Rapids, MI: Eerdmans, 1956), 295.

143 Mark R. Woodward, "Gifts for the sky people: Animal sacrifice, head hunting and power among the Naga of Burma and Assam," in *Indigenous Religions: A Companion*, edited by Graham Harvey (London: Cassell, 2000), 219.

144 Woodward, "Gifts," 223.

145 *Li Chi*, 25, in *The Way and Its Power: Lao Tzu's* Tao Tê Ching *and Its Place in Chinese Thought*, translated and edited by Arthur Waley (New York: Grove Press, [1934] 1958), 23.

146 Hebrews 9:9–10; 10:1–4.

147 Mark 14:36.

148 John 10:11, 18.

149 William Childs Robinson, "Wrath of God," in *Evangelical Dictionary of Theology*, second ed., edited by Walter A. Elwell (Grand Rapids: Baker, 2001), 1304.

150 *The Jewish Study Bible*, ed. Adele Berlin and Marc Zvi Brettler (Oxford: Oxford University Press, 2004), notes on Leviticus 26, p. 274.

151 Romans 2:4–11.

152 2 Thessalonians 2:10 NIV.

153 John 3:18, 36; 2 Thessalonians 2:10; Romans 5:9; 1 Thessalonians 1:10; 5:9.

154 Romans 3:25–26 NIV.

155 1 Timothy 2:6 NIV. The Greek word translated "ransom" is *antilutron*—a combination of the simple *lutron* "price of release, ransom" and the preposition *anti. Anti* often conveys the idea of substitution, as in Matthew 2:22, "Archelaus was reigning in Judea *in place of* [*anti*] his father Herod," or Luke 11:11, "Which of you fathers, if your son asks for a fish, will give him a snake *instead* [*anti*]?"

156 Galatians 3:13 NIV. The word translated "for" is *hyper* and not *anti*, but the idea of substitution still emerges.

157 Isaiah 53:3–12.

158 Acts 8:35.

159 Colossians 1:19–22.

160 Romans 5:10–11 NIV.

161 The most frequently noted is Tacitus, *Annals* 15.44—"Nero fastened the guilt and inflicted the most exquisite tortures on a class hated for their abominations, called Christians by the populace. Christus, from whom the name had its origin, suffered the extreme penalty during the reign of Tiberius at the hands of one of our procurators, Pontius Pilatus."

162 Romans 8:31–39.

163 Hebrews 2:14–15.

164 Harold S. Kushner, *How Good Do We Have To Be? A New Understanding of Guilt and Forgiveness* (Boston: Little, Brown and Co., 1996), 10.

165 "Scandal" in its sense of being "an obstacle in coming to faith and a cause of going astray in it." Gustav Stählin, "σκάνδαλον, σκανδαλίζω," in *Theological Dictionary of the New Testament*, edited by Gerhard Kittel and Gerhard Friedrich, translated by Geoffrey W. Bromiley, vol. 7, Σ (Grand Rapids: Eerdmans, 1971), 345.

166 Some Buddhists promote the contemplation of human corpses in various stages of decay in order to remind the observer that all things change and thereby promote detachment.

167 Qur'ān 4.157–8.

168 Daniel Ladinsky, preface to *The Gift: Poems by Hafiz the Great Sufi Master*, translations by Daniel Ladinsky (New York: Penguin Compass, 1999), 2.

169 1 Corinthians 1:18–25.

170 John Bowring, "In the Cross of Christ I Glory," 1825. Public domain.

171 Horatio G. Spafford, "It is Well With My Soul," 1873. Public domain.

172 Hans Küng, *On Being a Christian*, translated by Edward Quinn (New York: Doubleday, 1976), 408, 601–2.

9: The Wisdom of Folly

173 Compare this idea with the Native American Lenápe phrase *wemi tali*, which means "'All Where,' that is, 'Every Where,' The Every Where, or All That Is." As such, the *wemi tali* "is a single unity of which we, as humans, are just a part, and not the most significant part either." Jack D. Forbes, "Nature and Culture: Problematic Concepts for Native Americans," in *Indigenous Traditions and Ecology: The Interbeing of Cosmology and Community*, edited by John A. Grim. Religions of the World and Ecology, series editors Mary Evelyn Tucker and John Grim (Cambridge, MA: Harvard University Press, 2001), 110.

174 Citations from the *Daodejing* generally come from Ellen M. Chen, *The Tao Te Ching: A New Translation with Commentary* (St. Paul: Paragon, 1989). Those marked "Addiss" are from *Tao Te Ching Lao-Tzu*, translated by Stephen Adiss and Stanley Lombardo, introduction by Burton Watson, ink paintings by Stephen Addiss (Boston: Shambhala, 2007); those marked "Hua-Ching Ni" are from *The Complete Works of Lao Tzu: Tao Teh Ching & Hua Hu Ching*, translation and elucidation by Hua-Ching Ni (Santa Monica: SevenStar Communications, 1979, 1995); those marked "Lin" are from *Tao Te Ching: Annotated & Explained*, translation and annotation by Derek Lin, foreword by Lama Surya Das (Woodstock, VT: Skylight Paths, 2006); those marked "Man-Ho Kwok" are from *Tao Te Ching*, translated by Man-Ho Kwok, Martin Palmer, and Jay Ramsay, calligraphy by Kwok-Lap Chan (London: Vega, 2002); those marked "Waley" are from *The Way and Its Power: Lao Tzu's Tao Tê Ching and Its Place in Chinese Thought*, translated and edited by Arthur Waley (New York: Grove, [1934] 1958).

175 Adapted from [*Chuang Tzu*] in *The Sacred Books of China: The Texts of Tâoism*, translated by James Legge, Part 1: *The Tâo Teh* King, *The Writings of* Kwang-ȝze Books I–XVII. *The Sacred Books of the East*, edited by F. Max Müller, vol. XXXIX (Oxford: Clarendon, 1891), VI.7; 243–4.

176 Solala Towler, *Tales from the Tao: Inspirational Teachings from the Great Taoist Masters*, photographs by John Cleare (New York: Fall River, 2005), 2–3.

177 Chen, *Tao Te Ching*, 41, 127.

178 Chen, *Tao Te Ching*, 144.

179 Adapted from [*Chuang Tzu*] in Legge, *Texts of Tâoism*, XIV.4; 353.

180 Thomas Merton, *The Way of Chuang Tzu* (Boston: Shambhala, 2004 [1965]), 21.

181 Ursula K. Le Guin, *The Lathe of Heaven: A Novel* (New York: Scribner, 1971, 2008).

182 Chen, *Tao Te Ching*, 97–8.

183 Lin, *Tao Te Ching*, 34.

184 Adapted from [*Chuang Tzu*] in Legge, *Texts of Tâoism*, XV.3; 366.

185 Merton, *Chuang Tzu*, 19–20.

186 Chuang Tzu [Zhuangzi] is the name of both the sage and the book attributed to him. The same for the earlier Lao Tzu [Laozi].

187 Merton, *Chuang Tzu*, 105–8. Cp. Musō Soseki, *Dialogues in a Dream: The Life and Zen Teachings of Musō Soseki*, translated and annotated by Thomas Yūhō Kirchner (Somerville, MA: Wisdom Publications, 2015), 192: "In the days of old, Xu Yu, hearing that Emperor Tang Yao wished to hand over the throne to him, washed out his ears in the River Ying, and Chao Fu led his ox home so it would not drink of the water in which Xu had washed his ears."

188 Chen, *Tao Te Ching*, x.

189 Chen, *Tao Te Ching*, 42–3.

190 Lionel Giles, Introduction to *The Sayings of Lao Tzu*. In *Tao: The Way: The Sayings of Lao Tzu, Chuang Tzu, Lieh Tzu*. Translated by Lionel Giles and Herbert A. Giles. Edited by Shawn Conners. Special Edition Books. Kindle edition. Page 9 of 200; location 249 of 3514.

191 He Jianming, "Dialogue between Christianity and Taoism: The Case of Lin Yutang," in *Christianity and Chinese Culture* [Christianity and Chinese Culture: A Sino-Nordic Conference on Chinese Contextual Theology held in Lapland, Finland, August 13–17, 2003], edited by Miikka Ruokanen and Paulos Huang (Grand Rapids: Eerdmans, 2010), 126.

192 Confucius, *Genuine Living,* 5, in Archie J. Bahm, *The Heart of Confucius: Interpretations of* Genuine Living *and* Great Wisdom, with a foreword by Thomé H. Fang, and sixteen Ming-dynasty Confucian prints (Berkeley: Asian Humanities Press, 1969, 1992), 77.

10: Responding to Grace

193 *The Bhagavad Gita*, translated with a general introduction by Eknath Easwaran (Tomales, CA: Nilgiri Press, 1985), 1.21–3, 26–31, 36–47.

194 Many who comment on the *Gītā* speak of only the first three.

195 Vasudha Narayanan, *Hinduism—Origins, Beliefs, Practices, Holy Texts, Sacred Places* (Oxford: Oxford University Press, 2004), 21, 42.

196 Sri Swami Sivananda, *The Bhagavad Gita: Text, Word-to-Word Meaning, Translation and Commentary*, 14th ed. (Uttarakhand, India: Divine Life Society, 2013), xviii–xix. Transliteration and references have been omitted.

197 Thich Nhat Hanh, *Living Buddha, Living Christ*, introduction by Elaine Pagels, foreword by Brother David Steindl-Rast (New York: Riverhead Books, 1995), 25–6.

198 http://www.cbsnews.com/news/man-captured-by-terrorist-group-taliban-dilip-joseph-survived-to-tell-his-tale/?ftag=YHF4eb9d17, accessed 15 October 2014.

11: Living Trumps Talking

199 Adapted from Hirata Takashi, *Mumonkan, Zen no goruko*, vol. 18 (Tokyo: Chikuma shobō, 1969), 37–41, as cited in Albert Welter, "Mahākāśyapa's Smile: Silent Transmission and the Kung-an (Kōan) Tradition," in *The Kōan: Texts and Contexts in Zen Buddhism*, edited by Steven Heine and Dale S. Wright (New York: Oxford University Press, 2000), 75. The story is told with variations. In some a follower gives the

Buddha a flower as he ascends the dais to teach, in others the Buddha himself plucks a lotus and holds it dripping mud and water before the saṅgha. In some each disciple tries to explain what Śākyamuni means while in others they sit in mute incomprehension. Mahākāśyapa's smile indicates he alone understood what the Buddha meant, and when he did so the latter responded, "What can be said I have said to you, and what cannot be said, I have given to Mahākāśyapa."

200 "The opening of another's mind through one's own inner light is called 'the transmission of the lamp,' the lamp signifying the mind-light, enlightenment, transmitted by the master to his disciples. This inner illumination, transmitted from generation to generation, is the chief characteristic of the teachings of Ch'an." *Original Teachings of Ch'an Buddhism Selected from The Transmission of the Lamp*, translated with introductions by Chang Chung-Yuan (New York: Pantheon, 1969), xii.

201 *The Three Pillars of Zen—Teaching, Practice, and Enlightenment*, compiled and edited by Philip Kapleau, updated and revised (New York: Anchor, 1989, 2000), 102.

202 The analogy was proposed by Wu-men Hui-k'ai (1183–1260). See p. 76.

203 "Zen is founded upon the historical moment of the raising of the flower by Śākyamuni Buddha and the smile of comprehension of Mahākāśyapa" (Thich Thien-An, *Zen Philosophy, Zen Practice* [Emeryville, CA: Dharma Publishing, 1975], 156). "Zen" transliterates the Japanese pronunciation of the first syllable of *ch'an-na*. *Ch'an-na* is Chinese for the Sanskrit *dhyāna*, "meditation," uninterrupted contemplation beyond any memory of ego. *Samādhi* ("self-collectedness") is its final stage. The Pāli cognate is *jhāna*; the Korean word is *son*, the Vietnamese *thiên*.

204 Daisetz Teitaro Suzuki, *An Introduction to Zen Buddhism*, with a foreword by Carl Jung (New York: Grove Weidenfeld, 1964), 38–9. Buddhism is not the only, or perhaps even the chief, antecedent of Zen.

"Zen may therefore be regarded as the fullest development of Taoism by wedding it to the congenial Buddhist insights and the powerful Buddhist impulse of apostolic zeal. If Buddhism is the father, Taoism is the mother of this prodigious child. But there can be no denying that the child looks more like the mother than the father." John C.H. Wu, *The Golden Age of Zen*, with an introduction by Thomas Merton, second edition (New York: Doubleday, 1996), 31.

205 "Killing the Buddha" means "[e]radicating from the mind the notion of a Buddha as opposed to an ordinary being, ridding oneself of the idea that Shakyamuni Buddha is God or a super-being, obliterating the subtle pride which arises from kensho and leads one to think, 'Now I'm a Buddha.'" *Three Pillars*, 236, n. 21.

206 Suzuki, *Introduction to Zen*, 58–9.

207 Suzuki, *Introduction to Zen*, 33.

208 Thich Nhat Hanh, *Living Buddha, Living Christ* (New York: Riverhead Press, 1995), 141.

209 Osho, *Zen: Its History and Teachings* (Lewes, UK: Bridgewater, 2004), 19.

210 *Three Pillars of Zen*, 77.

211 *Three Pillars of Zen*, 160–1, 163–5.

212 *Three Pillars of Zen*, 276.

213 William Barrett, "Zen for the West," in Daisetz T. Suzuki, *Zen Buddhism: Selected Writings of D. T. Suzukim*, edited by William Barrett (Garden City, NY: Doubleday, 1956), xvii.

214 Kapleau, Editor's Preface to *Three Pillars of Zen*, xv.

215 *Original Teachings of Ch'an*, x.

216 Thien-An, *Zen Philosophy, Zen Practice*, 64–6.

217 Thien-An, *Zen Philosophy, Zen Practice*, 154–5.

218 The pictures are in the public domain in their country of origin and other countries and areas where the copyright term is the author's life plus 100 years or fewer. The introductions and verses may be found in Daisetz Teitaro Suzuki, *Manual of Zen Buddhism* (Kyoto: Eastern Buddhist Society, 1934; reprint edition, New York: Grove, 1960), 129–34.

219 See, e.g., http://www.sacred-texts.com/bud/mzb/oxherd.htm [From *The Manual of Zen Buddhism,* D.T. Suzuki. By Shubun (15th Century)]. See also http://www.iloveulove.com/spirituality/buddhist/tenbulls.htm Empty circle = #8.

220 Osho, *Zen*, 60.

221 Thien-An, *Zen Philosophy, Zen Practice*, 161.

222 *Three Pillars of Zen*, 27–8.

223 Koji Sato, *The Zen Life*, photographs by Sosei Kuzunishi, translated by Ryojun Victoria (New York: Weatherhill, 1972), caption to picture 63.

224 Sato, *Zen Life*, 178, 180.

225 For example, David Schak and Hsin-Huang Michael Hsiao write, "As her group formed, she resolved to maintain Sangha independence and instituted rules: no sutra chanting or Dharma ritual service for fees and no begging. 'Instead her followers took whatever handicrafts they could subcontract from factories to make a living, such as sewing paper bags and making baby shoes, so as to abide by the Zen master Baizhang's motto of "no toil, no meal," a slogan still prominent in the Tzu Chi

headquarters.' "Taiwan's Socially Engaged Buddhist Groups" *China Perspectives* 59 (May–June 2005), as found on http://chinaperspectives.revues.org/2803, ¶60, accessed 21 February 2013.

226 Thien-An, *Zen Philosophy, Zen Practice*, 156.

227 Thien-An, *Zen Philosophy, Zen Practice*, 163.

228 Thien-An, *Zen Philosophy, Zen Practice*, 155.

229 *Three Pillars of Zen*, 164.

230 *Sakkapañha Sutta: Sakka's Questions*, A God Consults the Buddha, in *The Long Discourses of the Buddha: A Translation of the Dīgha Nikāya*, translated by Maurice Walshe (Boston: Wisdom Publications, 1995), 328–9 [with ellipses and changes in capitalization]: Sakka, ruler of the gods, put his first question to the Lord: "By what fetters, sir, are beings bound whereby, although they wish to live without hate, harming, hostility or malignity, and in peace, they yet live in hate, harming one another, hostile and malign?" And the Lord replied: "Ruler of the Gods, it is the bonds of jealousy and avarice that bind beings so that, though they wish to live without hate, they yet live in hate, harming one another, hostile and malign." "But sir, what gives rise to jealousy and avarice?" "Jealousy and avarice, Ruler of the Gods, take rise from like and dislike." "But, sir, what gives rise to like and dislike?" "Desire." "What gives rise to desire?" "Thinking." Though the sutta takes thinking itself back to "the tendency to proliferation," the translator acknowledges that this last word is "difficult." However we understand "proliferation," the *Sakkapañha Sutta*, which long predates the rise of Zen, assigns to thinking a very negative role in relation to human happiness and goodness.

12: Wired to Connect

231 National Geographic, "Light at the Edge of the World," as seen on http://www.youtube.com/watch?v=ZQ50fOmSBrU, accessed 05 March 2013.

232 Daniel Goleman, *Social Intelligence: The New Science of Human Relationships* (New York: Bantam, 2006), 41–2, 56, 68.

233 Robert H. Stockman, *The Bahá'í Faith: A Guide for the Perplexed* (London: Bloomsbury, 2013), 143.

234 John Ebenezer Esslemont, *Bahá'u'lláh and the New Era*, http://reference.bahai.org/en/t/alpha.html, accessed 18 May 2013, pp. 9–10, 154–5, 159, 164–7. Minor spelling changes have been made, e.g., quaa → qua, one for all → once for all, hath → has, Islám → Islam, ajudicate → adjudicate, cöoperate → cooperate, cöordinated → coordinated, etc.

235 *Collection of Caodai Holy Messages* (*Thanh Ngon Hiep Tuyen*), edition 1968, translated by Hum D. Bui and Hong D. Bui, edited by NgaSharaNguyet Beck-Huy and Todd Berry (Chicago, 2006), on http://www.caodai.org/documents/pdf/caodai_holy_messages.pdf, accessed 30 May 2013.

236 Confucius, *Genuine Living*, in Archie J. Bahm, *The Heart of Confucius* , with a foreword by Thomé H. Fang, and sixteen Ming-dynasty Confucian prints (Berkeley: Asian Humanities Press, 1969, 1992), 78.

237 Howard Bloom, *The Lucifer Principle: A Scientific Expedition into the Forces of History* (New York: Atlantic Monthly Press, 1995), 126.

238 Walther Eichrodt, *Theology of the Old Testament*, translated by J.A. Baker (Philadelphia: Westminster, 1961), 1:134.

13: Disagreeing Agreeably

239 Jean C. Cooper, *An Illustrated Introduction to Taoism: The Wisdom of the Sages*, edited by Joseph A. Fitzgerald, foreword by William Stoddart (Bloomington, IN: World Wisdom, 2010), 9.

240 *Foxe's Book of Martyrs*, edited by Marie Gentert King (Old Tappan, NJ: Revell, 1968), 61–2.

241 John 17:21–3.

242 Ephesians 4:1–6.

243 2 Corinthians 6:14–7:1.

244 Matthew 13:24–30, 37–43.

245 1 Corinthians 5.

246 Acts 5:33–49.

247 1 Samuel 15:2–3.

248 Deuteronomy 13:1–11.

249 Acts 15:14.

250 Acts 15:5–29.

251 Hebrews 8:13.

252 Leviticus 24:11–6; Numbers 15:32–6; Deuteronomy 18:20; Matthew 13:24–30, 38–43.

253 Balthasar Hubmaier, "On Heretics and Those Who Burn Them," in *Balthasar Hubmaier: Theologian of Anabaptism*, translated and edited by H. Wayne Pipkin and John H. Yoder (Scottdale, PA: Herald Press, 1989), 58–66. Scripture references have been deleted. Article 22 is taken from *Anabaptist Beginnings (1523–1533): A Source Book*, Bibliotheca Humanistica & Reformatorica, vol XVI, edited by William R. Estep (Nieuwkoop: B. De Graaf, 1976), 51.

254 Micah 4:1–4.

255 Revelation 21:22–27.

256 Matthew 12:18–21, citing Isaiah 42:1–4.

257 D.A. Carson, "Matthew," in *The Expositor's Bible Commentary*, general editor Frank E. Gæbelein. Vol. 8: *Matthew, Mark, Luke* (Grand Rapids: Zondervan, 1984), 287.

258 Frederick Dale Bruner, *The Christbook* (Waco, TX: Word, 1987), 453–4.

259 Luke 9:54–6; 23:34; John 18:10–1.

260 2 Timothy 2:24–6; Titus 3:2–3; 1 Peter 3:15–6; James 3:8–10, 17–8.

261 See, for example, Acts 14:15 and 19:26.

262 Sūrah 2 *Al Baqarah*, āyah 256, and footnote 300 in 'Abdullah Yūsuf 'Alī, *The Meaning of The Holy Qur'ān*, 11th edition (Beltsville, MD: Amana, 1425 AN / 2004 AC), 106.

263 http://ammanmessage.com/media/openLetter/english.pdf, accessed 04 November 2013. Emphases in original.

264 Eknath Easwaran, *A More Ardent Fire—From Everyday Love to Love of God* (Tomales, CA: Nilgiri Press, 1979, 2000), 135–6.

265 Thich Thien-An, *Zen Philosophy, Zen Practice* (Emeryville, CA: Dharma Publishing, 1975), 61–2.

266 The ongoing violence by Hindus in the Indian state of Orissa and the rhetoric of Buddhist monk Wirathu in Myanmar are examples.

267 Paul Griffiths and Delmas Lewis, "On Grading Religions, Seeking Truth, and Being Nice to People—A Reply to Professor Hick," *Religious Studies* 19 (March 1983): 77.

268 Stephen Prothero, *God Is Not One: The Eight Rival Religions That Run the World—and Why Their Differences Matter* (New York: HarperOne, 2010).

14: The Earth Is Our Mother

269 Helena Norberg-Hodge [founder of the International Society for Ecology and Culture], cited in Greg Mortenson and David Oliver Relin, *Three Cups of Tea—One Man's Mission to Promote Peace . . . One School at a Time* (London: Penguin, 2006), 136.

270 Javier Galicia Silva, "Religion, Ritual, and Agriculture among the Present-Day Nahua of Mesoamerica," in *Indigenous Traditions and Ecology: The Interbeing of Cosmology and Community*, edited by John A. Grim. Publications of the Center for the Study of World Religions, Harvard Divinity School, general editor Lawrence E. Sullivan. Religions of the World and Ecology, series editors Mary Evelyn Tucker and John Grim (Cambridge, MA: Harvard University Press, 2001), 303–23.

271 Darrell Addison Posey, "Intellectual Property Rights and the Sacred Balance: Some Spiritual Consequences from the Commercialzation of Traditional Resources," in *Indigenous Traditions and Ecology*, 4–5.

272 Paul VanDevelder, "A Coyote For All Seasons," *Native Peoples* 11/4 (Summer 1998): 45–6, 48. The individual quoted in the latter paragraphs is Raymond Cross, a Mandan-Hidatsa Native American.

273 Fikret Berkes, Johan Colding, and Carl Folke, "Rediscovery of Traditional Ecological Knowledge as Adaptive Management," *Ecological Applications* 10/5 (Oct. 2000): 1254.

274 Berkes, et, al., "Rediscovery," 1259.

275 Alan Weisman, *The World Without Us* (New York: Thomas Dunne Books, 2007), 53–67.

276 Berkes, et. al, "Rediscovery," 1256–7, 1252, 1259.

277 Posey, "Intellectual Property Rights," in *Indigenous Traditions*, 4, 21.

279 http://www.dalailama.com/messages/environment/an-ethical-approach, accessed 03 Sept 2013.

279 http://www.ucsusa.org/about/1992-world-scientists.html, accessed 07 September 2013.

280 J. P. Williams, *Denying Divinity: Apophasis in the Patristic Christian and Soto Zen Buddhist Traditions* (Oxford: Oxford University, 2000), 194–5.

281 Raymond Cross, a Mandan-Hidatsa Native American, cited in Paul VanDevelder, "A Coyote For All Seasons," *Native Peoples* 11/4 (Summer 1998): 45.

282 Psalm 19:1–6 ESV.

283 Psalm 104:10–24, 31 ESV.

284 Job 38:4–7; 39:5–8, 19–30.

285 Revelation 11:18.

286 C.S. Lewis, *Perelandra* (New York: Macmillan, 1944), 183–4.

287 Lewis, *Perelandra*, 215–6.

288 Lynn White, Jr., "The Historical Roots of Our Ecologic Crisis," *Science* 155/3767 (10 March 1967): 1205, 1207.

289 Robert Siegel, *Alpha Centauri* (Westchester, IL: Cornerstone Books, 1980), 184.

290 Luther Standing Bear, *My Indian Boyhood*, new edition, introduction by Delphine Red Shirt (Lincoln: University of Nebraska, 1933, 2006), 12–3, 52–3.

291 Luther Standing Bear, *Land of the Spotted Eagle*, new edition, foreword by Richard N. Ellis, introduction by Joseph Marshall III (Lincoln: University of Nebraska, 1933, 2006), 192–3, 195.

292 Standing Bear, *Spotted Eagle*, 165–6.

293 Cited in Alexandra Fuller, "Life After Wounded Knee," photographs by Aaron Huey, *National Geographic* 222/2 (August 2012), 59.

294 John (Fire) Lame Deer and Richard Erdoes, *Lame Deer: Seeker of Visions* (New York: Simon & Schuster, 1972), 119–23, 137–8.

295 Fuller, "Wounded Knee," 48.

296 Cited in in Fuller, "Wounded Knee," 52.

15: Regardless of Size

297 Genesis 1:26–31.

298 Genesis 6:11, 13; 9:1–6 NIV.

299 Nicholas de Lange, *Judaism* (Oxford: Oxford University Press, 1986), 87.

300 Abraham Cohen, *Everyman's Talmud: The Major Teachings of the Rabbinic Sages*, foreword by Jacob Neusner (New York: Schocken, 1949, 1955), 211.

301 Isaiah 1:10–17.

302 Isaiah 58:1–10 NIV.

303 Amos 5:7–24 NIV.

304 Malachi 2:13–6 NIV.

305 Psalm 50:7–23 NIV.

306 Note that neither the rich nor the poor were to be favored in their lawsuits. The Tanakh is not a Robin Hood ideology. At the deepest level, rich and poor are equal (Exodus 23:3; 30:11–6; Proverbs 22:2).

307 Isaiah 1:17 NIV; Leviticus 19:9–10; Ruth 2:15–6 NIV.

308 Jeremiah 22:13–9 NIV.

309 Leviticus 25:10–23 NIV.

310 Isaiah 5:8–10 NIV.

311 Genesis 4:1 NIV.

312 Genesis 15:2–6 NIV.

313 Psalm 127; 128 NIV.

314 Genesis 18:17–9 NIV.

315 Deuteronomy 6:4–7 NIV.

316 Proverbs 1:8–9; 23:22–5 NIV.

317 Genesis 1:27; Numbers 27:1–8; Ruth 4:15 NIV.

318 Luther Standing Bear, *Land of the Spotted Eagle*, new edition, foreword by Richard N. Ellis, introduction by Joseph Marshall III (Lincoln: University of Nebraska, 1933, 2006), 123–5, 163–4.

16: Life Is Now

319 Huston Smith, Foreword to *The Three Pillars of Zen—Teaching, Practice, and Enlightenment*, compiled and edited by Philip Kapleau, updated and revised (New York: Anchor, 1989, 2000), xiii.

320 Editor's Introduction to Dogen, *Treasury of the True Dharma Eye: Zen Master Dogen's* Shobo Genzo, edited by Kazuaki Tanahashi (Boston: Shambhala, 2012), xxix.

321 Dōgen, recalling the words of his mentor Rujing in *Journal of My Study in China*, cited in the Editor's Introduction to *Treasury of the True Dharma Eye*, xxxix.

322 *Bhaddekaratta Sutta* A Single Excellent Night (131), in *The Middle Length Discourses of the Buddha: A Translation of the Majjhima Nikāya* [*MN*], translated by Bhikkhu Ñāṇamoli and Bhikkhu Bodhi, 3rd ed. (Boston: Wisdom Publications, 2005), 1039.

323 Bhante Henepola Gunaratana, *Mindfulness in Plain English* (Boston: Wisdom, 2002), 140.

324 The Sanskrit term for mindfulness is *smṛti*; in Pāli *sati*. The Pāli sūtras are *Satipaṭṭhāna* and *Mahāsatipaṭṭhāna*—Foundations of Mindfulness and Greater Discourse on the Foundations of Mindfulness, *MN* 10 and *DN* 22.

325 *Satipaṭṭhāna Sutta* The Foundations of Mindfulness (10), in *MN*, 147.

326 Thich Nhat Hanh, *The Heart of the Buddha's Teaching; Transforming Suffering into Peace, Joy, & Liberation: The Four Noble Truths, The Noble Eightfold Path, and Other Basic Buddhist Teachings* (New York: Broadway Books, 1998), 64–5.

327 Alan Watts, *The Way of Zen* (New York: Vintage, 1957), 124.

328 See also Masunaga Reiho, "The Standpoint of Dogen and his Ideas on Time," http://www.zenki.com/index.php?lang=en&page=Masunaga04, accessed 05 May 2014.

329 Keiji Nishitani, *Religion and Nothingness*, translated with an Introduction by Jan Van Bragt, Foreword by Winston L. King (Berkeley: University of California, 1982), 189.

330 Alan Watts, *The Way of Zen* (New York: Vintage, 1957), 82. See Dōgen *Shōbōgenzō*, 3 *Genjō Kōan* or *Actualizing the Fundamental Point*, 30–1.

331 Steven Heine, *Existential and Ontological Dimensions of Time in Heidegger and Dōgen*, SUNY Series in Buddhist Studies, edited by Kenneth Inada (Albany: State University of New York, 1985), 145.

332 Matthew 6:19–34.

333 John 9:4.

334 Matthew 25:21.

335 1 Corinthians 10:11.

336 1 Corinthians 11:26.

337 Titus 2:11–4.

338 Ecclesiastes 9:7–10; 12:1–7 NIV.

339 *Three Pillars of Zen*, 19.

The Journey

340 Albert Einstein to Hermann Weyl, April 8, 1918. Cited in Walter Isaacson, *Einstein: His Life and Universe* (New York: Simon & Schuster, 2007), 337.

341 Leo Kadanoff, cited in Melanie Mitchell, *Complexity: A Guided Tour* (Oxford: Oxford University, 2009), 37.

342 *Shōbōgenzō: The Treasure House of the Eye of the True Teaching: A Trainee's Translation of Great Master Dōgen's Spiritual Masterpiece*, translated by Hubert Nearman (Mount Shasta, CA: Shasta Alley Press, 2007), 106–18. http://www.shastaabbey.org/pdf/shobogenzo.pdf, accessed 16 May 2013.

ACKNOWLEDGMENTS AND CREDITS

Seeking permission has proved in itself to be an exercise in diversity. Several Buddhist publishers and one Hindu have been the most enthusiastic and generous. My desire to use a respected Jewish translation for citations from the Tanakh was stymied, whereas Christian Bible translators often grant generous permission. The Seuss estate disallowed the use of eleven words from one of its children's books. At any rate, the author gratefully acknowledges the following for permission to use their material:

Bukkyo Dendo Kyokai America, Inc., of Moraga, CA, for the use of "The Larger Sutra on Amitāyus," in *The Three Pure Land Sutras*, translated by Hisao Inagaki in collaboration with Harold Stewart, revised second ed., BDK English Tripiṭaka Series (Berkeley: Numata Center for Buddhist Translation and Research, 2003).

Dharma Publishing, for quotations from Thich Thien-An, *Zen Philosophy, Zen Practice* Emeryville, CA: Dharma Publishing, 1975.

Hongwanji International Center, for quotations from *The Collected Works of Shinran*, Jodo Shinshu Hongwanji-ha, Kyoto, Japan.

Native Peoples, for quotations from Paul VanDevelder, "A Coyote For All Seasons," *Native Peoples* 11/4 (Summer 1998).

Nilgiri Press, for quotations From *The Bhagavad Gita*, translated by Eknath Easwaran, founder of the Blue Mountain Center of Meditation, copyright 1985, 2007; reprinted by permission of Nilgiri Press, P.O. Box 256, Tomales, CA 94971, www.easwaran.org.

Paragon House, for use of Ellen M. Chen, *The Tao Te Ching: A New Translation with Commentary* (St. Paul: Paragon, 1989).

Shasta Abbey of Mt. Shasta, California, for the use of *Shōbōgenzō: The Treasure House of the Eye of the True Teaching: A Trainee's Translation of Great Master Dōgen's Spiritual Masterpiece*, translated by Hubert Nearman, 2007.

Wisdom Publications of Somerville, Massachusetts, for the use of *The Connected Discourses of the Buddha: A Translation of the Saṃyutta Nikāya*, translated by Bhikku Bodhi, 2000; *The Long Discourses of the Buddha: A Translation of the Dīgha Nikāya*, translated by Maurice Walshe,1995; *The Middle Length Discourses of the Buddha: A Translation of the Majjhima Nikāya*, translated by Bhikkhu Ñāṇamoli and Bhikkhu Bodhi, 3rd ed., 2005; *The Numerical Discourses of the Buddha: A Translation of the Aṅguttara Nikāya*, translated by Bhikkhu Bodhi, 2012.

The author further acknowledges permission to cite:

Excerpts from "Bahá'u'lláh and the New Era," reprinted with permission of the copyright owner, National Spiritual Assembly of the Bahá'ís of the United States © 1950-1995.

Excerpt from pp. 143–4 [354 words] from THE BEGINNING: CREATION MYTHS AROUND THE WORLD by MARIA LEACH and JAN BELL FAIRSERVIS, ILLUSTRATOR. Copyright © 1956 by Harper & Row, Publishers, Inc., renewed copyright © 1984 by MacDonald H. Leach. Reprinted by permission of HarperCollins Publishers.

From GOING HOME: JESUS AND BUDDHA AS BROTHERS by Thich Nhat Hanh, copyright © 1999 by Thich Nhat Hanh. Used by permission of Riverhead, an imprint of Penguin Publishing Group, a division of Penguin Random House LLC.

Hōnen's Senchakushū: *Passages on the Selection of the Nembutsu in the Original Vow (Senchaku hongan nembutsu shū*), translated and edited by the *Senchakushū* English Translation Project (Honolulu: University of Hawai'i, 1998).

Excerpts from Darrell Addison Posey, "Intellectual Property Rights and the Sacred Balance: Some Spiritual Consequences from the Commercialization of Traditional Resources"; and Javier Galicia Silva, "Religion, Ritual, and Agriculture among the Present-Day Nahua of Mesoamerica";

both contained in *Indigenous Traditions and Ecology: The Interbeing of Cosmology and Community*, edited by John A. Grim (Cambridge, MA: Harvard Divinity School, 2001), ISBN 0-945454-28-7.

Excerpt from the note on Leviticus 26:14–45, p. 274, in THE JEWISH STUDY BIBLE 1E edited by Adele Berlin and Marc Zvi Brettler (2004) © 2004 by Oxford University Press. Tanakh translation 1999 by Jewish Publications Society "By Permission of Oxford University Press, USA."

From LIVING BUDDHA, LIVING CHRIST by Thich Nhat Hanh, copyright © 1995 by Thich Nhat Hanh. Used by permission of Riverhead, an imprint of Penguin Publishing Group, a division of Penguin Random House LLC.

From *The Lotus Sutra*, translated by Burton Watson. Translations from the Asian Classics. Copyright © 1993 Columbia University Press. Reprinted with permission of the publisher.

PERELANDRA by C.S. Lewis copyright © C.S. Lewis Pte. Ltd. 1944. Extract reprinted by permission.

Excerpts from RIVER OF FIRE, RIVER OF WATER by Taitetsu Unno, copyright © 1998 by Taitetsu Unno. Used by permission of Doubleday, an imprint of the Knopf Doubleday Publishing Group, a division of Penguin Random House LLC. All rights reserved.

Excerpts from THE THREE PILLARS OF ZEN by Roshi P. Kapleau, copyright © 1989 by Roshi Philip Kapleau. Used by permission of Anchor Books, an imprint of the Knopf Doubleday Publishing Group, a division of Penguin Random House LLC. All rights reserved.

By Thomas Merton, from THE WAY OF CHUANG TZU, copyright © 1965 by The Abbey of Gethsemani. Reprinted by permission of New Directions Publishing Corp.

Excerpts from WHAT THE BUDDHA TAUGHT, copyright © 1959 by W. Rahula. Second and enlarged edition copyright © 1974 by W. Rahula. Used by permission of Grave/Atlantic, Inc. Any third party use of this material, outside of this publication, is prohibited.